The Expositor's Bible Commentary

with The New International Version

ROMANS

THE
Expositor's
Bible
Commentary
with The New International Version

ROMANS

Everett F. Harrison

ZondervanPublishingHouse
Grand Rapids, Michigan

A Division of HarperCollinsPublishers

General Editor:

FRANK E. GAEBELEIN
Former Headmaster, Stony Brook School
Former Coeditor, *Christianity Today*

Associate Editors:

J. D. DOUGLAS
Editor, *The New International
Dictionary of the Christian Church*

RICHARD P. POLCYN

Romans
Copyright © 1995 by Everett F. Harrison

Requests for information should be addressed to:
Zondervan Publishing House
Grand Rapids, Michigan 49530

Library of Congress Cataloging-in-Publication Data

The expositor's Bible commentary : with the New International Version of the Holy Bible /
Frank E. Gaebelein, general editor of series.
   p.   cm.
Includes bibliographical references and index.
Contents: v. 1–2. Matthew / D. A. Carson — Mark / Walter W. Wessel — Luke / Walter
L. Liefeld — John / Merrill C. Tenney— Acts / Richard N. Longenecker — Romans /
Everett F. Harrison — 1 and 2 Corinthians / W. Harold Mare and Murray J. Harris —
Galatians and Ephesians / James Montgomery Boice and A. Skevington Wood
   ISBN: 0-310-20109-8 (softcover)
   1. Bible N.T.—Commentaries. I. Gaebelein, Frank Ely, 1899–1983.
BS2341.2.E96 1995
220.7-dc 00   94-47450
                                                                           CIP

Printed in the United States of America

   96 97 98 99 00 / ❖ DH / 10 9 8 7 6 5 4 3 2

CONTENTS

PREFACE

The title of this work defines its purpose. Written primarily by expositors for expositors, it aims to provide preachers, teachers, and students of the Bible with a new and comprehensive commentary on the books of the Old and New Testaments. Its stance is that of a scholarly evangelicalism committed to the divine inspiration, complete trustworthiness, and full authority of the Bible. Its seventy-eight contributors come from the United States, Canada, England, Scotland, Australia, New Zealand, and Switzerland, and from various religious groups, including Anglican, Baptist, Brethren, Free, Independent, Methodist, Nazarene, Presbyterian, and Reformed churches. Most of them teach at colleges, universities, or theological seminaries.

No book has been more closely studied over a longer period of time than the Bible. From the Midrashic commentaries going back to the period of Ezra, through parts of the Dead Sea Scrolls and the Patristic literature, and on to the present, the Scriptures have been expounded. Indeed, there have been times when, as in the Reformation and on occasions since then, exposition has been at the cutting edge of Christian advance. Luther was a powerful exegete, and Calvin is still called "the prince of expositors."

Their successors have been many. And now, when the flood of new translations and their unparalleled circulation have expanded the readership of the Bible, the need for exposition takes on fresh urgency.

Not that God's Word can ever become captive to its expositors. Among all other books, it stands first in its combination of perspicuity and profundity. Though a child can be made "wise for salvation" by believing its witness to Christ, the greatest mind cannot plumb the depths of its truth (2 Tim. 3:15; Rom. 11:33). As Gregory the Great said, "Holy Scripture is a stream of running water, where alike the elephant may swim, and the lamb walk." So, because of the inexhaustible nature of Scripture, the task of opening up its meaning is still a perennial obligation of biblical scholarship.

How that task is done inevitably reflects the outlook of those engaged in it. Every biblical scholar has presuppositions. To this neither the editors of these volumes nor the contributors to them are exceptions. They share a common commitment to the supernatural Christianity set forth in the inspired Word. Their purpose is not to supplant the many valuable commentaries that have preceded this work and from which both the editors and contributors have learned. It is rather to draw on the resources of contemporary evangelical scholarship in producing a new reference work for understanding the Scriptures.

A commentary that will continue to be useful through the years should handle contemporary trends in biblical studies in such a way as to avoid becoming outdated when critical fashions change. Biblical criticism is not in itself inadmissible, as some have mistakenly thought. When scholars investigate the authorship, date, literary characteristics, and purpose of a biblical document, they are practicing biblical criticism. So also when, in order to ascertain as nearly as possible the original form of the text, they deal with variant readings, scribal errors, emendations, and other phenomena in the manuscripts. To do these things is essential to responsible exegesis and exposition. And always there is the need to distinguish hypothesis from fact, conjecture from truth.

The chief principle of interpretation followed in this commentary is the grammatico-historical one—namely, that the primary aim of the exegete is to make clear the meaning of the text at the time and in the circumstances of its writing. This endeavor to understand what in the first instance the inspired writers actually said must not be confused with an inflexible literalism. Scripture makes lavish use of symbols and figures of speech; great portions of it are poetical. Yet when it speaks in this way, it speaks no less truly than it does in its historical and doctrinal portions. To understand its message requires attention to matters of grammar and syntax, word meanings, idioms, and literary forms—all in relation to the historical and cultural setting of the text.

The contributors to this work necessarily reflect varying convictions. In certain controversial matters the policy is that of clear statement of the contributors' own views followed by fair presentation of other ones. The treatment of eschatology, though it reflects differences of interpretation, is consistent with a general premillennial position. (Not all contributors, however, are premillennial.) But prophecy is more than prediction, and so this commentary gives due recognition to the major lode of godly social concern in the prophetic writings.

THE EXPOSITOR'S BIBLE COMMENTARY is presented as a scholarly work, though not primarily one of technical criticism. In its main portion, the Exposition, and in Volume 1 (General and Special Articles), all Semitic and Greek words are transliterated and the English equivalents given. As for the Notes, here Semitic and Greek characters are used but always with transliterations and English meanings, so that this portion of the commentary will be as accessible as possible to readers unacquainted with the original languages.

It is the conviction of the general editor, shared by his colleagues in the Zondervan editorial department, that in writing about the Bible, lucidity is not incompatible with scholarship. They are therefore endeavoring to make this a clear and understandable work.

The translation used in it is the New International Version (North American Edition). To the International Bible Society thanks are due for permission to use this most recent of the major Bible translations. The editors and publisher have chosen it because of the clarity and beauty of its style and its faithfulness to the original texts.

To the associate editor, Dr. J. D. Douglas, and to the contributing editors—Dr. Walter C. Kaiser, Jr. and Dr. Bruce K. Waltke for the Old Testament, and Dr. James Montgomery Boice and Dr. Merrill C. Tenney for the New Testament—the general editor expresses his gratitude for their unfailing cooperation and their generosity in advising him out of their expert scholarship. And to the many other contributors he is indebted for their invaluable part in this work. Finally, he owes a special debt of gratitude to Dr. Robert K. DeVries, executive vice-president of the Zondervan Publishing House; Rev. Gerard Terpstra, manuscript editor; and Miss Elizabeth Brown, secretary to Dr. DeVries, for their continual assistance and encouragement.

Whatever else it is—the greatest and most beautiful of books, the primary source of law and morality, the fountain of wisdom, and the infallible guide to life—the Bible is above all the inspired witness to Jesus Christ. May this work fulfill its function of expounding the Scriptures with grace and clarity, so that its users may find that both Old and New Testaments do indeed lead to our Lord Jesus Christ, who alone could say, "I have come that they may have life, and have it to the full" (John 10:10).

FRANK E. GAEBELEIN

ABBREVIATIONS

A. General Abbreviations

A	Codex Alexandrinus	MT	Masoretic text
Akkad.	Akkadian	n.	note
א	Codex Sinaiticus	n.d.	no date
Ap. Lit.	Apocalyptic Literature	Nestle	Nestle (ed.) *Novum*
Apoc.	Apocrypha		*Testamentum Graece*
Aq.	Aquila's Greek Translation	no.	number
	of the Old Testament	NT	New Testament
Arab.	Arabic	obs.	obsolete
Aram.	Aramaic	OL	Old Latin
b	Babylonian Gemara	OS	Old Syriac
B	Codex Vaticanus	OT	Old Testament
C	Codex Ephraemi Syri	p., pp.	page, pages
c.	*circa*, about	par.	paragraph
cf.	*confer*, compare	‖	parallel passage(s)
ch., chs.	chapter, chapters	Pers.	Persian
cod., codd.	codex, codices	Pesh.	Peshitta
contra	in contrast to	Phoen.	Phoenician
D	Codex Bezae	pl.	plural
DSS	Dead Sea Scrolls (see E.)	Pseudep.	Pseudepigrapha
ed., edd.	edited, edition, editor; editions	Q	Quelle ("Sayings" source
e.g.	*exempli gratia*, for example		in the Gospels)
Egyp.	Egyptian	qt.	quoted by
et al.	*et alii*, and others	q.v.	*quod vide*, which see
EV	English Versions of the Bible	R	Rabbah
fem.	feminine	rev.	revised, reviser, revision
ff.	following (verses, pages, etc.)	Rom.	Roman
fl.	flourished	RVm	Revised Version margin
ft.	foot, feet	Samar.	Samaritan recension
gen.	genitive	SCM	Student Christian Movement Press
Gr.	Greek	Sem.	Semitic
Heb.	Hebrew	sing.	singular
Hitt.	Hittite	SPCK	Society for the Promotion
ibid.	*ibidem*, in the same place		of Christian Knowledge
id.	*idem*, the same	Sumer.	Sumerian
i.e.	*id est*, that is	s.v.	*sub verbo*, under the word
impf.	imperfect	Syr.	Syriac
infra.	below	Symm.	Symmachus
in loc.	*in loco*, in the place cited	T	Talmud
j	Jerusalem or	Targ.	Targum
	Palestinian Gemara	Theod.	Theodotion
Lat.	Latin	TR	Textus Receptus
LL.	Late Latin	tr.	translation, translator,
LXX	Septuagint		translated
M	Mishnah	UBS	The United Bible Societies'
masc.	masculine		Greek Text
mg.	margin	Ugar.	Ugaritic
Mid	Midrash	u.s.	*ut supra*, as above
MS(S)	Manuscript(s)	viz.	*videlicet*, namely

vol.	volume	Vul.	Vulgate
v., vv.	verse, verses	WH	Westcott and Hort, *The New Testament in Greek*
vs.	versus		

B. Abbreviations for Modern Translations and Paraphrases

AmT	Smith and Goodspeed, *The Complete Bible, An American Translation*	LB	The Living Bible
		Mof	J. Moffatt, *A New Translation of the Bible*
ASV	American Standard Version, American Revised Version (1901)	NAB	The New American Bible
		NASB	New American Standard Bible
		NEB	The New English Bible
Beck	Beck, *The New Testament in the Language of Today*	NIV	The New International Version
		Ph	J. B. Phillips *The New Testament in Modern English*
BV	Berkeley Version (The Modern Language Bible)		
		RSV	Revised Standard Version
JB	The Jerusalem Bible	RV	Revised Version — 1881–1885
JPS	*Jewish Publication Society Version of the Old Testament*	TCNT	Twentieth Century New Testament
KJV	King James Version	TEV	Today's English Version
Knox	R.G. Knox, *The Holy Bible: A Translation from the Latin Vulgate in the Light of the Hebrew and Greek Original*	Wey	*Weymouth's New Testament in Modern Speech*
		Wms	C. B. Williams, *The New Testament: A Translation in the Language of the People*

C. Abbreviations for Periodicals and Reference Works

AASOR	*Annual of the American Schools of Oriental Research*	BAG	Bauer, Arndt, and Gingrich: *Greek-English Lexicon of the New Testament*
AB	*Anchor Bible*		
AIs	de Vaux: *Ancient Israel*	BC	Foakes-Jackson and Lake: *The Beginnings of Christianity*
AJA	*American Journal of Archaeology*		
		BDB	Brown, Driver, and Briggs: *Hebrew-English Lexicon of the Old Testament*
AJSL	*American Journal of Semitic Languages and Literatures*		
AJT	*American Journal of Theology*	BDF	Blass, Debrunner, and Funk: *A Greek Grammar of the New Testament and Other Early Christian Literature*
Alf	Alford: *Greek Testament Commentary*		
ANEA	*Ancient Near Eastern Archaeology*	BDT	Harrison: *Baker's Dictionary of Theology*
ANET	Pritchard: *Ancient Near Eastern Texts*	Beng.	Bengel's *Gnomon*
		BETS	*Bulletin of the Evangelical Theological Society*
ANF	Roberts and Donaldson: *The Ante-Nicene Fathers*		
		BJRL	*Bulletin of the John Rylands Library*
ANT	M. R. James: *The Apocryphal New Testament*		
		BS	*Bibliotheca Sacra*
A-S	Abbot-Smith: *Manual Greek Lexicon of the New Testament*	BT	*Babylonian Talmud*
		BTh	*Biblical Theology*
AThR	*Anglican Theological Review*	BW	*Biblical World*
BA	*Biblical Archaeologist*	CAH	*Cambridge Ancient History*
BASOR	*Bulletin of the American Schools of Oriental Research*	CanJTh	*Canadian Journal of Theology*
		CBQ	*Catholic Biblical Quarterly*

MM	Moulton and Milligan: *The Vocabulary of the Greek Testament*
MNT	Moffatt: *New Testament Commentary*
MST	McClintock and Strong: *Cyclopedia of Biblical, Theological, and Ecclesiastical Literature*
NBÇ	Davidson, Kevan, and Stibbs: *The New Bible Commentary*, 1st ed.
NBCrev.	Guthrie and Motyer: *The New Bible Commentary*, rev. ed.
NBD	J. D. Douglas: *The New Bible Dictionary*
NCB	*New Century Bible*
NCE	*New Catholic Encyclopedia*
NIC	*New International Commentary*
NIDCC	Douglas: *The New International Dictionary of the Christian Church*
NovTest	*Novum Testamentum*
NSI	Cooke: *Handbook of North Semitic Inscriptions*
NTS	*New Testament Studies*
ODCC	*The Oxford Dictionary of the Christian Church*, rev. ed.
Peake	Black and Rowley: *Peake's Commentary on the Bible*
PEQ	*Palestine Exploration Quarterly*
PNFl	P. Schaff: *The Nicene and Post-Nicene Fathers* (1st series)
PNF2	P. Schaff and H. Wace: *The Nicene and Post-Nicene Fathers* (2nd series)
PTR	*Princeton Theological Review*
RB	*Revue Biblique*
RHG	Robertson's *Grammar of the Greek New Testament in the Light of Historical Research*
RTWB	Richardson: *A Theological Wordbook of the Bible*
SBK	Strack and Billerbeck: *Kommentar zum Neuen Testament aus Talmud und Midrash*
SHERK	*The New Schaff-Herzog Encyclopedia of Religious Knowledge*
SJT	*Scottish Journal of Theology*
SOT	Girdlestone: *Synonyms of Old Testament*
SOTI	Archer: *A Survey of Old Testament Introduction*
ST	*Studia Theologica*
TCERK	Loetscher: *The Twentieth Century Encyclopedia of Religious Knowledge*
TDNT	Kittel: *Theological Dictionary of the New Testament*
TDOT	*Theological Dictionary of the Old Testament*
Theol	*Theology*
ThT	*Theology Today*
TNTC	*Tyndale New Testament Commentaries*
Trench	Trench: *Synonyms of the New Testament*
UBD	*Unger's Bible Dictionary*
UT	Gordon: *Ugaritic Textbook*
VB	Allmen: *Vocabulary of the Bible*
VetTest	*Vetus Testamentum*
Vincent	Vincent: *Word-Pictures in the New Testament*
WBC	*Wycliffe Bible Commentary*
WBE	*Wycliffe Bible Encyclopedia*
WC	*Westminster Commentaries*
WesBC	*Wesleyan Bible Commentaries*
WTJ	*Westminster Theological Journal*
ZAW	*Zeitschrift für die alttestamentliche Wissenschaft*
ZNW	*Zeitschrift für die neutestamentliche Wissenschaft*
ZPBD	*The Zondervan Pictorial Bible Dictionary*
ZPEB	*The Zondervan Pictorial Encyclopedia of the Bible*
ZWT	*Zeitschrift für wissenschaftliche Theologie*

D. Abbreviations for Books of the Bible, the Apocrypha, and the Pseudepigrapha

OLD TESTAMENT

Gen	2 Chron	Dan
Exod	Ezra	Hos
Lev	Neh	Joel
Num	Esth	Amos
Deut	Job	Obad
Josh	Ps(Pss)	Jonah
Judg	Prov	Mic
Ruth	Eccl	Nah
1 Sam	S of Songs	Hab
2 Sam	Isa	Zeph
1 Kings	Jer	Hag
2 Kings	Lam	Zech
1 Chron	Ezek	Mal

NEW TESTAMENT

Matt	1 Tim
Mark	2 Tim
Luke	Titus
John	Philem
Acts	Heb
Rom	James
1 Cor	1 Peter
2 Cor	2 Peter
Gal	1 John
Eph	2 John
Phil	3 John
Col	Jude
1 Thess	Rev
2 Thess	

APOCRYPHA

1 Esd	1 Esdras
2 Esd	2 Esdras
Tobit	Tobit
Jud	Judith
Add Esth	Additions to Esther
Wisd Sol	Wisdom of Solomon
Ecclus	Ecclesiasticus (Wisdom of Jesus the Son of Sirach)
Baruch	Baruch
Ep Jer	Epistle of Jeremy
S Th Ch	Song of the Three Children (or Young Men)
Sus	Susanna
Bel	Bel and the Dragon
Pr Man	Prayer of Manasseh
1 Macc	1 Maccabees
2 Macc	2 Maccabees

PSEUDEPIGRAPHA

As Moses	Assumption of Moses
2 Baruch	Syriac Apocalypse of Baruch
3 Baruch	Greek Apocalypse of Baruch
1 Enoch	Ethiopic Book of Enoch
2 Enoch	Slavonic Book of Enoch
3 Enoch	Hebrew Book of Enoch
4 Ezra	4 Ezra
JA	Joseph and Asenath
Jub	Book of Jubilees
L Aristeas	Letter of Aristeas
Life AE	Life of Adam and Eve
Liv Proph	Lives of the Prophets
MA Isa	Martyrdom and Ascension of Isaiah
3 Macc	3 Maccabees
4 Macc	4 Maccabees
Odes Sol	Odes of Solomon
P Jer	Paralipomena of Jeremiah
Pirke Aboth	Pirke Aboth
Ps 151	Psalm 151
Pss Sol	Psalms of Solomon
Sib Oracles	Sibylline Oracles
Story Ah	Story of Ahikar
T Abram	Testament of Abraham
T Adam	Testament of Adam
T Benjamin	Testament of Benjamin
T Dan	Testament of Dan
T Gad	Testament of Gad
T Job	Testament of Job
T Jos	Testament of Joseph
T Levi	Testament of Levi
T Naph	Testament of Naphtali
T 12 Pat	Testaments of the Twelve Patriarchs
Zad Frag	Zadokite Fragments

E. Abbreviations of Names of Dead Sea Scrolls and Related Texts

CD	Cairo (Genizah text of the) Damascus (Document)	1QSa	Appendix A (Rule of the Congregation) to 1QS
DSS	Dead Sea Scrolls	1QSb	Appendix B (Blessings) to 1QS
Hev	Nahal Hever texts	3Q15	Copper Scroll from Qumran Cave 3
Mas	Masada Texts		
Mird	Khirbet mird texts	4QFlor	Florilegium (or Eschatological Midrashim) from Qumran Cave 4
Mur	Wadi Murabba'at texts		
P	Pesher (commentary)		
Q	Qumran	4Qmess ar	Aramaic "Messianic" text from Qumran Cave 4
1Q,2Q,etc.	Numbered caves of Qumran, yielding written material; followed by abbreviation of biblical or apocryphal book.	4QPrNab	Prayer of Nabonidus from Qumran Cave 4
QL	Qumran Literature	4QTest	Testimonia text from Qumran Cave 4
1QapGen	Genesis Apocryphon of Qumran Cave 1	4QTLevi	Testament of Levi from Qumran Cave 4
1QH	*Hodayot* (Thanksgiving Hymns) from Qumran Cave 1	4QPhyl	Phylacteries from Qumran Cave 4
1QIsa[a, b]	First or second copy of Isaiah from Qumran Cave 1	11QMelch	Melchizedek text from Qumran Cave 11
1QpHab	Pesher on Habakkuk from Qumran Cave 1	11QtgJob	Targum of Job from Qumran Cave 11
1QM	*Milhamah* (War Scroll)		
1QS	*Serek Hayyahad* (Rule of the Community, Manual of Discipline)		

TRANSLITERATIONS

Hebrew

א = '	ד = d	י = y	ס = s	ר = r
ב = b	ה = h	כ = k	ע = $'$	שׂ = $ś$
ב = $ḇ$	ו = w	כ = $ḵ$	פ = p	שׁ = $š$
ג = g	ז = z	ל = l	פ = $p̄$	ת = t
ג = $ḡ$	ח = $ḥ$	מ = m	צ = $ṣ$	ת = $ṯ$
ד = d	ט = $ṭ$	נ = n	ק = q	

(ה)ֳ = $â$ (h)	ֳ = $ā$	ֲ = a	ֳֵ = e
ֵי = $ê$	ֵ = $ē$	ֶ = e	ֳֵ = e
ֳִ = $î$		ִ = i	ֵ = e (if vocal)
וֹ = $ô$	ֹ = $ō$	ֹ = o	ֳֵ = o
וּ = $û$		וּ = u	

Aramaic

' b g d h w z $ḥ$ $ṭ$ y k l m n s ' p $ṣ$ q r $ś$ $š$ t

Arabic

' b t $ṯ$ $ǧ$ $ḥ$ $ḫ$ d $ḏ$ r z s $š$ $ṣ$ $ḍ$ $ṭ$ $ẓ$ ' $ǵ$ f q k l m n h w y

Ugaritic

' b g d $ḏ$ h w z $ḥ$ $ḫ$ $ṭ$ $ẓ$ y k l m n $s̀$ ' $ǵ$ p $ṣ$ q r $š$ t $ṯ$

Greek

α	—	a	π	—	p	αι — ai
β	—	b	ρ	—	r	αυ — au
γ	—	g	σ,ς	—	s	ει — ei
δ	—	d	τ	—	t	ευ — eu
ε	—	e	υ	—	y	ηυ — ēu
ζ	—	z	φ	—	ph	οι — oi
η	—	ē	χ	—	ch	ου — ou
θ	—	th	ψ	—	ps	υι — hui
ι	—	i	ω	—	ō	
κ	—	k				ῥ — rh
λ	—	l	γγ	—	ng	‘ — h
μ	—	m	γκ	—	nk	
ν	—	n	γξ	—	nx	ᾳ — ā
ξ	—	x	γχ	—	nch	ῃ — ē
ο	—	o				ῳ — ō

ROMANS

Everett F. Harrison

ROMANS

Introduction

1. Background

By common consent, Romans is the greatest of Paul's letters, and the Roman church became one of the major centers of Christendom, yet next to nothing is known about the circumstances surrounding the founding and early history of this church. The apostle does not deal with these things in the course of his letter. Luke provides no help beyond mentioning that Aquila and Priscilla, with whom Paul lived and labored at Corinth, had recently come from Italy (Acts 18:2). He says nothing about Paul's witnessing to them, so the presumption is that they were already believers. The expulsion of Jews from Rome by order of the emperor Claudius was dictated, according to the historian Suetonius (*Claudius* 25), by "disturbances at the instigation of Chrestus." Since the confusion of "i" and "e" was not unknown in Latin renditions of Greek, it is possible to conclude from this statement that the Roman Jews had become unusually agitated and disorderly over the proclamation in their midst of Jesus as the Christ (Christus), provoking the emperor to take action against them. But the stir could have been caused by messianic fervor with revolutionary overtones. At any rate, it is probable that by the fifth decade of the first century the Christian faith had gained a foothold in the capital of the empire. According to Ambrosiaster (4th century), the Roman church was not established by an apostle (which removes Peter from consideration) but by unnamed Hebrew Christians. By the time Paul wrote, it had become famous far and wide for its faith (1:8).

2. Authorship

From the postapostolic church to the present, with almost no exception, the Epistle has been credited to Paul. If the claim of the apostle to have written the Galatian and Corinthian letters is accepted, there is no reasonable basis for denying that he wrote

3

Romans, since it echoes much of what is in the earlier writings, yet not slavishly. A few examples must suffice: the doctrine of justification by faith (Rom 3:20–22; Gal 2:16); the church as the body of Christ appointed to represent and serve him through a variety of spiritual gifts (Rom 12; 1 Cor 12); the collection for the poor saints at Jerusalem (Rom 15:25–28; 2 Cor 8–9). Understandably, Paul makes fewer references to himself and to his readers in Romans than in 1 and 2 Corinthians and Galatians, since he had not founded the Roman church and guided its struggles to maturity as he had the others.

3. Date and Place of Origin

Fixed dates for the span of Paul's labors are few, but one of them is the summer of A.D. 51, when Gallio arrived in Corinth to serve as proconsul of Achaia. After this the apostle stayed in the city "some time" (Acts 18:18). Possibly in the spring of 52 he went to Caesarea and Jerusalem, stopping at Antioch on the way back and probably spending the winter of 52 there. Presumably, his return to Ephesus was in the spring of 53, marking the beginning of a three-year ministry there (Acts 20:31). At the end of 56 he spent three months in Corinth (Acts 20:3), starting his final trip to Jerusalem in the spring of 57. When he wrote Romans the fund for the Jerusalem church seems to have been finally completed (Rom 15:26ff.). This may indicate a date in early 57 rather than late 56 for the writing of the letter. (The fund was incomplete when Paul, on the way from Ephesus to Corinth, wrote 2 Cor 8–9.)

Corinth is the most likely place of composition, since Phoebe of nearby Cenchrea was apparently entrusted with the carrying of the letter (Rom 16:1, 2). The mention of Gaius as Paul's host (Rom 16:23) confirms this conclusion, Gaius having been one of the most prominent of converts during the apostle's mission at Corinth (1 Cor 1:14). Cenchrea is a less likely possibility. Paul would not naturally have gone there except to board ship. At that juncture a plot against his life forced him to change his plan (Acts 20:3). Thus it is hard to imagine Paul finding time or peace of mind at Cenchrea for composing a book like Romans. A Macedonian origin has also been claimed for the books, with Romans 15:25 as support (cf. NEB). But the verb can be understood futuristically: "I am about to go."

4. Destination

The titles of the Pauline Epistles are not part of the text, so the superscription "The Letter of Paul to the Romans" cannot be attributed to the apostle but must be taken as reflecting the understanding of the church as a whole sometime during the second century. Yet, since the intended readers are located at Rome by the writer (Rom 1:7, 15), all doubt about the destination would seem to be removed.

Strange to say, however, a few manuscript authorities (G, Origen, Ambrosiaster) lack the words "in Rome." One important witness, P[46], has the closing doxology of 16:25–27 at the end of chapter 15. This feature, plus the failure of the words "in Rome" to appear in a few manuscripts, as noted above, has led some scholars to follow the suggestion of T.W. Manson.[1] He thinks that P[46] reflects the letter as Paul wrote it to the Roman church,

---

[1] *Studies in the Gospels and Epistles* (Philadelphia: Westminster Press, 1962), pp. 225–241.

but that the apostle at the same time sent a copy, minus the indication of Roman destination and with chapter 16 added, to the church at Ephesus. This would mean that the people mentioned in the closing chapter were living at Ephesus rather than at Rome. Attractive though this view is, it has not been universally received, because a good case can be made for a Roman destination for chapter 16.[2]

5. Occasion and Purpose

These two items are so closely related as to warrant considering them together. When Paul's Ephesian ministry had continued for more than two years, with tremendous impact on the city and province, he sensed that it would soon be time for him to move to another field of labor. It may be that for some time he had been looking westward toward Rome (see "many years" in Rom 15:23). Now the conviction grew that he must act by beginning to plan for work in the West (Acts 19:21). He had already preached the gospel in the strategic centers of population in the East and his restless spirit yearned to reach out to places where Christ was not known. He would go through Rome to Spain to plant the gospel there (Rom 15:22–24).

The question naturally arises, Why did this plan dictate the writing of a letter such as Romans? Why not send a note by Phoebe simply to inform the church that he would be coming to them in a short time? Two things should be said about this.

First, since Paul hoped to go beyond Rome even as far as Spain, he evidently expected to have in the Roman church a base of missionary operation comparable to Antioch in the East. If this was to be realized, he needed to share with the church a rather complete exposition of the gospel he had been preaching for over twenty years. By putting this exposition in writing and sending it ahead, he would give the Christian community in Rome an opportunity to digest the message and be ready to share in the extension of the gospel to the West.

Another factor may have entered in. The very passage that sets forth his plan and purpose is followed by one requesting prayer for his safety and success as he went on to Judea prior to leaving for Rome. Particularly ominous is his expressed need to be delivered from unbelievers in Judea (Rom 15:31). The plot by Jews at Corinth against his life (Acts 20:3) may already have been made and become an omen of future events. Possibly at this point intimations from the Holy Spirit began to warn him about the imprisonment and afflictions that awaited him (Acts 20:23). What if he should not live to declare the gospel in the West? Then he must write a letter so systematic and comprehensive that the church would be able intelligently to continue his work, proclaiming the very gospel he was spelling out for them, taking it in his stead to the farthest reaches of the empire. For all he knew at the time, this letter might be in a sense his last will and testament, a precious deposit bequeathed to the church and through it to the community of the faithful everywhere.

Manson's theory that the apostle provided a copy of the letter to go to Ephesus would fit into this concept, such a copy being intended as a lasting memorial to him and a blueprint for intensified evangelization by his friends in the yet unreached regions of the East. But believers at Ephesus must already have been well informed about the

---

[2]For a fuller discussion, see the present writer's *Introduction to the New Testament* (Grand Rapids: Eerdmans, 1971 ed.), pp. 307–311.

gospel after Paul's long ministry in their midst. So Manson's conclusion is speculative.

We should not overlook the distinct possibility that in addition to its evangelistic function Romans may have been designed to meet needs within the congregation, for, alongside its kerygmatic materials, it abounds in teaching. The degree to which Paul was familiar with conditions within the church at Rome may be debatable, but it is highly probable that he knew a good deal about them. Beginning at least from the time of his contact with Priscilla and Aquila at Corinth, he doubtless had a fairly continuous stream of information about the church, especially during his stay at Ephesus, since travel to and from Rome was relatively easy. The number of people listed in chapter 16 suggests many individual sources of information.

Yet for Paul to exhibit on the surface too intimate a knowledge of conditions in the church would be indelicate and might even betray the confidence of his informers. Likewise, to deal with these problems too directly and pointedly would be unseemly in view of his personal detachment from the Roman situation. Consequently, the interpreter is tempted to see in passages that are broad and general in their statement a penetrating relevance the Christians at Rome could hardly avoid seeing as a reference to themselves, compelling them to wonder at the unexpected discernment of an apostle who had not set foot in their city. Especially pertinent in this connection is the tension between Jew and Gentile within the church, two groups that may be approximately identified with the weak and the strong (see 15:1–8). Then there is the warning not to be lifted up with pride because of Israel's being set aside (11:20, 21), followed by a reminder that this setting aside is temporary (11:25, 26). The very fact that Jew and Gentile (rather than mankind) are given so much prominence in the main theme (1:16) and in the section that demonstrates the need for salvation (1:18–3:20) argues for the impact on the apostle of this tension at the time of writing.

6. Literary Form

Of the four types of writing found in the NT (Gospel, Acts, Epistle, Apocalypse) the epistle is by far the most common. The word itself is a transliteration of the Greek *epistolē*, meaning a communication, usually of a written nature. Romans bears this label in 16:22. Paul uses the word fairly often in reference to his correspondence with churches (e.g., 1 Cor 5:9; Col 4:16; 1 Thess 5:27). There is also a reference to his writings in 2 Peter 3:16.

The appropriateness of using "epistle" to describe Paul's written works has been challenged in modern times by Adolph Deissmann,[3] who contended for a distinction between epistle and letter, based not on the form but on the intent of the author. He reasoned that the epistle has a public character, often being of an official nature, intended to be preserved for posterity, whereas the letter is a private communication, dealing with matters of the moment and not expected to survive for scrutiny by future generations. Furthermore, Deissmann pictured Paul as a rough artisan possessed of little literary skill and requiring the aid of a secretary in composing his letters. Such a view is certainly not in accord with the judgment even of Paul's opponents (2 Cor 10:10). C.H. Dodd exposed the fallacy of this view when he acutely observed, "That [Paul] was not born to a proletarian status seems clear from the tone of his letters. A man born to manual

---

[3]*Bible Studies* (Edinburgh, 1901), pp. 3–59; *Paul* (London, 2nd. ed., 1926), pp. 3–26.

labour does not speak self-consciously of 'labouring with my own hands.' " [4] The very fact that we can speak of a Pauline style shows in itself that even when Paul used an amanuensis the mold of his thinking was well preserved. A passage such as 1 Corinthians 13 can hardly be attributed to an assistant.

Deissmann's weakness was his failure to recognize the wide gap between the letters found in the nonliterary papyri and the letters of Paul. The latter are not properly classed as private correspondence; indeed, even the most personal, the letter to Philemon, was directed also to the church that met in his house. So we must conclude that so far as Paul's writings are concerned, the line between private and public letters cannot be sharply drawn. One may with perfect propriety describe them either as letters or as epistles. As letters, they are direct, unstilted, relevant to the needs of the moment; as epistles they convey in elevated and beautiful expression the timeless truth of the gospel intended by God for all generations.

Many have observed that Romans is almost like an essay, showing comparatively little attention to the personal needs and pressing problems of the readers, and in this respect is strikingly different from 1 Corinthians, for example. Such a difference is not unexpected, since Paul did not found the Roman church and was doubtless acquainted with only a limited number of its constituency (ch. 16). But the difference should not be overstated, because there are indications that Paul is to some extent addressing himself to the situation of his readers. For example, he would hardly have allowed himself to discuss the problem of the strong and the weak (14:1–15:7) at such length had he not learned that this was a matter of concern to the Roman church. Again, his warning about "those who cause divisions and put obstacles in your way" (16:17) could reflect awareness of actual threats to the unity and soundness of the church. The source of his information could have been one or more of the friends listed by name in the closing chapter.

7. Theological values

Romans satisfies the craving of the human spirit for a comprehensive exposition of the great truths of salvation set out in logical fashion, supported and illumined by OT Scripture. The systematic element includes due attention to doctrine and life—in that order, because right relations must be established with God before one can live so as to please him and mediate his blessings to others.

The question as to what is most central to the Pauline theology has been long debated. Some have said that it is justification by faith. Others have insisted that the life "in Christ" is the secret, for it lifts one out of the rigidity and barrenness of legal terminology, disclosing the positive and dynamic relationship the believer may have with God's Son. Fortunately, we do not have to choose between these two, because both are important in Paul's presentation. Without justification there can be no life in Christ (5:18), and such life in turn confirms the reality of the justification.

Salvation is the basic theme of Romans (cf. 1:16)—a salvation presented in terms of the righteousness of God, which, when received by faith, issues in life (1:17). It is helpful to realize that salvation, righteousness, and life are eschatological terms. The apostle talks about salvation with a future reference (13:11). Righteousness, too, in the absolute sense, belongs only to the perfected state. Again, life comes to fullness of meaning only in terms

---

[4] *New Testament Studies* (Manchester, England: Manchester Univ. Press, 1953), p. 71.

of the future (6:22; cf. Mark 10:29, 30). Yet all these future realities are to be entered into and enjoyed during the earthly pilgrimage of the saints. Salvation is a present reality (10:10). So is righteousness (4:3–5). So is life (6:23; 8:2). In the last analysis, only the grace of God permits us to participate now in that which properly belongs to the future.

Though Romans does not give special instruction about the Trinity, it clearly delineates the respective responsibilities of the members of the Godhead. The gospel, which is the theme of the letter, is called the gospel of God at the very beginning (1:1) before it is called the gospel of his Son (1:9). God's righteousness must be reckoned with, both by sinner and by saint, for it is the basis of judgment as well as of salvation. The Son of God is held up to view also from the first, because the gospel centers in him (1:3). He is the one through whom the grace of God is mediated to sinful humanity in justification, reconciliation, and redemption. The man Christ Jesus is set over against the first Adam as the one who has succeeded in undoing the ruin wrought by the fall (5:12–21) and who now sustains and preserves all who put their trust in him (5:10). The Spirit's role is to nurture the new creation life of the children of God by providing assurance of their sonship (8:16), release from the bondage of sin (8:2–4), effectiveness in prayer (8:26, 27), experience of the love of God (5:5) and of other joys of spiritual life (14:17), crowned by a confident hope that the bliss of the better state that is to come will be realized (8:23; 15:13). The Spirit also provides the dynamic for Christian service (15:19).

It is not possible, however, to claim for the Epistle a complete coverage of doctrine. Though salvation is central in Romans, its climax in terms of the coming of the Lord is not unfolded to any extent (13:11), though the glorification of the saints is included (8:18, 19, 23). Furthermore, though the word "church" appears five times in chapter 16, it is not a theme for definitive instruction per se. Too much can be made of this seeming incompleteness, however. From chapters 9 to 11 it appears that Paul is deeply concerned about the composition of the church, how Jew and Gentile relate to it in the divine plan. Again, any attempt to deal with the concept of "covenant" is lacking, for the two references (9:4; 11:27) say nothing about the new covenant in Christ (contrast with 2 Cor 3 and Gal 3–4). That there should be no mention of the Lord's Supper may seem strange, especially since baptism is mentioned (6:4). But in Romans Paul is not concerned with ecclesiology, at least not in the sense of giving it specific (as opposed to incidental) treatment. Despite these omissions, it remains true that nowhere else in Scripture is the subject of salvation dealt with in such breadth and thoroughness.

In the so-called practical section of the Epistle (chs. 12–15) the effect of these great truths ("the mercies of God") is set forth in terms of transformed conduct. Christians have a life to live in this world as well as a faith to hold and a fellowship to enjoy. Paul was pastor as well as preacher. In Romans, as in his other letters, his theological teaching was given not merely for the sake of information, but to build up and encourage the people of God.

8. Canonicity

Since ancient authorities regularly include Romans without question, no problem exists in this area. Marcion had it in his list, as did the Canon of Muratori. Although its position in the various lists is not uniform, from the fourth century onward and even in the third (P[46] of the Chester Beatty Papyri collection), Romans stands at the head of the Pauline Epistles. Since it was not the first to be written, its position may be taken as testimony to a growing awareness in the church of its cardinal importance.

9. Special Problems

Only one problem will be dealt with here, a question that has divided students of Romans through the years. It is the problem of the composition of the church at Rome. Were the believers mainly Gentiles or were Jewish Christians in the majority? At the outset, Paul considers his readers Gentiles (1:13) and this should be decisive unless contrary evidence of the strongest sort can be adduced. Such evidence is sometimes held to be available at the point where the apostle speaks of Abraham as "our forefather" (4:1) and in the passage where he treats the law (presumably Mosaic) and says that his readers know it (7:1ff.). Neither of these constitutes compelling evidence.

As to the former item, it means no more than does the apostle's allusion to "our forefathers" in 1 Corinthians 10:1, an obvious reference to Israel in a letter intended for a Gentile church. Paul was careful to teach the spiritual kinship that existed between the Israel of the past and the people of God in the Christian dispensation. In the case of Abraham, this is spelled out clearly when he calls Abraham "the father of all who believe but have not been circumcised" (Rom 4:11). As to the familiarity of Roman Christians with the Mosaic law, two things need to be observed. One is that Paul feels perfectly free to quote the law and other portions of the Hebrew Scriptures even when writing to Gentile churches—e.g., Galatians and Corinthians. Many Gentile converts to the gospel had previously attended the synagogue as God-fearers and there had heard the OT read and expounded.

The second consideration is that in writing to the Galatian churches about the purpose of the law, Paul affirms that it "was put in charge to lead us to Christ" (Gal 3:24). Though Gentiles were not under the law, they were to profit from it as a guide leading and impelling them to Christ as Savior. With consistency, Paul preserves the same stance in writing to the church at Rome.

There remains, however, the awkward fact that the apostle devotes three chapters (9–11) to the nation of Israel. The failure of this people as a whole to turn to Jesus as the Messiah was a source of deep grief to him. One may well ask, Was it not to inform and comfort a church essentially in the same position as himself that he discusses this matter at such length? Not necessarily. Here one can ask a counter question: Would Paul be at pains to warn Gentile believers in direct terms not to take their position for granted and lapse into a false security (11:13ff.) if he were writing for the benefit of a chiefly Hebrew-Christian group?

Going back to the solid fact that Paul addresses the church as Gentile in character (1:13), we must ask ourselves whether chapters 9 to 11 might have a special purpose as addressed to Gentile believers. These people could certainly learn much from the passage—viz., the obvious advantages God had given the Jew, his own sovereignty in setting them apart as his chosen people, his righteousness in cutting them off so far as national privilege was concerned, and his faithfulness to covenant commitments to be seen when the nation by repentance and faith would be restored. Gentile believers could find much here to warn them and much to lead them to prayer and witness on behalf of Israel. When these considerations are added to the generous use of the OT in the development of the theme of Romans, it becomes clear that Paul is concerned lest Gentile Christianity should lose sight of its heritage in OT history and revelation.

10. Bibliography

BOOKS

Barclay, William. *The Letter to the Romans*. Philadelphia: Westminster Press, 1955.
Barrett, C.K. *A Commentary on the Epistle to the Romans*. New York: Harper and Brothers, 1957.
Barth, Karl. *A Shorter Commentary on Romans*. Richmond: John Knox Press, 1959.
_____. *The Epistle to the Romans*. Oxford University Press, E.T. 1933.
Best, Ernest. *The Letter of Paul to the Romans*. Cambridge: Cambridge University Press, 1967.
Black, Matthew. *Romans*. NCB. Greenwood: Attic Press, 1973.
Bruce, F.F. *The Epistle of Paul to the Romans*. TNTC. Grand Rapids: Eerdmans, 1963.
Calvin, John. *Commentary on the Epistle of Paul the Apostle to the Romans*. Grand Rapids: Eerdmans, 1947.
Cranfield, C.E.B. *A Commentary on Romans 12–13*. Edinburgh: Oliver and Boyd, 1965.
Denney, James. *St. Paul's Epistle to the Romans*. EGT (vol. II). London: Hodder and Stoughton, 1917.
Dodd, C.H. *The Epistle of Paul to the Romans*. Moffatt NT Com. New York: Harper and Brothers, 1932.
Field, Frederick. *Notes on the Translation of the New Testament*. Cambridge: Cambridge University Press, 1899.
Gifford, E.H. *The Epistle of St. Paul to the Romans*. London: John Murray, 1886.
Godet, F. *Commentary on St. Paul's Epistle to the Romans*. Edinburgh: T. & T. Clark, 2 vols. E.T. 1883–84.
Haldane, Robert. *Exposition of the Epistle to the Romans*. New York: Robert Carter and Bros., 1860.
Hodge, Charles. *A Commentary on the Epistle to the Romans*. New York: Armstrong, 1896.
Hunter, A.M. *The Epistle to the Romans*. London: SCM Press, 1955.
Käsemann, Ernst. *An die Römer*. Handbuch z. NT. Tübingen: J.C.B. Mohr, 1973.
_____. *New Testament Questions Today*. Philadelphia: Fortress Press, E.T. 1969.
Knox, John. *The Epistle to the Romans*. IB vol. 9. New York: Abingdon Press, 1954.
Lagrange, M.J. *Épître aux Romains*. Paris: Gabalda. 6th ed., 1950.
Leenhardt, Franz J. *The Epistle to the Romans*. London: Lutterworth Press, E.T. 1961.
Liddon, H.P. *Explanatory Analysis of St. Paul's Epistle to the Romans*. London: Longman, Green and Co., 1893.
Luther, Martin. *Commentary on the Epistle to the Romans*. Grand Rapids: Zondervan, E.T. 1954.
Meyer, H.A.W. *Critical and Exegetical Handbook to the Epistle to the Romans*. New York: Funk and Wagnalls, E.T. 1884.
Michel, Otto. *Der Brief and die Römer*. Göttingen: Vandenhoeck & Ruprecht, 1955.
Moule, Handley C.G. *Epistle of St. Paul to the Romans*. 5th ed. New York: Armstrong, 1902.
Munck, Johannes. *Christ and Israel; an Interpretation of Romans 9–11*. Philadelphia: Fortress Press, E.T. 1967.
_____. *Paul and the Salvation of Mankind*. Richmond: John Knox Press, E.T. 1959.
Murray, John. *The Epistle to the Romans*. NIC. Grand Rapids: Eerdmans, 1968.
Nygren, Anders. *Commentary on Romans*. Philadelphia: Muhlenberg Press, E.T. 1949.
Richardson, Peter. *Israel in the Apostolic Church*. Cambridge: Cambridge University Press, 1969.
Sanday, William and Headlam, Arthur C. *A Critical and Exegetical Commentary on the Epistle to the Romans*. ICC. Edinburgh: T. & T. Clark, 5th ed., 1925.
Schlatter, A. *Gottes Gerechtigkeit*. Stuttgart: Calwer Verlag, 1952.
Shedd, William G.T. *A Critical and Doctrinal Commentary upon the Epistle of St. Paul to the Romans*. New York: Scribner's, 1879.
Stifler, James M. *The Epistle to the Romans*. New York: Revell, 1897.
Thomas, W.H. Griffith. *St. Paul's Epistle to the Romans*. 3 vols. London: The Religious Tract Society, n.d.
Ziesler, J.A. *The Meaning of Righteousness in Paul*. Cambridge: Cambridge University Press, 1972.

ARTICLES

Borg, Marcus. "A New Context for Romans xiii." NTS 19 (Jan. 1973) 205–218.
Bring, Ragnar. "Paul and the Old Testament." ST 25 (1971) 21–60.
Danker, F.W. "Romans V.12: Sin under Law." NTS 14 (April 1968) 424–439.
Dinkler, Erich. "The Historical and Eschatological Israel in Romans Chapters 9–11: A Contribution to the Problem of Predestination and Individual Responsibility." JR 36 (1956) 109–127.
Donfried, Karl Paul. "A Short Note on Romans 16." JBL 89 (1970) 441–449.
Reumann, John. "The Gospel of the Righteousness of God." INT 20 (1966) 432–452.

11. Outline

    I. Introduction (1:1–15)

       A. Salutation (1:1–7)

       B. Paul and the Church at Rome (1:8–15)

   II. Theme: The Gospel As the Revelation of God's Righteousness (1:16, 17)

  III. The Need for Salvation: The Plight of Mankind (1:18–3:20)

       A. In the Pagan World (1:18–32)

       B. Principles of Judgment (2:1–16)

       C. Specific Guilt of the Jew (2:17–3:8)

       D. Summary (3:9–20)

   IV. Justification: The Imputation of Righteousness (3:21–5:21)

       A. The Description of Justification (3:21–26)

       B. The Availability of Justification Through Faith Alone (3:27–31)

       C. The Illustration of Justification From the Old Testament (4:1–25)

          1. The case of Abraham (4:1–5)

          2. The case of David (4:6–8)

          3. The promise to Abraham—apart from circumcision (4:9–12)

          4. The promise to Abraham—apart from the law (4:13–17)

          5. Abraham's faith the standard for every believer (4:18–25)

       D. The Benefits of Justification (5:1–11)

       E. The Universal Applicability of Justification (5:12–21)

    V. Sanctification: The Impartation of Righteousness (6:1–8:39)

       A. The Believer's Union With Christ in Death and Resurrection Life (6:1–14)

          1. The statement of the fact (6:1–10)

          2. The appeal based on the fact (6:11–14)

       B. Union With Christ Viewed As Enslavement to Righteousness (6:15–23)

       C. Union With Christ Viewed As Deliverance From Law (7:1–6)

       D. The Relationship Between Law and Sin (7:7–25)

       E. The Blessings of Life in the Spirit (8:1–39)

          1. Liberation by the Spirit from the law of sin and death (8:1–11)

          2. Additional ministries of the Spirit (8:12–27)

          3. The security and permanence of the life of the redeemed (8:28–39)

   VI. The Problem of Israel: God's Righteousness Vindicated (9:1–11:36)

       A. Paul's Sorrow Over Israel's Condition (9:1–5)

       B. God's Choice of Israel Based on Election, not on Natural Generation or Works of Merit (9:6–13)

       C. God's Freedom to Act in His Own Sovereign Right (9:14–29)

Text and Exposition

I. Introduction

A. *Salutation*

1:1-7

> ¹Paul, a servant of Christ Jesus, called to be an apostle and set apart for the gospel of God—²the gospel he promised beforehand through his prophets in the Holy Scriptures ³regarding his Son, who as to his human nature was a descendant of David, ⁴and who through the Spirit of holiness was declared with power to be the Son of God by his resurrection from the dead: Jesus Christ our Lord. ⁵Through him and for his name's sake, we received grace and apostleship to call people from among all the Gentiles to the obedience that comes from faith. ⁶And you also are among those who are called to belong to Jesus Christ.
>
> ⁷To all in Rome who are loved by God and called to be saints:
>
> Grace and peace to you from God our Father and from the Lord Jesus Christ.

1 As in all his letters, Paul uses his Roman name. The shift from "Saul" occurs in the biblical context where he came in contact with a Roman official (Acts 13:6–12). Paul's relation to Christ is primary, so to express his attachment to his Lord he uses the term "servant." Some prefer the rendering "slave," but this could suggest an unwilling attachment. In Israel the citizenry regarded themselves as servants of their king, even though they were free men. Since this word *doulos* is used of Christ in relation to the Father (Phil 2:7), where "slave" would be inappropriate, the translation "servant" is altogether fitting here. By beginning in this fashion, the writer is putting himself on the same plane as his readers. He does not seek to dominate them. If "servant" expresses Paul's commitment to Christ, "apostle" sets forth his authority as Christ's appointee—his right not only to preach the gospel (believers in general could do that) but to found and supervise churches and if necessary discipline them. But this authority carries with it responsibility, for he must give account of the conduct of his mission (1 Cor 4:1–4).

Paul has been "set apart" for the gospel of God. As a Pharisee he had been set apart to a life of strict observance of Jewish law and custom. Now his life work is to further the gospel, the good news that God has for man. It is most natural to locate the time of this setting apart at Paul's conversion and commission (Acts 9:15; Gal 1:12).

2 Before the historic events providing the basis for the gospel message unfolded, God "promised" the good news in the prophetic Scriptures. Promise means more than prophecy, because it commits the Almighty to make good his word, whereas a prophecy could be just an advance announcement of something that would happen. The concept permeates this Epistle (4:13–25; 9:4; 15:8). God did not invent the gospel to cover up disappointment over Israel's failure to receive the Lord Jesus. Nor did Paul create the gospel, which was "his" (2:16; 16:25) in an entirely different sense. The reference to Scripture prepares the reader for rather copious use of the OT, beginning with 1:17.

3,4 The gospel centers in God's Son, who had this status before he took "human nature" and who, in becoming man, became not only an Israelite (9:5) but a son of David (Matt 1:1; Luke 1:32; Acts 13:22, 23; 2 Tim 2:8), a qualification he needed as Messiah (Isa 11:1).

By beginning with the sonship, Paul guards his whole statement from doing service for a heretical adoptionist Christology. The period of Christ's earthly life and ministry was followed by another phase—that which resulted from his resurrection. "With power" may belong with "declared," but may with greater warrant be joined with "Son of God," indicating the new quality of life Jesus had after his resurrection (Phil 3:10; Col 1:29).

"Spirit of holiness" is a unique expression generally regarded as a Semitism conveying the same concept as "Holy Spirit." There may be a suggestion here that Jesus, anointed and sustained by the Holy Spirit in the days of his flesh, was acknowledged by the fact of resurrection to have successfully endured the tests and trials of his earthly life, having been obedient even to death. By resurrection he has become a life-giving spirit (1 Cor 15:45). His rising was indeed "from the dead." But Paul says more, namely, "of the dead," suggesting that Christ is the forerunner of others in this transformation (cf. 1 Cor 15:20, 21).

Another approach emphasizes the balanced construction of *kata pneuma* placed over against *kata sarka*, suggesting that the person of the Son is in view throughout (cf. 1 Tim 3:16). This could yield the conclusion that the human nature of Jesus was so holy, so absolutely free of sin, that death could not hold him (cf. Acts 2:24). On this view, there is no mention of the Holy Spirit.

Appropriately, Jesus Christ is now described as "our Lord." Though the title was fitting during his earthly ministry, it attained more frequent use and greater meaning following the resurrection (Acts 2:36; 10:36). Notable is the fact that in this initial statement about the gospel nothing is said concerning the redeeming work of Christ, which is reserved for later consideration (3:21-26; 4:25; 5:6-21). It was the infinite worth of the Son that made his saving work possible.

5-7 Now the apostle returns to his responsibility to proclaim the good news (cf. v.1). Two problems present themselves here, and they are somewhat related. Who is indicated by "we," and how should one understand the phrase "all the Gentiles"? Clearly, in using "we," Paul cannot be including his readers, because they did not possess apostleship. Could he be referring to other apostles, of whom the Roman believers must have heard? This is a possibility, though it is an unexpected development and is not amplified. The problem is complicated by the mention of the intended sphere of labor— "among all the Gentiles." This wording makes the limitation of the "we" to Paul (as a literary plural) natural, since the Gentiles constituted his special field of labor (cf. 15:16, 18, where the word "obey" corresponds to the word "obedience" in this passage). On the other hand, "all the Gentiles" can equally well be rendered, "all the nations" or "all peoples" (cf. Matt 28:19). This would favor the wider reference of "we" to all the apostles, since Israel would be included as one of the peoples. It is difficult to decide this question.

The desired response to the gospel message is "obedience that comes from faith." (For obedience, see 15:18; 16:26 and for faith, 1:16, 17; 10:17.) Paul's readers were not called, as he was, to apostleship; they were called "to belong to Jesus Christ" and to be "saints," the common term designating believers. This term has almost the same force as the expression Paul uses for himself—"set apart" (v.1). While it does not indicate actual condition (as opposed to position), it carries the aroma of holiness to which every child of God is called (6:19, 22).

At length the apostle is ready to extend a greeting to his readers—"grace and peace." Ordinary letters of that period usually contained a single word meaning "greeting" (as in James 1:1). Paul, however, is partial to terms with theological import. He desires for his readers a continuing and deepening experience of spiritual blessing that only God can bestow. Father and Son are the joint benefactors. While the NT contains several explicit statements of the deity of our Lord, in addition it has many that imply his godhood, as in this case. People may long for grace and peace, but only God can grant such gifts. The rich meaning of these terms will emerge as Paul uses them in the body of his work.

Notes

3,4 A frequently expressed opinion holds that Paul is here making use of a Christological formula not original with him but presumably known to the Roman church. This judgment is based on the absence of mention of the Davidic descent in the Pauline Epistles (2 Tim 2:8 is regarded as deutero-Pauline), the unparalleled use of "Spirit of holiness," and likewise the use of ὁρίζω (*horizō*—a word attributed to Paul in Acts 17:31 but not appearing in his writings), the absence of any reference to the death of Christ, etc. Unquestionably, there are brief creedal statements in Paul (e.g., 1 Cor 8:6), and there may be enough data to warrant the conclusion in this case that the passage is pre-Pauline. However, it is worth noting that in Acts 13:33–35 Paul is credited with emphasizing in close connection with each other three items found in Romans 1:3, 4, namely, the sonship of the Messiah, his relation to David, and his resurrection from the dead.

B. *Paul and the Church at Rome*

1:8–15

> [8]First, I thank my God through Jesus Christ for all of you, because your faith is being reported all over the world. [9]God, whom I serve with my whole heart in preaching the gospel of his Son, is my witness how constantly I remember you [10]in my prayers at all times; and I pray that now at last by God's will the way may be opened for me to come to you.
> [11]I long to see you so that I may impart to you some spiritual gift to make you strong—[12]that is, that you and I may be mutually encouraged by each other's faith. [13]I do not want you to be unaware, brothers, that I planned many times to come to you (but have been prevented from doing so until now) in order that I might have a harvest among you, just as I have had among the other Gentiles.
> [14]I am obligated both to Greeks and non-Greeks, both to the wise and the foolish. [15]That is why I am so eager to preach the gospel also to you who are at Rome.

8–10 The salutation has been unusually long and now, instead of moving to his theme at once the apostle still lingers over introductory matters. Doubtless he felt the need of getting acquainted, so to speak, by unburdening his own heart about what his readers mean to him. It is a shining example of his pastoral concern mingled with gracious sensitivity in dealing with the saints.

First of all, Paul must express his thanks to God for his readers. This was customary, and he omitted an expression of thanks only in writing the Galatians. His thanksgiving for the Roman believers is based on their faith (cf. Eph 1:15, 16; Col 1:3, 4; and 1 Thess 1:3).

Not without reason Paul has become known in Christendom as the apostle of faith. To him, faith was the basic Christian virtue, and he was eager to commend it. Here the commendation is exceedingly generous, even hyperbolic. The whole world has heard of their faith (cf. 1 Thess 1:8). It was Paul's habit to praise believers when this was in order. If rebuke had to be given, it would find a more ready reception if the way was prepared by heartfelt appreciation. Paul's statement about his thanksgiving is followed by a statement concerning his prayer—both intercession for them and a special plea that his hope of coming to be with them, providing it is God's will, shall be realized.

But why should Paul find it necessary to summon God as his witness that he had been faithful in praying for the Roman believers? There are two reasons. For one thing, he had been praying "constantly." The Greek word denotes "repeatedly," meaning that there is no great length of time between prayers. This seems almost too much to expect of a man who did not know most of these people. Furthermore, as he will tell his readers later (15:25), he is about to leave for Jerusalem, and this could give the appearance of his not putting the Roman believers first in his plans. Here, as elsewhere, when Paul calls God as his witness, it is because the thing he is claiming seems difficult to believe.

11–13 The apostle confesses to a great desire to see his readers, not simply that he might come to know them personally, but that he might minister to them. By "spiritual gift" we are probably not to understand something charismatic (the purpose, "to make you strong," is not favorable to such a view), since Paul does not specify any particular gift and avoids the plural (cf. 1 Cor 12:1). Moreover, his own prominence in the contemplated bestowal hardly makes room for the specialized gifts of the Spirit (cf. 1 Cor 1:7). But no sooner has this sentiment been expressed than it is halfway recalled, being revised because it seems to suggest that blessing will flow only one way, from Paul to the church. So he alters his language to make room for mutual encouragement and upbuilding. Faith is basically one, but to see it at work in one individual after another, in various ways, adds zest to Christian fellowship. Paul himself needed this.

As he had prayed constantly for the Romans, so he had planned many times to visit them, but again and again the plan had to be set aside. There is no intimation of Satanic opposition as in the case of the Thessalonian church (1 Thess 2:18), so we are left with the supposition that his work in the East had involved him so completely that he did not see his way clear to break away for the projected trip to Rome.

His hope to have "a harvest" among his readers should not be interpreted narrowly, as though he is hinting that some in their ranks are not genuinely saved. His use of the word "Gentiles" instead of "churches" may be a pointer for us, hinting that "among you" is a reference to the community rather than to the church specifically, and that the fruit he envisions is the reaching of the unsaved. This would not exclude fruit-bearing in the sense of the development of the saints in character (Gal 5:22, 23), but the other meaning seems the more obvious.

14,15 Paul looks forward to his visit, but he also considers it an obligation. On what is this based? He has already laid the groundwork for such a statement by acknowledging that he is Christ's servant (v.1) and that he has been given a charge to take the gospel to all peoples (v.5). In mentioning "Greeks and non-Greeks" he seems to have in mind all non-Jewish members of the human race. He is carrying forward the term he has just used at the end of the previous verse—*Gentiles*.

The Hellenistic writers Philo and Josephus tended to think of the Jews as a third group. Philo in particular had the concept that the Jews, with their special religious advantages, were destined to be the people who, by means of their universal faith, could unify these two diverse groups. In classical and even in early Hellenistic times, the Greeks were prone to include the Latins among the *barbaroi*. But by the time of Paul this was no longer the case. The Romans had become the caretakers of Hellenic civilization. This being so, it is probable that in using *barbaroi* Paul had in mind the territory beyond Rome to the West, where he hoped to go. At the same time, when v.15 is taken into account, it should be granted that he would not have to look beyond Rome itself with its diverse population to find representatives of both groups.

The "wise" are not being equated with the Greeks, for this would mean that non-Greeks are being dubbed "foolish," which would be unwarranted. The wise are perishing in the midst of their worldly wisdom (1 Cor 1:18–21), and the foolish in their abject simplicity. Both need the gospel.

How heartwarming is the apostle's attitude toward his obligation! Instead of considering it a burden he must bear, a duty he must carry out, he is "eager" to fulfill it. If one has the finest intellectual and formal preparation for preaching but is lacking in zeal, he cannot hope for much success. The call to preach and the need for the message together constitute the preacher's compelling incentive to proclaim the message of salvation.

Notes

14 When the word rendered "non-Greeks" is transliterated, it yields "barbarians" (βάρβαροι, *barbaroi*). As one can see, the first two syllables are the same, which points to the original force of this word as indicating a stammerer. Later it came to mean non-Greeks, those who did not use the Greek language. A further development was its application to uncivilized people, taking on the meaning of savage, which is the usual connotation of the word "barbarian" today

II. Theme: The Gospel As the Revelation of the Righteousness of God

1:16,17

[16]I am not ashamed of the gospel, because it is the power of God for the salvation of everyone who believes: first for the Jew, then for the Gentile. [17]For in the gospel a righteousness from God is revealed, a righteousness that is by faith from first to last, just as it is written: "The righteous will live by faith."

16 Having confessed his fervent desire to preach the gospel at Rome, Paul goes on to give a reason for his zeal. He has no sense of reserve about his mission. He does not in any way consider his task unworthy or one that will prove to be illusory. He is ready to challenge the philosophies and religions in Rome that vie for the attention of men, because he knows on the basis of his experience in the East that God's power at work in the proclamation of the good news is able to transform lives. The Greek word for "power" (*dynamis*) has sometimes elicited the reaction that the gospel is dynamite! This is quite out of place, for the emphasis is not on blowing false religions out of the way or blasting a trail of success for the true faith or even on delivering people from habits they have been unable to shake off. Paul himself goes on to explain in what sense

"power" is to be understood. The stress falls not on its mode of operation but on its intrinsic efficacy. It offers something not to be found anywhere else—a righteousness from God. More about that directly.

Closer at hand is the linkage between power and salvation. Judaism was prone to think of the law as power, but this is not affirmed in Scripture. As for salvation, the OT is clear in its teaching that whether it is conceived of physically as deliverance (Exod 14:13) or spiritually (Ps 51:12), it comes from the Lord. This is maintained in the NT as well, and is affirmed in Paul's statement that the gospel is "the power of God" for salvation. So if the apostle permits himself to say that if he himself saves anyone (1 Cor 9:22), it is only in the sense that he is Christ's representative who is able to point out the way to his fellowmen.

Salvation is a broad concept. It includes the forgiveness of sins, but involves much more, because its basic meaning is soundness or wholeness. It promises the restoration of all that sin has marred or destroyed. It is the general term that unites in itself the particular aspects of truth suggested by justification, reconciliation, sanctification, and redemption. But its efficacy depends on man's willingness to receive the message. "Everyone who believes" will benefit equally. This sweeping declaration ties in with the previous statement (concerning Greeks and non-Greeks) and now includes both the Jew and the Gentile. The Jew receives "first" consideration. This does not mean that every Jew must be evangelized before the gospel can be presented to Gentiles. But it does mean that God, after having dealt in a special way with the Jew in OT days and having followed this by sending his Son to the lost sheep of the house of Israel, could not pass by this people. To them was given the first opportunity to receive the Lord Jesus, both during his ministry (John 1:11) and in the Christian era (Acts 1:8; 3:26). Paul himself followed this pattern (Acts 13:45, 46: 28:25, 28). It is a case of historical priority, not essential priority, for the Jew who is first to hear the gospel is also the first to be judged for his sins (2:9).

17 Next, the apostle passes to an explanation of his statement that the gospel means salvation for those who receive it by faith. The reason given is that this salvation discloses "a righteousness from God." Paul is dependent here on the OT (Isa 46:12, 13, KJV, NASB; 61:10). "In the Hebrew tradition, early and late, God's righteousness is the way he acts, and notably the way he acts in maintaining the covenant" (Ziesler, p. 186). Such an idea was quite foreign to Greek thought. Clearly, the character of God is involved in the sense that what he does and provides must be in keeping with his nature (cf. 3:26). But just as clearly, the expression must go beyond this to include the activity of God. The gospel would not be the good news if it simply disclosed the righteousness of God. Such a message would scarcely demand faith. In view of man's sinful state, it could well create fear. But if salvation as God provides it and offers it is fully in keeping with his righteous character, then it has integrity. If it satisfies God, man can be content with it.

Returning to the idea of activity, we should look at Paul's statement in Philippians 3:9, where he contrasts his pre-Christian state, in which he had a righteousness based on observance of the law, with his present situation, in which he rests on a righteousness which is of (from) God, based on faith. In summary, God's righteousness in this context, while it has an implied reference to his character, stresses divine provision. What this entails will be unfolded in due course. Paul had already taught that Christ was the medium for the bringing of righteousness from God to sinful man (1 Cor 1:30; 2 Cor 5:21).

Somewhat baffling is the twofold reference to faith—lit. "from faith to faith" (Gr., *ek pisteōs eis pistin*); cf. NIV "by faith from first to last." We should try to determine first of all whether these two prepositional phrases are to be joined to the verb "revealed," or whether they should be taken with God's righteousness as indicating how that righteousness is to be received. Position in the sentence may be said to favor the former alternative, but the resultant sense is obscure. Furthermore, when Paul restates the theme of his letter (3:21, 22) in such a way as to take account of the intervening material, he mentions God's righteousness as manifested (answering to "revealed" in 1:17), then repeats the word "righteousness" and characterizes it as a righteousness through faith (*dia pisteōs*) and for all who believe. These phrases are probably to be understood as a recapitulation of what has been said in 1:17.

Assuming, then, that we are to connect the statement about faith with God's righteousness, we must still inquire into the distinctives of the two phrases involving faith. Among the numerous suggestions are these: from the faith of the preacher to the faith of the hearer; from OT faith to NT faith (based on the quotation immediately following); entirely from faith; and from faithfulness (God's) to faith (man's), as Barth interprets it (*The Epistle to the Romans*, 1933). These various renderings understand "from" as a point of departure. This would be entirely legitimate if the preposition were *apo*, but it is *ek*, which Paul uses repeatedly with faith when indicating the basis on which God grants justification (3:26; 5:1; Gal 2:16) or righteousness (9:30; 10:6), a fact that incidentally shows how readily the term "righteousness" can take on the force of "justification." The really troublesome element here is the second phrase—"for faith." Perhaps what it conveys is the necessity of issuing a reminder to the believer that justifying faith is only the beginning of Christian life. The same attitude must govern him in his continuing experience as a child of God.

It remains to treat the quotation from another standpoint—the order of the words. Is it "The righteous shall live by faith" or "The one who is just by virtue of faith shall live"? Since the apostle quotes the same passage in Galatians 3:11 to show that one is not justified by law but rather by faith, it is probable that he intends the reference in the same way here. Since the quotation is used in Romans at the very beginning, where he confronts the problem of man's getting right with God, the wording that fits most closely the movement of thought should be chosen. At this point Paul is not concerned with how the justified man lives, but how the sinner can be considered just (righteous) in the sight of God. Righteousness as a matter of ethical conduct is reserved for later treatment (chs. 6–8). Ethical righteousness depends on right relation to God, so the latter merits priority of treatment.

It could be argued, of course, that Paul ought to have changed the order of the words to bring this out, and since he did not, the wording of the quotation, "The righteous will live by faith," should be retained. Apparently he was not desirous of disturbing the form of a familiar quotation. We know that he would endorse the truth that the Christian is not only justified by faith but is also expected to live by faith in order to please God. Such an emphasis has its place, but only when the initial problem of the sinner has been met. The liberty involved in using a quotation in a way somewhat different from its original setting is necessitated by the progress of revelation. It was practiced also in Judaism before Paul's time, as we know from the Dead Sea Scrolls. The Qumran group applied Habakkuk 2:4 to their own situation by an interpretative elaboration. "But the righteous through his faithfulness shall live. This refers to all in Jewry who carry out the Law" (*Commentary on the Book of Habakkuk*). Here the passage is made to do service in behalf of the special type of piety, grounded in the study of the Torah, which distinguished the Qumran community.

Notes

17 Of the various efforts to handle the two phrases, Barth's is the most intriguing. It has an element of plausibility in that πίστις (*pistis*) can mean "faithfulness" as well as "faith," and this could be the sense of the LXX rendering of Habakkuk 2:4, the passage from which Paul proceeds to quote. The LXX reading can be translated, "The just shall live by my faithfulness" or "The just shall live by faith in me" (cf. the construction in Rom 3:26). There is no doubt that the Hebrew אֱמוּנָה (*ʾemunāh*) means "faithfulness," but the Hebrew text reads "his faithfulness" and refers this to the just man, not to God. It is likely that Paul is reaching beyond faithfulness to what underlies it, namely, faith. He uses *pistis* in Romans 3:3 when writing of God's faithfulness, but when he states his theme, the argument requires him to insist on the more fundamental concept of faith. The very fact that in the previous verse he has posited faith (in its verbal form) as the necessary condition for receiving salvation creates a presumption that faith in v.17 will have the same connotation.

III. The Need for Salvation: The Plight of Mankind (1:18–3:20)

Instead of plunging at once into an exposition of the gospel, Paul launches into a lengthy exposure of the sinfulness of man. This is sound procedure, for until men are persuaded of their lost condition they are not likely to be concerned about deliverance. So Paul undertakes to demonstrate in the human situation a grievous lack of the righteousness God requires. "Within the action of the divine righteousness there is a place for deliverance and for condemnation, a place for salvation and for punishment" (David Hill, *Greek Words and Hebrew Meanings* [Cambridge: Cambridge University Press, 1967], p. 90).

A. *In the Pagan World*

1:18–32

18The wrath of God is being revealed from heaven against all the godlessness and wickedness of men who suppress the truth by their wickedness, 19since what may be known about God is plain to them, because God has made it plain to them. 20For since the creation of the world God's invisible qualities—his eternal power and divine nature—have been clearly seen, being understood from what has been made, so that men are without excuse.

21For although they knew God, they neither glorified him as God nor gave thanks to him, but their thinking became futile and their foolish hearts were darkened. 22Although they claimed to be wise, they became fools 23and exchanged the glory of the immortal God for images made to look like mortal man and birds and animals and reptiles.

24Therefore God gave them over in the sinful desires of their hearts to sexual impurity for the degrading of their bodies with one another. 25They exchanged the truth of God for a lie, and worshiped and served created things rather than the Creator—who is forever praised. Amen.

26Because of this, God gave them over to shameful lusts. Even their women exchanged natural relations for unnatural ones. 27In the same way the men also abandoned natural relations with women and were inflamed with lust for one another. Men committed indecent acts with other men, and received in themselves the due penalty for their perversion.

28Furthermore, since they did not think it worthwhile to retain the knowledge of God, he gave them over to a depraved mind, to do what ought not to be done. 29They have become filled with every kind of wickedness, evil, greed and depravity. They are full of envy, murder, strife, deceit and malice. They are gossips, 30slanderers, God-haters, insolent, arrogant and boastful; they invent ways of doing evil; they disobey their parents; 31they are senseless, faithless, heartless, ruthless. 32Although they know God's righteous decree that those who do such things deserve death, they not only continue to do these very things, but also approve of those who practice them.

18 At the outset it is important to observe the correlation between righteousness and wrath. Both are represented as *being* revealed. As previously observed, full salvation in terms of divine righteousness awaits the future, being eschatological in nature; but it also belongs to the present and is appropriated by faith. Similarly, wrath is an even more obviously eschatological concept, yet it is viewed here as parallel to the manifestation of righteousness, belonging therefore to the present age. It is "being revealed." This means that the unfolding of history involves a disclosure of the wrath of God against sin, seen in the terrible corruption and perversion of human life. This does not mean that the price of sin is to be reckoned only in terms of the present operation of wrath, for there is a day of judgment awaiting the sinner (2:5). But the divine verdict is already in some measure anticipated. "We think that Paul regards the monstrous degradation of pagan populations, which he is about to describe, not as a purely natural consequence of their sin, but as a solemn intervention of God's justice in the history of mankind, an intervention which he designates by the term *paradidonai—to give over*" (Godet, in loc.).

"God's wrath is being revealed from heaven." The two factors, the designation of the wrath as God's and the addition of the words "from heaven" make it difficult to accept the view of C.H. Dodd (pp. 20–24). He observes that Paul never uses the verb *be angry* with God as its subject. Further, in the Pauline corpus "the wrath of God" appears elsewhere only in Ephesians 5:6 and Colossians 3:6. Otherwise we encounter "wrath" or "the wrath," which appear intended to describe "an inevitable process of cause and effect in a moral universe" (p. 23). But it is precarious to make much of the fact that God is not linked with wrath in every Pauline reference. The context usually makes it clear when the divine wrath is intended. In the passage before us the words "from heaven" are decisive. As G. Dalman points out, the phrase as used in the Gospels means *from God* (*The Words of Jesus* [Edinburgh: T. & T. Clark, 1909], p. 219). Furthermore, since there is a wrath to come that will inevitably involve God, there is no reason why he should not involve himself in manifesting his wrath in the present. Human objection to the idea of the wrath of God is often molded, sometimes unconsciously, by human experience of anger as passion or desire for revenge. But this is only a human display of wrath, and one that is corrupted. God's wrath is not temperamental (cf. 13:4, 5, where its judicial character is evident).

The object of the divine wrath is twofold—"all the godlessness and wickedness of men." Paul explicates the first term in vv.19–27 and the second in vv.28–32. "Godlessness" means a lack of reverence, an impiety that arrays man against God, not simply in terms of neglect but also of rebellion. "Wickedness" means injustice, relating to the vitiating of man's conduct toward his fellows. The two together serve to denote the failure of mankind in terms of the requirements of the two tables of the Decalogue. No distinction is made here between Jews and Gentiles, since "men" is broad enough to include the human race. These are the very areas in which the prophets found fault with Israel. But as the thought unfolds, the culprit appears much more sharply in terms of Gentiles than of Jews.

They "suppress the truth by their wickedness." R.C.H. Lenski observes, "Whenever the truth starts to exert itself and makes them feel uneasy in their moral nature, they hold it down, suppress it. Some drown its voice by rushing into their immoralities; others strangle the disturbing voice by argument and by denial" (*The Interpretation of St. Paul's Epistle to the Romans* [Columbus: Wartburg Press, 1945]). Presumably, the truth referred to here is basically the truth about God (cf. v.25). Suppression of the truth implies knowledge of the truth, and what this involves is explained in the sequel.

19,20 The creation bears clear witness to its Maker, and the evidence is "plain to them." Here Paul enters upon a discussion of what is usually designated natural revelation in distinction from the special revelation that comes through the Scriptures. Four characteristics are noted. First, it is a clear testimony set before the eyes of men, as the word "plain" implies. Second, from the use of "understood," the revelation does not stop with perception, but is expected to include reflection, the drawing of a conclusion about the Creator. Third, it is a constant testimony, maintained "since the creation of the world" (cf. Acts 14:17). Fourth, it is a limited testimony in that it reflects God in certain aspects only—namely, "his eternal power and divine nature." One has to look elsewhere for the disclosure of his love and grace—i.e., to Scripture and especially to the revelation of God in his Son (John 1:14). Natural revelation is sufficient to make man responsible, but is not by itself sufficient to accomplish his salvation. The element of power is common to the two spheres of nature (v.20) and grace (v.16). Acquaintance with it in the former area should prepare men to expect it in the latter. But they have failed and are left without excuse. It is characteristic of man in his sinful state that he knows much more truth than he translates into fitting response.

21-23 Despite the knowledge of God conveyed to them through the creation, men failed to act on it. They "neither glorified him as God nor gave thanks to him." Liddon affirms that these two obligations "embrace the whole cycle of the soul's duty towards God" (in loc.). Man is a religious being, and if he refuses to let God have the place of preeminence that is rightfully his, then he will put something or someone in God's place.

"Their thinking became futile." The suggestion that emerges from this statement is that mythology and idolatry grew out of man's insistent need to recognize some power in the universe greater than himself, coupled with his refusal to give God the place of supremacy. He had to make a substitution. It is highly suggestive that the verb "to become futile" yields a noun form that was used for idols (Acts 14:15). Idols are unreal and unprofitable, and their service can only lead to futility and further estrangement from the true and living God. Pertinent is Daniel's rebuke of Belshazzar (Dan 5:23).

This abandonment of God in favor of inferior objects of worship is traced in a descending scale. "Mortal man" is the first substitution. The Creator is forsaken in preference for the creature. Scripture shows us the deification of man in the case of Nebuchadnezzar. The colossus that appeared in his dream was interpreted by Daniel as pointing to the king himself so far as the head of gold was concerned (Dan 2:38). Wasting no time, the monarch erected an immense statue of gold and compelled his subjects to prostrate themselves before it (Dan 3:1). In Paul's day the cult of Caesar had spread throughout the empire. Before long, Caesar and Christ would be competing for the homage of society. In modern times the western world has outgrown crass idolatry, but humanism has subtly injected the worship of man without the trappings. God is quietly ruled out and man is placed on the throne.

The next stage is worship of the animal kingdom. Verse 23 owes its wording largely to Psalm 106:20. The immediate context refers to the sin of Israel in making a calf at Horeb and bowing down to this molten image. Paul makes one change in the text of the psalm, which reads: "And they changed their glory for the likeness of an ox that eats grass." To the psalmist God is the glory of the Israelites. Paul seems to make the glory of God his spirituality, in contrast to any attempt to express his excellence in physical terms. God's majesty may well be included here. Whereas Paul is dealing with a characteristic sin of paganism, he resorts to OT history for an illustration. God did not and could not condone idolatry in the people he had chosen. His judgment fell heavily when there was no repentance, even to the point of desolation and deportation from the land he had given Israel.

According to the prophetic word, the worship of man and beast will merge during the tribulation period. We read of the beast who will control the world, and we encounter this significant statement; "If anyone has insight, let him calculate the number of the beast, for it is man's number" (Rev 13:18).

24,25 The opening word "therefore" carries the reader all the way back to the mention of the revelation of God's wrath, taking in also what lies between. The false worship just pictured is God's judgment for abandoning the true worship. Man's religion in its various cultic forms is a species of punishment for spurning the revelation God has given of himself in nature.

This should dispose of the naive notion that religion as such is necessarily a beneficial thing for mankind. On the contrary, it is in many cases a means of keeping people so occupied that they never arrive at a confrontation with the true God.

"God gave them over" becomes a refrain (vv.24, 26, 28). For a nuance of the term, see 1 Corinthians 5:5; 1 Timothy 1:20. The same expression is used of God's judgment on Israel for idolatry (Acts 7:42). In our passage the reference is principally to Gentiles (Israel was largely purged of this sin by means of the captivity in Babylon). We are not told how this giving over was implemented, but most likely we are to think of it in negative terms—i.e., that God simply took his hands off and let willful rejection of himself produce its ugly results in human life. There is no suggestion here of direct intervention such as was granted to Israel by sending prophets to expostulate with God's people concerning their unfaithfulness.

At this point a problem must be faced. How is it that we have a reference to sexual immorality in v.24 and again in vv.26, 27? Is this a case of repetition? No, the immorality lies in different areas. The earlier reference is to cultic prostitution, the latter to immoral relations in ordinary life. In reading the OT it is sometimes difficult to determine which type is intended. Fertility cults made use of prostitutes, based on a definite rationale. "This religion was predicated upon the belief that the processes of nature were controlled by the relations between gods and goddesses. Projecting their understanding of their own sexual activities, the worshipers of these deities, through the use of imitative magic, engaged in sexual intercourse with devotees of the shrine, in the belief that this would encourage the gods and goddesses to do likewise. Only by sexual relations among the deities could man's desire for increase in herds and fields, as well as in his own family, be realized" (O.J. Baab, *IDB* 3:932–933). How true is the observation that "their foolish hearts were darkened." Paul was no stranger to the matter he discusses here. Writing from Corinth, where the temple of Aphrodite housed hundreds of cult prostitutes, he must have been keenly aware of this scourge that affected the moral life of the city so adversely.

"They exchanged the truth of God for a lie." Many versions are content to render it thus, but the definite article precedes "lie" and probably should be brought out in the translation. This is *the* lie above all others—the contention that something or someone is to be venerated in place of the true God. Bengel in his *Gnomon* makes the laconic observation that this is "the price of mythology." According to the prophetic word, history will repeat itself in that when the man of lawlessness is revealed and demands to be worshiped, men will follow him and reap ruin because they have refused the truth and have believed the lie (2 Thess 2:3–12). There, too, God gives them over to strong delusion (v.11).

In the passage we are considering, the indictment is that by a wretched exchange men came to worship and serve "created things rather than the Creator." An alternative translation is possible: "more than" in place of "rather than." But the flow of the argument demands the latter. It is not that men grant God a relative honor in their devotion, but none at all. They have wholly rid themselves of him by substituting other objects in his place. This should be sufficient to banish the notion that in the practice of idolatry men simply use the idol as a means of worshiping God (cf. Hos 14:3). Contemplating this abysmal betrayal, the apostle cannot resist an outburst to counteract it. The Creator "is forever praised." God's glory remains, even though unacknowledged by many of his creatures.

26,27 For the second time the sad refrain is sounded—"God gave them over"—this time to immorality, with emphasis on perversion in sexual relations. The sequence Paul follows—idolatry, then immorality—raises a question as to the possibility that a connection between the two is being suggested. What is that connection? Sanday and Headlam make a helpful suggestion. "The lawless fancies of men invented their own divinities. Such gods as these left them free to follow their own unbridled passions" (in loc.). Men went so far as to project their own license onto their gods, as a perusal of the Homeric poems readily reveals. Gifford observes, "The sin against God's nature entails as its penalty sin against man's own nature" (in loc.). Paul's use of "exchanged" is suggestive. The first exchange, that of the truth for the lie, is followed by another—the upsetting of the normal course of nature in sexual relations. Instead of using the ordinary terms for men and women, Paul substitutes "males" and "females." The irony is that this sort of bestiality finds no counterpart in the animal kingdom. Perversion is the unique contrivance of the human species. In bringing this discussion to a close, the apostle uses two expressions, "received" and "due penalty," which in the original involve the idea of recompense, the punishment being in keeping with the offense. These terms serve to underscore the principle of *lex talionis* contained in the words "Because of this, God gave them over. . . ." Sexual deviation contains in itself a recompense, a punishment for the abandonment of God and his ways. This need not demand the conclusion that every homosexual follows the practice in deliberate rebellion against God's prescribed order. What is true historically and theologically is in measure true, however, experientially. The "gay" facade is a thin veil for deep-seated frustration. The folly of homosexuality is proclaimed in its inability to reproduce the human species in keeping with the divine commandment (Gen 1:28). To sum up, what men do with God has much to do with their character and life style. Godet put it well when he said, "A law broods over human existence, a law which is at the same time a divine act: Such as thou makest thy God, such wilt thou make thyself" (in loc.). Throughout the passage man is represented as active—seeing, thinking, doing. He is not represented as victimized, as taken captive against his will, as the dupe of evil influences from outside himself. "Sin comes from the mind, which perverts the judgment. The effect of retribution is to abandon the mind to that depravity" (Henri Maurier, *The Other Covenant* [New York: Newman Press, 1968], p. 185).

28–32 Here the second key word of v.18 ("wickedness" or "injustice") reappears, indicating that this section is to be given over almost totally to a picture of the havoc wrought in human relations because of suppressing the knowledge of God. In the original there is a word play—men disapproved of retaining God in their knowledge, so God in turn gave them over to a "depraved" (lit. "disapproved") mind, which led them in turn to commit all kinds of sin. It is God's function to judge, but men have usurped that prerogative in order to sit in judgment on him and dismiss him from their lives. Sometimes this has taken the form of open and public expression, as in the French and Bolshevik revolutions. The prior emphasis on the mind is in accord with our Lord's appraisal, who traced the wellspring of sinful acts to the inner life rather than to environmental factors (Mark 7:20–23). The depraved mind is explained in terms of what it approves and plans—"to do what ought not to be done," that is, what is "offensive to man even according to the popular moral sense of the Gentiles, i.e., what even natural human judgment regards as vicious and wrong" (H. Schlier, TDNT 3:440).

Scholars have found it difficult to detect any satisfactory classification in the long list of offenses included here, which only confirms the fact that sin is irrational in itself and disorderly in its effects. It can be pointed out, however, that the initial group contains broad, generic descriptions of sin. The first of these, "wickedness" (*adikia*), by its derivation, is the antithesis of righteousness, denoting the absence of what is just. The term "iniquity" expresses it rather well. It necessitates the creation of laws to counteract its disruptiveness, lest society itself be rendered impossible. The next term, "evil," denotes what is evil not in the sense of calamity, but with full ethical overtones, signifying what is sinister and vile. This is the term used when the devil is called "the evil one." The third word, "greed," indicates the relentless urge to acquire more (cf. Col 3:5). "Depravity" is an attempt to render *kakia*, a term which indicates a condition of moral evil, emphasizing its internal and resident character or as Trench describes it, "the evil habit of mind." It is related to the word translated "malice" in our text, but the latter goes further, denoting malignity, a mind-set that attributes evil motives to others without provocation. Among the final twelve descriptions, "God-haters" stands out, since it alone is related directly to an attitude toward the Almighty. But it is not isolated, not introduced without reason. The hatred that vents itself on God readily finds objects of its displeasure among his creatures. When man comes to the place of worshiping himself, overweening and insolent pride is the inevitable attitude assumed toward his fellows. Some of the descriptions Paul uses here are not found again in his writings or elsewhere in the NT, but four of them occur in 2 Timothy 3:2, 3 in predictions of the state of society in the last days.

The final item in the indictment is climactic (v.32). It is prefaced by the reminder that men have not lacked a sufficient knowledge of God's "righteous decree" or requirement (for this word see 2:26; 8:4). If the knowledge of his power and deity (v.20) was sufficient to obligate men to worship God with gratitude for his benefits, the knowledge of his righteousness, innate in their very humanity, was sufficient to remind them that the price of disobedience would be death. Yet men were not deterred from their sinful ways by this realization. In fact, they were guilty of the crowning offense of applauding those who practiced wickedness in its various manifestations. Instead of repenting of their own misdeeds and seeking to deter others, they promoted wrongdoing by encouraging it in their fellows, allying themselves with wanton sinners in defiant revolt against a righteous God.

Some questions need to be raised about vv.18–32. Since the use of the past tense predominates in this section, are we to conclude that Paul has in view some epoch in the past when sin manifested itself with special intensity? This is unlikely, for he moves now and again to the present tense also. The conclusion is that the description fits his own time as well as earlier ages. If this were not so, the passage could scarcely deserve a place in the development of the theme.

Another problem is raised by the sweeping nature of the charge made in this portion of the letter. Are we to think Paul is accusing every pagan of this total list of offenses? Such a conclusion is unwarranted. Sinful man is capable of committing all of them, but not every individual is necessarily guilty of every one.

A further query concerns the originality of the presentation. Was the apostle dependent on earlier sources? Somewhat the same ground is covered in the intertestamental work entitled *Wisdom*, a product of Hellenistic Judaism. It reproaches the nations for their idols and, like Paul, notes a connection between idolatry and fornication (14:12). But the development of the thought is not fully the same, for a resort to idolatry is related to men's ignorance of God (13:1), whereas Paul emphasizes a limited knowledge of God gleaned from his works. In another Jewish source the forsaking of the Lord by the Gentiles is noted as resulting in sexual perversion.

> Sun and moon and stars change not their order; so do ye also change not the law of God in the disorderliness of your doings. The Gentiles went astray, and forsook the Lord, and changed their order, and obeyed stocks and stones, spirits of deceit. But ye shall not be so, my children, recognizing in the firmament, in the earth, and in the sea, and in all created things, the Lord who made all things, that ye become not as Sodom, which changed the order of nature (*Testament of Napthali* 3:2–4).

Undoubtedly, the synagogues of the Dispersion made use of material of this kind in trying to proselytize Gentiles.

B. *Principles of Judgment*

2:1–16

¹You, therefore, have no excuse, you who pass judgment on someone else, for at whatever point you judge the other, you are condemning yourself, because you who pass judgment do the same things. ²Now we know that God's judgment against those who do such things is based on truth. ³So when you, a mere man, pass judgment on them and yet do the same things, do you think you will escape God's judgment? ⁴Or do you show contempt for the riches of his kindness, tolerance and patience, not realizing that God's kindness should lead you to repentance?

⁵But because of your stubbornness and your unrepentant heart, you are storing up wrath against yourself for the day of God's wrath, when his righteous judgment will be revealed. ⁶God "will give to each person according to what he has done." ⁷To those who by persistence in doing good seek glory, honor and immortality, he will give eternal life. ⁸But for those who are self-seeking and who reject the truth and follow evil, there will be wrath and anger. ⁹There will be trouble and distress for every human being who does evil: first for the Jew, then for the Gentile; ¹⁰but

glory, honor and peace for everyone who does good: first for the Jew, then for the Gentile. [11]For God does not show favoritism.

[12]All who sin apart from the law will also perish apart from the law, and all who sin under the law will be judged by the law. [13]For it is not those who hear the law who are righteous in God's sight, but it is those who obey the law who will be declared righteous. [14](Indeed, when Gentiles, who do not have the law, do by nature things required by the law, they are a law for themselves, even though they do not have the law, [15]since they show that the requirements of the law are written on their hearts, their consciences also bearing witness, and their thoughts now accusing, now even defending them.) [16]This will take place on the day when God will judge men's secrets through Jesus Christ, as my gospel declares.

In turning to this section, one can recognize considerable resemblance to 1:18–32. Human inadequacy in the light of divine standards continues to characterize the discussion (cf. 2:1, "no excuse," with 1:20, "without excuse"). The indictment continues to be stated first in broad terms, with no indication whether the people in view are Jews or Gentiles (cf. 1:18; 2:1), but as the picture unfolds, the Jew takes shape before our eyes just as the Gentile has come into focus in the previous section. Likewise, in both portions, general terms for sin are followed by very specific accusations (cf. 1:18 with 1:23, 26–32 and 2:1–16 with 2:17–29).

1–4 A stylistic change occurs here as the apostle enters into dialogue with an imagined interlocutor who has absorbed what was said up to this point and shows by his attitude that he is in hearty agreement with the exposure of Gentile wickedness. That Paul had experienced such encounters in his missionary preaching is hardly open to doubt. We have an echo here of just such occasions.

The implication in the opening verse is that a Jewish auditor, heartily endorsing the verdict rendered concerning the Gentiles, fails to realize his own plight. True judgment rests on the ability to discern the facts in a given case. If one is able to see the sin and hopelessness of the Gentile, he should logically be able to see himself as being in the same predicament. But he is so taken up with the faults of others that he does not consider his own failures (cf. Matt 7:2, 3). The charge that he who passes judgment does the same things he sees in others is enlarged in 2:17–24. There is a real sting in the allegation "you ... do the same things," for the word "do" is the term used in 1:32 for the practices of the benighted Gentile. Paul repeats it in v.2. As he moves to state the first of the principles of divine judgment, he carries the observer with him. Surely this man will agree ("we know") that when God pronounces judgment on those who make a practice of indulging in sin, his judgment is based on truth. This has no reference to the truth of the gospel, but simply means that the judgment is reached on the basis of reality, on the facts of the case, not on the basis of appearances or of a man's pretensions. "Do you think you will escape God's judgment?" Two words are emphatic here, "think" and "you." Paul is reading the inmost thoughts of the Jew, whom he understands thoroughly from his own pre-Christian experience. That Judaism could be guilty of such complacency is clear from a passage in *Wisdom* that follows immediately on the portion already noted about pagan idolatry and immorality. "But thou, our God, art gracious and true, longsuffering, and in mercy ordering all things. For even if we sin, we are thine, knowing thy dominion; but we shall not sin, knowing that we have been accounted thine: for to be acquainted with thee is perfect righteousness" (15:1–3).

Paul carries the probing deeper still (v.4), suggesting that in addition to self-righteousness with its accompanying false security there is an ignoring and despising of the fact that God, to be true to himself, must bring sin into judgment. There is even a scornful attitude toward God's forbearance with his people Israel, as though that forbearance were but a confirmation of their security, if not a sign of weakness on God's part. "Because sentence against an evil deed is not executed speedily, the heart of the sons of men is fully set to do evil" (Eccl 8:11). God's kindness toward Israel, noted here, is noted again at a later point in Romans (11:22).

In this passage "tolerance" and "patience" seem to be explanatory of "kindness," which is repeated as the governing thought. The word rendered "tolerance" has the idea of self-restraint. In classical Greek it is used of a temporary truce. "Patience" is literally "longspiritedness." The intent of the kindness is to give opportunity for repentance (cf. 2 Peter 3:15), a term that occurs only here in Romans, though it must have been often on Paul's lips in preaching (Acts 20:21). In this Epistle he places greater emphasis on faith.

5–11 The apostle speaks plainly in order to startle the Jew out of his lethargy of self-deception. What the nation is doing by its stubbornness and impenitence is to invite retribution, which is slowly but surely building up a reservoir of divine wrath that will be crushing when it breaks over the guilty in the day of reckoning. Then the judgment will be revealed, patent to all, in contrast to the indirect working of God's wrath in the present scene, as depicted in chapter 1. At that time a second principle of divine judgment will become apparent, emphasizing performance: "to each person according to what he has done," literally, "according to his works." Profession does not take the place of production. This is very close in sense to the first principle. In view of the comprehensiveness of the passage as a whole, it will hardly do to explain this day of wrath as the destruction of Jerusalem in A.D. 70. The explicit statement that God "will give to each person according to what he has done" points to the final reckoning. National judgment fits into a temporal scheme, but personal judgment belongs to the frontier of the ages to come. The use of the word "day" is decisive enough to settle the issue.

In amplifying this second principle of judgment Paul makes room for only two broad classes—those who persist in doing good and those who follow an evil course (vv.7, 8, 9, 10). The first group, pictured as seeking glory, honor, and immortality, are promised eternal life. Because of the further statement of v.10 that some are to receive glory, honor, and peace, it is tempting to suppose that in v.7 the corresponding three items stated there are the things to be received and that the seeking has eternal life as its object, but this is not permitted by the construction in the Greek. What can the apostle mean by his breathtaking assertion about attaining eternal life? At the very least, it is safe to say that he is not contradicting what he says later about the impossibility of having salvation by means of the works of the law (3:20). Far from teaching a system of salvation by works, the statement of v.7, rightly understood, teaches the opposite. "The reward of eternal life . . . is promised to those who do not regard their good works as an end in themselves, but see them as marks not of human achievement but of hope in God. Their trust is not in their good works, but in God, the only source of glory, honour, and incorruption" (Barrett, in loc.). Paul is simply portraying the motivation and the tenor of the life that will culminate in eternal fellowship with God. As applied to the "seeker" (cf. Acts 17:27), the principle commits God to honor the moral aim and provide the means for making a decision, as we see in the case of the Ethiopian eunuch (Acts 8) and Cornelius (Acts 10). Both were seekers making use of the light they had. The good works the believer performs do not bring him salvation, but they attest the salvation he has received by faith (6:22), and therefore have an essential function (cf. Eph 2:8–10).

On the other side of the ledger we find a pattern of evil defined in terms of self-seeking and rejection of the truth leading to divine wrath in terms of trouble and distress. In the statement "who reject the truth and follow evil" (better, "wickedness") we detect a distinct echo of 1:18. Destiny does not depend on whether one is Jew or Gentile. The Jew is mentioned first simply because of God's prior dealing with him in history. Mention of the two divisions of mankind leads naturally to the pronouncement of the third principle: God's judgment is impartial. He "does not show favoritism" (v.11). This is the truth that Peter learned in the Cornelius incident (Acts 10:34). Paul's explanation of what it involves belongs to the following paragraph.

12–16 The principle of impartiality has to face a problem as soon as the two groups, Jews and Gentiles, are considered together. God has not dealt with them in similar fashion. To the Jew he has given a revelation of himself in Scripture that has been denied the Gentile. But in this section Paul will show that the Gentile does have *a* law, and this suffices as a basis for judgment. Before discussing this law, however, Paul sees in it no power to save, for "all who sin apart from the law will also perish apart from the law." The Gentile does not perish for the reason that he lacks the law which the Jew possesses, but because he sins. In speaking of the Jew, Paul says he "will be judged" by the law, but this does not imply exoneration, for no Jew has succeeded in keeping the law.

The expression "all who sin under the law" could strike a Jewish reader as incongruous, but Paul is linking sin with law deliberately in order to prepare the way for his next statement to the effect that the righteous are not those who "hear the law." We have a reminder in James 1:22–24 of the ease with which the Jew could hear the law read and go away without any effect on his life and conduct. Those who will be "declared righteous" are the doers of the law (v.13). This is the first occurrence in Romans of the important expression "be declared righteous." Full treatment of this matter must wait until we encounter the term again in chapter 3. Sometimes the verb *dikaioō* may have a general, as opposed to a theological, frame of reference, as in the statement "Wisdom is proven right by all her children" (Luke 7:35), where vindication is clearly intended. But the passage before us is dealing with law, sin, and judgment, so that the full theological significance of the word should be retained.

Paul's purpose is to undercut the position of the Jew who is counting on his (limited) obedience to the law for acceptance with God. His compliance would have to be perfect if he were to be declared righteous by an absolutely righteous God (cf. Luke 10:28; contrast Luke 8:12). By analogy, the Gentile is in essentially the same position, seeing that he also is not without law, as Paul goes on to indicate. The future tense of the verb ("will be declared righteous") favors the conclusion that final judgment is in view. Paul is not raising false hopes here; on the contrary, he is dashing them—in keeping with the movement of thought. Only after the flimsy edifice of humanly contrived righteousness has been leveled will the apostle be ready to put in its place the sturdy foundation of the justification provided by God in Christ. Though Paul usually uses the verb "justify" in a realized and positive sense (e.g., 3:24), here the frame of reference is eschatological and negative.

The opening word of v.14—"indeed"—is important as showing that in the discussion of the Gentile situation to which Paul now turns he has in mind a presentation designed to counter the boastfulness of the Jew. He seems anxious to avoid the impression that he is discussing the Gentiles in their entirety (he says "Gentiles," not "the Gentiles"). He is thinking of them in individual terms, not as masses. Furthermore, if he encompassed all men save the Jews in his statement, the contrast with the adverse picture of pagans in chapter 1 would be so startling as to suggest contradiction. There are Gentiles who, despite their apparent disadvantage in not possessing the Mosaic law, "do by nature" what the law requires.

What are these things? Presumably, they are not matters peculiar to the law of Moses, but moral and ethical requirements widely recognized and honored in mankind general-ly. It is a commonplace of rabbinic teaching that Abraham kept the laws of Sinai long before they were given. Philo taught a correspondence between the law and nature, saying that Moses "wished to show that the enacted ordinances are not inconsistent with nature" (*On Abraham*, 5). Again, Philo notes that Moses begins his work with an account of the creation of the world, "implying that the world is in harmony with the Law, and the Law with the world, and that the man who observes the law is constituted thereby a loyal citizen of the world, regulating his doings by the purpose and will of Nature, in accordance with which the entire world itself also is administered" (*On the Creation*, 3).

Paul states that such men as he has in mind are "a law for themselves." By no means does he intend to say that they are indifferent to any law except that which they invent in their self-interest. On the contrary, he goes on to say that they are governed by the law that is written on their hearts. This ought not to be confused with the promise of the law written in the heart as depicted in Jeremiah 31:33, because if that were the case, as Nygren observes, Gentiles "would indeed have the law, and that in a more intimate way than the Jew had it" (in loc.). Paul is not asserting this. Rather, he is insisting that the basic requirements of the law are stamped on human hearts. Presumably, he can say this because man is made in the image of God. C.S. Lewis begins his argument in *The Case for Christianity* by pointing out that when quarrels develop between people, the thing to be determined is who is in the right and who is in the wrong. The parties may differ radically as to their respective positions on this issue, but they are very clear that there is a right and there is a wrong. Similarly, despite the great differences in laws and customs among peoples around the world, what unites them in a common humanity is the recognition that some things are right and others are wrong.

An additional element that belongs to the equipment of the Gentiles is conscience (v.15). The translation speaks of their consciences as "bearing witness." In the Greek text there is an emphasis that does not appear in the translation—bearing witness *with*; so one must ask, With what? Only one answer seems possible, namely, with the require-ments of the law written on the heart. The two function together. In the OT the word "conscience" does not appear. Perhaps this is due to the Jews' overwhelming awareness of the regulating power of revealed truth. However, the operation of conscience is recognized (e.g., Gen 42:21; 2 Sam 24:10), even though the word is lacking.

Paul's fairly frequent use of the term "conscience" indicates his indebtedness to his Greek environment and the desirability of capitalizing on a concept that was familiar to his Gentile churches. With reference to the passage we are considering, C.A. Pierce writes, "That the everyday language of the Gentiles contains a word for confessing to feelings of pain on commission or initiation of particular acts—feelings which carry with them the conviction that the acts ought not to have been committed—is first-hand evidence that the Gentiles are subject, by nature, to a 'natural law' as the Jews, by vocation, to the Torah" (*Conscience in the New Testament* [London: SCM Press, 1955], p. 86). So it can be maintained that the function of conscience in the Gentile is parallel to the function of the law for the Jew. The way conscience operates is described as a process of accusation or defense by the thoughts of a man, the inner life being pictured as a kind of debating forum, so that at times he finds himself exonerated at the bar of conscience, at other times convicted of wrong.

"This will take place on the day when God will judge men's secrets" (v.16). The difficulty to be faced here is the determination of *what* will take place. Does Paul mean that only at the judgment will conscience be engaged in the manner he has just indicated? This would seem to be a severe limitation, unless the intent is to indicate a heightened operation of this God-given monitor as the soul faces the divine assize. It is possible that vv.14, 15 should be regarded as a parenthesis, in which case what takes place on the day of judgment is the declaration of righteousness (or otherwise) referred to in v.13. This interpretation makes good sense, but it has the disadvantage of making a rather unexpected connection, because of the length of the intervening material.

God's judgment will include men's "secrets" (cf. 1 Cor 4:5). This is the only court able to assess them. Many an act that seems entirely praiseworthy to those who observe it may actually be wrongly motivated, and contrariwise some things that seem to men to merit stern disapproval may pass muster in this supreme court because the intention behind the deed was praiseworthy. The Jew theoretically admitted judgment and certainly welcomed it in the case of the Gentile, while trying to shield himself behind his privileged position. The non-Jew admitted the reality of judgment implicitly by the very process of reasoning that either accused or excused his conduct. What the Gentile did not know was the item included here—that God will judge "through Jesus Christ" (John 5:27; Acts 17:31).

Some interpreters have seen in the closing statement, "as my gospel declares," a fourth principle of judgment intended to be linked with the three we have noted. This is more understandable if one works from a literal rendering of the text—"according to my gospel." But to make the gospel, in the sense of its content, to be the criterion for judgment *in this context* is clearly wrong, for Paul is not dealing with the gospel in this chapter. What he is saying is that the gospel he preached includes the prospect of judgment and that it will be conducted through the mediation of Christ.

C. Specific Guilt of the Jew

2:17–3:8

> [17]Now you, if you call yourself a Jew; if you rely on the law and brag about your relationship to God; [18]if you know his will and approve of what is superior because you are instructed by the law; [19]if you are convinced that you are a guide for the blind, a light for those who are in the dark, [20]an instructor of the foolish, a teacher of infants, because you have in the law the embodiment of knowledge and truth— [21]you, then, who teach others, do you not teach yourself? You who preach against stealing, do you steal? [22]You who say that people should not commit adultery, do you commit adultery? You who abhor idols, do you rob temples? [23]You who brag about the law, do you dishonor God by breaking the law? [24]As it is written: "God's name is blasphemed among the Gentiles because of you."
>
> [25]Circumcision has value if you observe the law, but if you break the law, you have become as though you had not been circumcised. [26]If those who are not circumcised keep the law's requirements, will they not be regarded as though they were circumcised? [27]The one who is not circumcised physically and yet obeys the law will condemn you who, even though you have the written code and circumcision, are a lawbreaker.
>
> [28]A man is not a Jew if he is only one outwardly, nor is circumcision merely outward and physical. [29]No, a man is a Jew if he is one inwardly; and circumcision is circumcision of the heart, by the Spirit, not by the written code. Such a man's praise is not from men, but from God.

3:1What advantage, then, is there in being a Jew, or what value is there in circumcision? 2Much in every way! First of all, they have been entrusted with the very words of God.

3What if some did not have faith? Will their lack of faith nullify God's faithfulness? 4Not at all! Let God be true, and every man a liar. As it is written:

"So that you may be proved right in your words and prevail in your judging."

5But if our unrighteousness brings out God's righteousness more clearly, what shall we say? That God is unjust in bringing his wrath on us? (I am using a human argument.) 6Certainly not! If that were so, how could God judge the world? 7Someone might argue, "If my falsehood enhances God's truthfulness and so increases his glory, why am I still condemned as a sinner?" 8Why not say—as we are being slanderously reported and as some claim that we say—"Let us do evil that good may result"? Their condemnation is deserved.

Two main developments are discernible in this passage. In 2:17–29 the advantage of the Jew in terms of his possession of the law and the distinctive mark of circumcision is seen as offset by his boastfulness and his fruitlessness. In 3:1–8 a new factor is introduced: Israel's failure to respond to God in terms of trust and obedience, justifying the visitation of his wrath upon them.

17–24 Here Paul begins to engage in dialogue with a representative Jew, and his razor-sharp irony is superb for its deftness. He proceeds to build up the Jew, citing his various distinctives and appearing to appreciate them (vv.17–20), only to swing abruptly into a frontal assault by exposing the inconsistency between his claims and his conduct (vv.21–24). The Jew was characterized by his reliance on the law, given by God through Moses. It came as the result of a relationship with God enjoyed by no other people. In Paul's time some of the leaders of Judaism were making such extravagant statements about the law as to put it virtually in the place of God. Many Jews were trying to keep the law for its own sake, to honor the law rather than its giver. This tendency was even more developed after the fall of Jerusalem, when the law became the rallying point for a nation that had lost its holy city and its temple.

Paul concedes that the use of the law will bring knowledge of God's will and a recognition of its superior teaching. But this is not all, for the Jew thinks that this advantage makes *him* superior to the Gentile. We can paraphrase here: "You come to the Gentile and propose yourself as a guide for his blindness (when, as a matter of fact, as I have already shown, he has a light and a law as well as you). You come to the Gentile as though he were dumb and childish, giving you the whip hand, which you thoroughly relish. To you they are mere infants, knowing next to nothing." By employing terms actually used by the Jews for the Gentiles, one after the other, not once suggesting that the Gentile has anything to his credit, but invariably magnifying the Jew, Paul has succeeded in exposing Jewish pride and boasting as utterly ridiculous.

21–24 Abruptly the shadow-boxing turns aggressive and the blows become lethal as the Jew is confronted by the disparity between what he teaches others as the will of God and his own manner of life. The thrust loses nothing of its forthrightness by being posed in a series of questions, for the effect is to turn the complacent Jew back on himself to search his own soul.

The indictment is summarized by the general charge of breaking the very law the Jew boasts of (v.23). In fact, the failure is so notorious that even non-Israelites notice the discrepancy. At this point Paul introduces a quotation from Isaiah 52:5. God has been obliged to chasten his disobedient people by permitting them to go into captivity, where their captors make sport of their God who was apparently unable to prevent their deportation (cf. Ezek 36:20, 21). But there also the fault lay not with God but with his people who had refused to take his law seriously.

25–27 If the law was the major distinctive of the Jews, a close second was circumcision. As with the law, so with circumcision, the nation was guilty of placing unwarranted confidence in the rite. Jewish tradition pictures Abraham as sitting at the gate of Gehenna to insure that no circumcised person be allowed to enter perdition (Gen R xlviii). The view that only circumcised children shared in the world to come was commonly held. Circumcision was to Jewry what baptism is to those who maintain baptismal regeneration. In dividing men into two classes, circumcised and uncircumcised, the Jews were in effect indicating those who were saved and those who were not.

But Paul's contention is that circumcision and observance of the law cannot be separated. If one has the symbol of Judaism and lacks the substance, of what value is the symbol? Society has laws that demand that the labeling of a can or bottle match the contents. How much more should there be correspondence in the spiritual realm! If a Gentile should manifest success in observing the law, the lack of circumcision is surely not so important as to discount his spiritual attainment (cf. the line of thought in 2:14). In fact, says Paul, one can go a step further (v.27) and say that the circumcised may find himself on a lower plane than the despised Gentile, because if the latter obeys the law that the Jew takes for granted instead of taking it seriously, then the Gentile will "condemn" him. This does not involve the bringing of any charge, but is a specialized use of the word "condemn" to indicate the effect created by one who surpasses another despite his inferior status or limited advantage (cf. Matt 8:11, 12; 12:41). The Gentile appears in a more favorable light than the Jew.

Some difficulty besets the attempt to understand the phrase in the Greek, which reads, "through letter and circumcision" (v.27). Calvin's attempt to handle the matter by combining the two to make them mean a literal circumcision in contrast to what is spiritual (in loc.) is hardly satisfactory. When Paul wants to make explicit the fact of literal circumcision, he uses the qualifying phrase "in the flesh"—NIV, "physically" (v.28). The basic problem, however, centers in the force of the preposition *dia*, which is normally rendered "through" in a construction such as the verse presents. But does it mean "through" in the sense of instrumentality or in the less common sense of indicating attendant circumstance? An example of the latter usage is in Romans 4:11, where Abraham is spoken of as the father of all who believe "through" circumcision. Clearly, this refers not to instrumentality but to the status of these people at the time they believe. NIV adopts this understanding in v.27—"even though you have . . ."—and this is the common interpretation. The factor that makes one hesitate is Paul's shift from *nomos* (law) to *gramma* (letter). One can detect in Paul's use of the latter term in v.29 and in 2 Corinthians 3:6 a somewhat pejorative connotation—what is written, laid down as law, but lacking any accompanying enablement. If taken in this sense in the passage before us, something of the force of instrumentality may be detected. G. Schrenk writes,

> When we are told in v.27 that the Jew *dia grammatos kai peritomēs* is a transgressor of the law, the *dia* cannot just be translated 'in spite of' as though to denote an accompanying circumstance; it must also be given an instrumental significance. It is precisely through what is written and through circumcision that the Jew is a transgres-

sor. He is to see that his true position involves possession of the *gramma* and the *peritomē*, but with no genuine fulfilment of the Law, since neither what is written nor circumcision leads him to action (TDNT, 1:765).

In the immediate context (v.23) Paul uses *dia* with the instrumental sense in raising the question of the Jew's dishonoring of God "through the transgression of the law." The transgression of the law is common to both statements.

28,29 That this portion is intended as a conclusion to the discussion of the law and circumcision is evident, for both are mentioned, though the law is referred to in terms of "letter," as in v.27. There was plenty of background for Paul's appeal for circumcision of the heart (e.g., Deut 30:6; Jer 4:4; 9:25, 26). A real Jew, says Paul, is one who has circumcision of the heart, accomplished "by the Spirit, not by the written code" (cf. 2 Cor 3:6). How striking this is! The law is part of the Scripture that the Spirit has inspired, yet there is no hint here that the true Jew is one in whom the Spirit has made the teaching of the law dynamic. By the avoidance of any such suggestion Paul prepares the way for his treatment of the law in chapter 7. He goes on to note that a Jew transformed by the Spirit would really be living up to the name he bears, for "Jew" comes from Judah, which means "praise." He would be praiseworthy in the eyes of God, fulfilling what the law requires but cannot produce (cf. 8:3, 4). Paul writes, of course, as a Christian, as one who has suffered much for his faith from his countrymen. But these closing verses of the chapter show that for all the bluntness of his references to the Jew he is not motivated by a desire to belittle his nation on account of the treatment he has received. He rather seeks their highest good (cf. 9:1–3; 10:1).

In 3:1–8 the subject of the guilt of the Jew is continued, but now with an emphasis on the element of unbelief and also on a sophistical claim of immunity from divine judgment on the plea that God's faithfulness is thrown into bolder relief by human failure. What reasonable basis remains for acting in judgment?

3:1–4 These opening words reflect the devastating attack the apostle has launched. "What advantage, then, is there, in being a Jew"? Although the term "the circumcision" (the definite article is used) is one that could serve to denote Israel (cf. 4:9), clearly that is not the case here, for that would involve tautology. The previous context makes the reference to the rite of circumcision natural. "Much in every way" suggests a manifold advantage, made explicit by "first of all." There seems no doubt that this suggests an enumeration, but Paul proceeds no further than his first point. The reader is kept waiting a long time for any resumption, but eventually the full list is provided (9:4, 5).

For present consideration the chosen advantage is that this nation has been "entrusted with the very words of God." The Greek *logia* is related to *logoi* (e.g., John 14:24) but has a specialized meaning. "Oracles" is the usual rendering. It has this meaning in classical Greek, where it is used especially for divine utterances, often for those preserved and handed down by earlier generations. Jewish writers used it both for pagan oracles, which they considered false, and for revelations from the God of Israel. LXX usage makes it evident that two elements could belong to a *logion:* a disclosure of what God proposes to do (especially in terms of prediction, as in Num 24:16ff.) or a pronouncement of the duty laid upon man in view of the divine will or promise (e.g., Ps 119:67).

To be "entrusted" with the divine oracles obviously means more than to be the recipient of them. Actually it means more even than to be the custodian and transmitter of them. What is called for, in the light of the meaning of *logia*, is faith and obedience.

35

Just at this point the Jew failed (v.3). Paul has already dealt sufficiently with Jewish failure in terms of the law, but here he deals with it in terms of God's revealed purpose. He is considerate in saying that "some did not have faith." One is reminded of 1 Corinthians 10, where the same author says that some became idolaters, some murmured, etc. Actually, only two men of the exodus generation pleased God and were permitted to enter the promised land. Paul is recognizing the concept of the faithful remnant in Israel. Is the rendering "did not have faith" acceptable here, or should one regard the RSV translation, "were unfaithful," as preferable? The problem is to determine which fits better with the contrasting term, "God's faithfulness." We should recall that the oracles of God summon both to faith (in their promissory character) and to faithfulness (in their legislative aspect). From the Jewish standpoint, a *logion* could involve both *halakhah* and *haggada*—something to be done and something to be believed (*haggada* embraced the promises and much else). But since Paul has dealt with obligation already in chapter 2, we should probably think here in terms of emphasis on the area of belief. Of course, the two concepts of faith and faithfulness are closely related. Barrett's rendering, "proved unbelieving," fits the context.

We should understand "the faithfulness of God" in terms of the covenant aspect of God's dealings with Israel. There are really two sides to this faithfulness, the one positive, the other negative, in line with a similar duality in connection with the righteousness of God (1:17, 18). That the negative aspect is before us here is evident from the mention of his wrath (v.5). This is in harmony with a frequent emphasis in the prophets. When Israel fractured the Sinaitic covenant, God's very faithfulness compelled him to judge his people by sending them into captivity. The positive aspect (which we might have expected from v.1 but which is deferred) will appear in the sustained discussion of God's dealings with Israel (chs. 9–11).

As might be expected, Paul vigorously rejects any suggestion that God could fail in terms of his faithfulness (v.4). The concept of his fidelity is carried forward by the use of a closely related term. He is "true" to his covenant promises because he is true in himself. If one had to choose between the reliability of God and of man, he would have to agree with the psalmist when he declared in his disillusionment concerning his fellows, "Every man [is] a liar" (Ps 116:11). One of the best men in Israel's history, declared to be the man after God's own heart, proved a disappointment. After being chastened for his sin and refusal to confess it for a long period, David was ready to admit that God was in the right and he was in the wrong (Ps 51:4).

5-8 The supposition that human wrong could serve to display the righteousness of God may have been suggested by the passage from Psalm 51 that has just been cited. Is it not possible (so the question goes) that since human failure can bring out more sharply the righteousness of God, the Almighty ought to be grateful for this service and soften the judgment that would otherwise be due the offender? The question is one a Jew might well resort to in line with his thought that God would go easy on his covenant people. So Paul speaks for a supposed interlocutor. The mention of wrath ties in with 2:8, 9.

Paul's explanatory statement, "I am using a human argument," is due to his having permitted himself to use the word "unjust" of God, even though it is not his own assertion. "If that were so," that is, if God were unjust, he would not be qualified to judge the world. There is no attempt to establish his qualifications, since the readers, at least, are not in doubt on a point of this sort about which Scripture is so clear.

Once more the apostle entertains a possible objection (vv.7, 8). The thought is closely related to what has been stated in v.4, as the similarity in language indicates. Though the construction is somewhat rough, the general sense is clear enough. Speaking for an objector, Paul is voicing the hoary adage that the end justifies the means. He has evidently had to cope with this in his own ministry, and he will be dealing with it again in a different context (6:1). Here he is content to turn the tables on the objector. If anyone claims that his falsehood, which throws into sharp relief the truthfulness of God, promotes his glory and should therefore relieve the sinner of condemnation, let him ponder the apostolic verdict—his "condemnation is deserved."

Notes

2:22 One item calls for investigation, namely, the query "Do you rob temples?" (ἱεροσυλεῖς, *hierosyleis*). A cognate of the same word occurs in Acts 19:37 (ἱεροσύλους, *hierosylous*), where it covers sacrilege in the general sense of desecrating sacred things. But in this passage in Romans a precise, strong contrast is intended. The Jew who has been taught to abhor idols is charged with laying hands on them for the sake of profit. This may sound inconceivable, but if the robbery was directed at the offerings brought to the idol, this was tantamount to robbing the idol and thereby desecrating the temple. Ancient temples were repositories of treasure and were therefore a source of temptation to the avaricious (cf. Jos. Antiq. 4:207).

3:5 David Daube has examined the expression κατὰ ἄνθρωπον λέγω (*kata anthrōpon legō*, "I speak according to man") in the light of rabbinic usage and has concluded that it is a technical term in Paul's writing. "It constitutes an apology for a statement which, but for the apology, would be too bold, almost blasphemous" (*The New Testament and Rabbinic Judaism* [London: The Athlone Press, 1956], p. 396).

D. Summary

3:9-20

⁹What shall we conclude then? Are we any better? Not at all! We have already made the charge that Jews and Gentiles alike are all under sin. ¹⁰As it is written:

> "There is no one righteous, not even one;
> 11   there is no one who understands,
>   no one who searches for God.
> ¹²All have turned away
>   and together become worthless.
> There is no one who does good,
>   not even one."
> ¹³"Their throats are open graves;
>   their tongues practice deceit."
> "The poison of vipers is on their lips."
> 14   "Their mouths are full of cursing and
>   bitterness."
> ¹⁵"Their feet are swift to shed blood;
> 16   ruin and misery mark their paths,
> ¹⁷and the way of peace they do not know."
> 18   "There is no fear of God before their eyes."

¹⁹Now we know that whatever the law says, it says to those who are under the law, so that every mouth may be silenced and the whole world held accountable

to God. ²⁰Therefore no one will be declared righteous in his sight by observing the law; rather through the law we become conscious of sin.

9 Questions both of text and of punctuation confront us at this point. (Concerning punctuation, see Note.) As to text, we need have no hesitation in accepting *proechometha*, rendered "Are we any better?" Other renderings of this word are possible. The basic idea of the verb is "to stand out," "excel," or "surpass," and this is the most likely sense here. There is a difficulty, to be sure, in that the word could be either middle or passive voice. If it is to be taken as middle in force as well as in form, the sense will be, "Do we have a defense?" or "Do we excuse ourselves?" But the middle may well be used here in an active sense, as is often done with other verbs. If taken as a passive, the sense will be, "Are we excelled?"

Assuming that Paul is identifying himself here with the Jews, of whom he has been speaking, the question would suggest that the indictment of the Jew has been so severe as to open the possibility that the Gentile is actually in a better position. But insufficient ground has been provided in the foregoing passage to suggest such a possibility. So the best conclusion is that Paul intends to question whether the Jew has an edge over the Gentile. His answer, "Not at all," registers an emphatic denial. Such a denial may seem to be in conflict with the statements in vv.1, 2, and for this reason some would render it, "Not absolutely." But there he deals with the distinctive position of the Jew in the divine economy; here he is dealing with the Jew's moral and spiritual fitness, how he stands before God in terms of fulfilling his God-given role.

Paul backs up his denial of Jewish superiority by reminding his readers of the charge he has been bringing, "that Jews and Gentiles alike are all under sin." To be under sin is to be under its sway and condemnation. It is noteworthy that in his discussion of sin up to this point Paul does not charge the Jew with the death of Christ as he does in 1 Thessalonians 2:15. He could have included the Gentile also (cf. Acts 4:27, 28) and made this a clinching factor in the case against mankind, but he did not. Perhaps this is because few Jews and still fewer Gentiles were involved in effecting the death of the Lord Jesus. Paul is basing his case on a much wider sampling of human character and conduct. The specific episode of Calvary is not needed to make the verdict certain, but can be held in reserve to be used with objectors, if need be.

10–18 However, there is another argument waiting to be brought into play to seal the verdict. It is the testimony of Scripture. Writing to those who are for the most part Gentiles, Paul does not set down Scripture first and then work from that as a base for exposition (which is the method used in the Epistle to the Hebrews), but he uses only a minimum of reference to the OT to substantiate what he has established. Leaving Scripture to the conclusion of the argument is calculated to increase the respect of the Gentile for it as being able to depict man's condition accurately and faithfully. Both Jews and early Christians were in the habit of drawing up collections of Scripture passages relating to various topics in order to use them as proof texts for instruction or argumentation. It is not known whether the present collection, taken mostly from the Psalms, is the work of Paul or whether he is utilizing something previously formulated.

The present catena serves a double purpose: to affirm the universality of sin in the human family and to assert its inroads upon every facet of individual and corporate life. "There is no one righteous, not even one." The language is devastatingly clear and sharp. No exception is allowed. Again, it can be put positively: "All have turned away," which seems to echo the thought of chapter 1 that men had opportunity to know God but discarded him to their own detriment and confusion. Paul wants the full impact to register. He does not turn aside to answer the objection that the OT speaks of righteous men and in fact recognizes them as a class over against the wicked (Ps 1) or as individuals (Job 1:8). From the standpoint of the divine righteousness, they all fall short, as Paul has affirmed of both the Jew and the Gentile, whether under the law or lacking it.

The latter half of the catena, beginning with v.13, reflects the second emphasis, namely, the ramifications of sin in human life. So far as relationship with God is concerned, the rupturing power of sin has been noted (vv.11, 12). But what effect does sin have on the sinner? The effect is total, because his entire being is vitiated. Observe at this point the various members of the body referred to: the throat, the tongue, and the lips (v.13); the mouth (v.14); the feet (v.15); and the eyes (v.18). This list serves to affirm what theologians speak of as total depravity, i.e., not that man in his natural state is as bad as he can possibly be, but rather that his entire being is adversely affected by sin. His whole nature is permeated with it. Human relations also suffer, because society can be no better than those who constitute it. Some of the obvious effects—conflict and bloodshed—are specified (vv.15–17).

The chain of Scriptures closes with a statement of the root difficulty: "There is no fear of God before their eyes" (v.18). This is the same observation gleaned from the study of chapter 1. Getting out of step with God is the cause of conflict and chaos in human relations.

19,20 In these closing statements of the indictment, the apostle may be reading the mind of a Jew who questions the legitimacy of appealing to passages of the sort he has used, on the ground that men in general are in view—or at any rate, Jews who by their very godlessness are not representative of the nation as a whole. But the stubborn fact is that whatever the law says, it says to those who are under the law (v.19). The first clause must refer to the law in the broad sense of the OT revelation (cf. 1 Cor 14:21), for to refer it to the Pentateuch or to its legislative portions would destroy the continuity of thought in the passage. As already observed, the string of quotations derives from the hagiographa and the prophets. "Under the law" is more literally "in the law"; so the thought is probably not so much that the Jew is under the law's authority and dominion in the legal sense as that he is involved in Scripture, which has relevance to him at every point. Otherwise the shift in meaning of *nomos* (law) is very abrupt. Yet the legislative aspect of the law is involved by virtue of being a part of Scripture.

"So that every mouth may be silenced." When human achievement is measured against what God requires, there is no place for pride or boasting but only for silence that lends consent to the verdict of guilty. In the various biblical scenes of judgment, the silence of those who are being judged is a notable feature (e.g., Rev. 20:11–14). Questions may be raised for the sake of clarification of the reason for the verdict (Matt 25:41–46), but when the explanation is given, no appeal is attempted. The Judge of all the earth does right (Gen 18:25).

In making these statements (v.19) the apostle has been occupied with the Jew because Scripture has been at issue, but suddenly he makes a statement that involves all mankind. He pictures the "whole world" as "accountable to God." This seems to be a *non sequitur*. How can Jewish failure in terms of what Scripture requires lead to the involvement of the remainder of the human race? Two possibilities come to mind. One is that the Jewish nation is being regarded as a test case for all peoples. If given the same privileges enjoyed by Israel, the rest would likewise have failed. Their human nature is no different from that of the sons of Abraham. Another possibility, which is the more likely explanation, is that the failure of the non-Jews is so patent that it is not a debatable subject; it can be taken for granted as already established (1:18-32). Once it has been determined that the record of the Jew is no better, then judgment is seen as universally warranted.

The final word to the Jew (v.20) is designed to rob him of any fancied support in the Mosaic law, the word "law" being used as in the second occurrence in v.19. Justification before God cannot be attained by attempted observance of the law, however much man may take satisfaction in that. As Jesus pointed out, no one had succeeded in keeping the law (John 7:19).

For the first time in Romans we encounter the expression "by works of law" (cf. v.28) which has such prominence in Galatians (2:16; 3:2, 5, 10). Part of the verse—"no one will be declared righteous in his sight"—is a quotation from Psalm 143:2, in which a change in the Greek text is made from "no one living" to "no flesh" (NIV simply has "no one"), an alteration designed to bring out the frailty and inability of man with respect to meeting God's requirements (cf. 8:3). The practical result of working seriously with the law is to "become conscious of sin" (cf. 5:20; 7:7-11). How startling it is to contemplate the fact that the best revelation man has apart from Christ only deepens his awareness of failure. The law loudly proclaims his need for the gospel.

Notes

9 As far as punctuation is concerned, the first three words of the Gr. text could be taken together, yielding some such tr. as "Wherein, then, are we excelled?" But οὐ πάντως (*ou pantōs*, "not at all") does not properly answer this question, so the double question should be retained. Uncertainty as to the meaning of προεχόμεθα (*proechometha*) accounts for the interpretative variant reading προκατέχομεν περισσόν (*prokatechomen perisson*), supported principally by D* G ψ 104 and having the meaning, "Why, then, are we especially superior?"

IV. Justification: The Imputation of Righteousness (3:21-5:21)

A. *The Description of Justification*

3:21-26

21But now a righteousness from God, apart from law, has been made known, to which the Law and the Prophets testify. 22This righteousness from God comes through faith in Jesus Christ to all who believe. There is no difference, 23for all have sinned and fall short of the glory of God, 24and are justified freely by his grace through the redemption that came by Christ Jesus. 25God presented him as a sacrifice of atonement, through faith in his blood. He did this to demonstrate his justice, because in his forbearance he had left the sins committed beforehand unpunished—26he did it to demonstrate his justice at the present time, so as to be just and the one who justifies the man who has faith in Jesus.

To help his readers follow his train of thought, the apostle reverts to the term he used in stating the theme of the letter in 1:17—God's righteousness. He repeats also the necessity for faith (cf. 1:16) and then summarizes the material from 1:18-3:20 by the reminder that there is no difference between Jew and Gentile so far as sin is concerned. Having done this, he goes on to give a rich exposition of salvation through the use of various theological terms, with principal attention to justification.

21 God's righteousness, that is, his method of bringing men into right relation to himself, is "apart from law," which is agreeable to the declaration that the law operates in quite another sphere—viz., to make those who live under it conscious of their sin (v.20). God's righteousness "has been made known" (literally, "has been manifested"). The perfect tense, in contrast to the present tense in 1:17, where the current proclamation of the gospel requires it, draws attention to the appearing of Jesus Christ in the arena of history (cf. 2 Tim 1:10) or, more specifically, points to the fulfillment of God's saving purpose in him. Yet even before the initial appearing of the Savior, this method of making men right with himself was operating in principle, as "the Law and the Prophets"—a summary term for the OT—testify. This observation prepares the reader for the recital of God's dealings with Abraham and David to be considered in the following chapter.

22 God's righteousness becomes operative in human life "through faith in Jesus Christ." This statement is more explicit than the initial mention of faith in connection with the gospel (1:16, 17), since it specifies the necessary object of faith, even Jesus Christ. A problem lies beneath the surface, however, in that the literal wording is "through faith of Jesus Christ." This raises the possibility that our Lord's own faith, or more precisely, his faithfulness in fulfilling his mission, is the thought intended (G. Howard in ExpT 85 [April 1974] 212–15). The word *pistis* evidently means faithfulness in 3:3. However, a glance at Mark 11:22 makes it clear that the *pistis* of God may mean faith *in* God, as the situation there requires. What should settle the matter in this passage (Rom 3:22) is the precedent in Galatians 2:16, where we find the identical phrase "through faith of Jesus Christ" followed by the explanatory statement, "we believed in Christ Jesus." Consequently, the NIV translation should be regarded as legitimate and preferable.

Incidentally, it is never said that men are saved on account of their faith in Christ, a construction that might encourage the notion that faith makes a contribution and has some merit. On the contrary, faith is simply "the hand of the heart" (Godet). It takes what God bestows but adds nothing to the gift. All recipients of salvation are shut up to faith, for "there is no difference," a repetition of the verdict of 3:9.

23 The reason all must come to God through faith in Christ is that "all have sinned and fall short of [or 'lack,' as in Mark 10:21] the glory of God." This glory cannot be eschatological, as in 5:2, since even believers, for whom the sin problem has been solved, lack the future glory now. The suggestion that the glory is God's approbation or praise (Denney) is unlikely, since this meaning of *doxa*, common in Luke, is somewhat rare in Paul. C.H. Dodd seeks to link the glory with the image of God in man (cf. 1 Cor 11:7) which is marred by sin. This is suggestive, but it would be more acceptable if Paul had used the past tense ("have fallen short") to match the sense in the previous statement about sin. Possibly the best interpretation is to associate the glory with the divine presence and the privilege man originally had of direct communion with God. This ever-present deprivation is depicted in the restriction of the glory to the holy of holies in the tabernacle and the denial of the right of access to the people save through the high priest once a year. God's glory is the majesty of his holy person. To be cut off from this fellowship is *the* great loss occasioned by sin.

41

24 At first glance it seems that Paul is committing himself to a doctrine of universal salvation, that all who have sinned are justified. That impression is certainly incorrect. The problem can be handled in either of two ways. One method is to suppose that the reader is intended to supply something along this line. "Since all have sinned, all must be justified—if they are to be saved—by God's free grace." The other method is to understand that the last statement in v.22 and all of v.23 should be regarded as semi-parenthetical, so that the statement about being justified is to be joined to "all who believe."

In confronting justification, we encounter the leading doctrinal contribution of Romans. How to be just in God's sight has been the age-old problem of man (Job 9:2; 10:14). To get at the meaning of the doctrine, some attention must be given to terminology. In classical Greek the verb *dikaioō* was sometimes used to mean "do right by a person, give him justice." As a result, it could be used in the sense of "condemn." But in its biblical setting it is used in the opposite sense, namely, "to acquit" (Exod 23:7; Deut 25:1). It is clear both from the OT and the NT that *dikaioō* is a forensic term; it is the language of the law court. But to settle on "acquittal" as the meaning of justification is to express only a part of the range of the word, even though an important part (Acts 13:39).

There is a positive side that is even more prominent in NT usage—"to consider, or declare to be, righteous." The word does not mean "to make righteous," that is, to effect a change of character. Because he considered it ethically deplorable that God should account righteous those who have been and to some extent continue to be sinful, Goodspeed defied the linguistic evidence and rendered *dikaioō* "to make upright." He failed to realize that the question of character and conduct belongs to a different area, namely, sanctification, and is taken up by Paul in due course, whereas justification relates to status and not to condition. For a clear statement on this, see R. Bultmann, *Theology of the New Testament* (New York: Scribner, 1951), 1:276.

In the background is the important consideration, strongly emphasized by Paul, that the believer is "in Christ," a truth to be unfolded at a later stage in Paul's presentation and summarized by him in 8:1 (cf. 1 Cor 1:30; 2 Cor 5:21). Nowhere is this better stated than in his declaration, ". . . that I may gain Christ and be found in him, not having a righteousness of my own that comes from the law, but that which is through faith in Christ" (Phil 3:8, 9). To be justified includes the truth that God sees the sinner in terms of his relation to his Son, with whom he is well pleased.

Though justification has much in common with forgiveness, the two terms ought not to be regarded as interchangeable, because even though forgiveness of sins can be stated in comprehensive fashion (Eph 1:7; 4:32) its continuing aspect, related to confession (1 John 1:9), sets it somewhat apart from justification, which is a once-for-all declaration of God on behalf of the believing sinner.

Sinners are justified "freely," i.e., as a gift. The same word is used in John 15:25, where it bears a somewhat different but not unrelated meaning—"without reason." God finds no reason, no basis, in the sinner for declaring him righteous. He must find the cause in himself. This truth goes naturally with the observation that justification is offered by God's grace. Perhaps the best synonym we have for it is "lovingkindness" (*passim* in the Psalms, KJV). It is a matter not simply of attitude but also of action, as the present verse attests. Grace (*charis*) lies at the basis of joy (*chara*) for the believer and leads to thanksgiving (*eucharistia*). If "freely" is the manner in which justification operates, and grace is its basis, "the redemption that came by Christ Jesus" is the means a gracious God employed to achieve this boon for mankind. The benefit that redemption brings in this life, according to Ephesians 1:7, is forgiveness of sins, and this is applicable in our passage. Another aspect, belonging to the future, is the redemption of the body, which will consummate our salvation (8:23; Eph 4:30).

25 "God presented him as a sacrifice of atonement." Some would object to the rendering "presented" on the ground that a public exhibition of the person of Jesus has something almost theatrical about it, and that for this reason the alternative rendering "purposed" (literally, "set before himself") might be preferred. However, there are words in the passage that express manifestation: "made known" (v.21) and "demonstrate" (vv.25, 26); so the objection is unwarranted. Also it should be pointed out that the emphasis on faith (v.25) suggests that the real force in "presented" is not so much the actual exhibition of Christ on the cross as in the proclamation of the gospel that makes his saving work central. That very proclamation emphasizes that Christ, under God, has become "a sacrifice of atonement." This language is an attempt to render the Greek *hilastērion*, which in form is an adjective that could be taken either as masculine or neuter. If the former, it refers back to "him" (Christ); if the latter, it requires something to be supplied, unless the liberty is taken to give it the force of a noun, as is done when it is considered the equivalent of "propitiation" (*hilasmos*), which occurs in 1 John 2:2; 4:10.

In LXX the first occurrence of *hilastērion* (Exod 25:17) has reference to a propitiatory lid or cover, usually translated "mercy seat." In the following context of Exodus 25 it occurs several times, each time without the word "lid." The only other occurrence in the NT (Heb 9:5) is a clear allusion to the mercy seat of the tabernacle. But can we be sure that Romans 3:25 has the same frame of reference? For one thing, the Hebrews passage has the definite article, whereas the reference in Romans does not. This is not an insuperable objection, for if Paul is intent on stressing that Christ is the antitype of the OT mercy seat, he would naturally omit the article so as to avoid identifying Christ with a material object.

More significant is the objection that whereas Hebrews is filled with references to the sanctuary and its ritual, Romans is not. This is true, but the contrast should not be overdrawn (cf. Rom 12:1). Again, it has been objected that any reference to the mercy seat is incongruous, since that article was withheld from public view and access. But the objection ignores the movement of thought in Hebrews 9, which emphasizes that the death of Christ opened up what had formerly been concealed and inaccessible to the people. As far as Romans is concerned, the word "presented" is a signpost suggesting a similar concept here. T.W. Manson remarks, "The mercy-seat is no longer kept in the sacred seclusion of the most holy place: it is brought out into the midst of the rough and tumble of the world and set up before the eyes of hostile, contemptuous, or indifferent crowds" (JTS 46 [1945] 5). Indeed, Christ has become the meeting place of God and man where the mercy of God is available because of the sacrifice of the Son.

Nygren supports the mercy seat interpretation by noting that the very terms used by Paul in the passage before us tally with the OT setting in Exodus 25—the manifestation of God, his wrath, his glory, the blood, and the mercy seat or propitiatory (p. 157).

Some scholars prefer the view that "propitiatory" requires a complement such as "sacrifice," which the reader is expected to supply, especially since the blood of Christ is mentioned here. But the very phrase "in his blood" tends to make such an addition needless. It remains, however, a viable option.

On the basis of the use of the word *hilastērion* on inscriptions of the *koine* period, A. Deissmann maintained that the word should be rendered "a votive offering" or "a propitiatory gift" (*Bible Studies* [Edinburgh: T. & T. Clark, 1901], pp. 124–135). His comment is, "The crucified Christ is the votive gift of the Divine Love for the salvation of men." But the examples he gives from pagan sources are all concerning votive gifts brought by men, designed to propitiate the deity, whereas Christ is set forth by God as propitiatory. The difference is very real.

In recent years considerable attention has been given to the conclusions of C.H. Dodd on the word in question (*The Bible and the Greeks* [London: Hodder and Stoughton, 1935], pp. 82–95). Dodd's contention is that when the LXX translators used the verb *hilaskesthai* ("to make propitiation") and its derivatives to render the Hebrew root *kipper* they did not attach to the word the classical sense of propitiation but rather gave it the force of expiation, that which is involved in the removal of sin's guilt (in contrast to the appeasement of wrath, which is inherent in the concept of propitiation). Admitting faint traces of propitiation in the OT data, he nevertheless advocates that when the subject of the verb is human, the idea is simply that of making expiation, and when the subject is divine, the concept is that of forgiveness.

Leon Morris (*The Apostolic Preaching of the Cross* [Grand Rapids: Eerdmans, 1955]) worked through the same OT materials and came out with different results, which may be summarized in two observations. First, Dodd ignored the fact that the verb *hilaskesthai*, which he would render "forgive" in reference to God, is used repeatedly in situations where the context makes it clear that the wrath of God is a factor, so that propitiation is actually involved (p. 138). Second, the argument from context is also important for the interpretation of the Romans passage, because the first main section of the book (1:18–3:20) is permeated with the concept of the divine wrath along with the emphasis on judgment. The word "wrath" (*orgē*) is found four times here (1:18; 2:5, 8; 3:5). Under these circumstances it would be strange for Paul to give a statement of the remedy for man's sin and unrighteousness without indicating that the wrath of God has been satisfactorily met by his own provision. There is no term in 3:21–26 that conveys this idea if it is not to be found in *hilastērion* (p. 169). An independent study by David Hill (*Greek Words*, pp. 23–48) leads to conclusions substantially in agreement with Morris's position.

The phrase "through faith in his blood" (v.25) poses a problem. This translation suggests that the believer's faith is to be placed in the blood of Christ, and the sequence of terms favors this. However, it has been pointed out that there is no example of Paul's calling for faith in a thing rather than a person, unless we allow the gospel to be included in this category. So if the translation is allowed to stand, it has to be regarded as anomalous. Furthermore, in the immediate context the idea of putting faith *in* is expressed without a preposition by using the genitive case (3:22, 26). The alternative suggestion is to place a comma after "faith," thus separating the clauses and making both dependent on *hilastērion*.

The remainder of v.25 deals with the necessity of the propitiatory provision in terms of God's justice (the same word in the original as "righteousness"). The character of God needs justification for his passing over "sins committed beforehand"—that is, in the ages prior to the cross. His "forbearance" is not to be thought of as sentimentality or weakness but as an indication that meeting the demands of his righteous character would be accomplished in due season. This happened at the cross. The Greek *paresis* (rendered "left ... unpunished") is close to *aphesis* ("forgiveness") in meaning, but with an appreciable difference in that *paresis* denotes a temporary remission of a debt (see Milligan and Moulton under *paresis*), which fits the situation here exactly. The full penalty for sin was not exacted, in line with God's forbearance.

26 Now the bearing of the cross on God's dealings with men "at the present time" is unfolded. It amounts to a declaration that God is at once just in himself and justifying in his activity on behalf of mankind. "It is something new, when absolute justice is said to be shown in the atonement through the sacrificial death of Jesus . . . and when God is called 'faithful and just to forgive our sins' (1 John 1:9), dikaios combining the ideas of judgment and salvation" (G. Schrenk, S.V. "Righteousness" in Bible Key Words. [New York: Harper and Brothers, 1951], p. 21).

Notes

21-24 In his important study of righteousness in Paul, Ziesler (in loc.) concludes that whereas the verb δικαιόω (dikaioō) is essentially forensic in meaning ("to justify"), the noun δικαιοσύνη (dikaiosynē) and the adjective δίκαιος (dikaios) describe "behaviour within relationship" and so are basically ethical in their import. This position is open to the criticism that it too sharply distinguishes the force of the noun and the adjective from that of the verb. In other words, the noun and the adjective are capable of carrying the forensic connotation also. See the review article by Nigel M. Watson in NTS 20 (Jan. 1974) 217-228.

22 Instead of "unto all" (εἰς πάντας, eis pantas), a few Fathers have "upon all" (ἐπὶ πάντας, epi pantas). A group of MSS (ℵ plus many cursives and Fathers) combine the two readings (cf. KJV).

24 We are confronted by a major theological concept. The Gr. term ἀπολύτρωσις (apolytrōsis) has as its kernel the word λύτρον (lytron), "ransom," used by Jesus of his own self-giving in behalf of the many (Mark 10:45). Paul does not use this word, though ἀντίλυτρον (antilytron) appears once (1 Tim 2:6). The word "redemption" has its OT background chiefly in the deliverance of Israel from Egypt (Exod 6:6; 15:13) and is used often without any reference to sin or the payment of a ransom. But something of the idea of the cost involved continues to cling to the word even though unexpressed. In our passage, the term may be said to connote "deliverance through the substitutionary death of Jesus, the emphasis being all the time on liberation" (David Hill, Greek Words and Hebrew Meanings [Cambridge: Cambridge University Press, 1967], p. 76).

B. The Availability of Justification Through Faith Alone

3:27-31

27Where, then, is boasting? It is excluded. On what principle? On that of observing the law? No, but on that of faith. 28For we maintain that a man is justified by faith apart from observing the law. 29Is God the God of Jews only? Is he not the God of Gentiles too? Yes, of Gentiles too, 30since there is only one God, who will justify the circumcised by faith and the uncircumcised through that same faith. 31Do we, then, nullify the law by this faith? Not at all! Rather, we uphold the law.

27-30 The opening words suggest that the paragraph is designed especially for the Jew, for even though boasting is not confined to the Jew, it has already been noticed as a distinct tendency in his case (2:17, 23). Paul asks on what principle (literally, "through what sort of law") boasting is excluded. But does "principle" convey the idea adequately? Certainly nomos is used in this sense later on (e.g., 7:21, 23). The use of the word nomos, so familiar to the Jew and so treasured by him, is calculated to catch his eye and make him think. Perhaps something between "law" and "principle" is needed here, something special in the sense of what is ordained by God (see TDNT IV, p. 1071). God has ordained faith as the sole condition of receiving salvation, and that provides no basis for boasting, seeing that in the last analysis it, like the salvation it embraces, is the gift of God (Eph 2:8, Gr.). Paul could speak of the righteousness he sought through law keeping as his own righteousness (Phil 3:9), but he cannot so speak of the righteousness he has in Christ. Once more he insists on justification by faith apart from law keeping. This may appear to bring him into contradiction with his assertion in 2:13. Paul would no doubt respond by saying that everything depends on the right motive. To glory over one's achievement ruins the whole enterprise: it becomes an affront to God, its value is gone. Read Galatians 3:12 in this connection.

Again Paul moves to catch the eye of his Jewish reader by appealing to his awareness that God is one (vv.29, 30; cf. Deut 6:4). The Jew, surrounded by pagan idolatry, proudly repeated his monotheistic confession. Paul now turns it to good account. Logically, if God is one, if he alone is God, then we can expect him to employ only one method to bring humanity to himself. Faith is the condition for receiving salvation on the part of Jew and Gentile alike (v.30). Neither has any advantage over the other. The Gentile must come "by that same faith" required of the Jew (cf. 1:16; Gal. 2:15, 16). It is doubtful that the difference in prepositions used with faith implies any basic distinction in God's dealings with the two groups.

31 The final verse of the chapter has elicited many interpretations, attesting its difficulty. That view is most likely to be correct that accords most closely with the foregoing material.

Paul has twice mentioned law observance (vv.27, 28) as not entering at all into justification, which is by faith apart from works of the law. May we draw the conclusion, then, that the law is useless? By no means, the apostle would answer, for the operation of faith really upholds or establishes the law. The gospel establishes the law in that the latter is vindicated. The law has fulfilled a vital role by bringing an awareness of sin (v.20). A broken law made the redeeming work of Christ at the cross necessary (vv.24, 25). One who sees that the cross was a divine necessity will never feel that he can make himself approved by God by fulfilling the law's demands. If that were possible, Christ would have died in vain. Since the death of Christ was in terms of God's righteousness (v.26), this means that the demands of the law have not been set aside in God's plan of salvation. It is not damaging to this position that "law" lacks the article here, for the same is true in 5:20.

Other views should be noticed briefly. One is that v.31 is intended to provide a transition to chapter 4, where Abraham's justification is explained. On this view "law" simply means Scripture, or more specifically, the Pentateuch. This view gets support from v.21 with its mention of "the Law and the Prophets." Something of a disadvantage is involved, however, in that v.31 in Greek speaks of "law" rather than of "*the* law" (the article is omitted). Further, it is doubtful that the material of the following chapter can be said to uphold the law.

Another possibility is that Paul is striking out against antinomianism. If his statement had occurred in the course of his argument in chapters 6 to 8, this would be quite apparent, but it is less likely here. Still another view is that Paul means to say that the moral standards of the law are maintained under the gospel, thus anticipating the truth stated in 8:4. In line with this is Luther's interpretation that to establish the law means to fulfill it through faith. But again, this anticipates what is developed only later on. The view that Paul means to say that we establish the law because under the gospel Christ keeps it for us is unsupported by anything in the passage. Doubtful also is the contention of H.J. Schoeps that Paul "implies that faith is the true content of the law" (*Paul* [Philadelphia: Westminster Press, 1961], p. 210). This runs counter to the argument in the preceding context.

C. *The Illustration of Justification From the Old Testament* (4:1–25)

The fact that in the gospel a righteousness from God is *revealed* (1:17) could suggest that justification is a new thing, peculiar to the Christian era. To discover that it was already present in the OT serves to engender confidence in an ongoing purpose of God and in the basic unity of the Bible. "It is essential for the structure of faith that behind the appearance of Christ in an historical perspective a preceding activity of God appears" (L. Goppelt, "Paul and Heilsgeschichte," INT 21 [1967] 325).

Paul's fourth chapter is devoted almost exclusively to Abraham and God's dealings with him. The NT writers seem to turn to Abraham almost instinctively when discussing faith (Heb 11; James 2). If Paul can establish as true that the father of the nation of Israel was justified by faith rather than by works, he will have scored heavily, especially with his Jewish readers.

1. *The case of Abraham*

4:1–5

¹What then shall we say that Abraham, our forefather, discovered in this matter? ²If, in fact, Abraham was justified by works, he had something to boast about—but not before God. ³What does the Scripture say? "Abraham believed God, and it was credited to him as righteousness."

⁴Now when a man works, his wages are not credited to him as a gift, but as an obligation. ⁵However, to the man who does not work but trusts God who justifies the wicked, his faith is credited as righteousness.

1–5 In calling Abraham "our forefather," the apostle is not turning aside to address Jewish believers only, because he makes the point in this chapter that Gentile believers also have a stake in Abraham (v.16). What had Abraham "discovered" about getting into right relation to God? Since the word is in the perfect tense, there is a hint that what he learned or experienced has value for future generations. Picking up the matter of boasting from 3:27, Paul naturally links works with it, but denies that it is possible to boast of works "before God." Abraham was not guilty of pharisaic folly. Justification is for the glory of God, not of man. To show that Abraham's close relation to God was not based on works, a simple appeal to Scripture is sufficient. That appeal was the more necessary because Judaism even before Paul's day was laying great store by Abraham's piety and was grounding it in his obedience. "Was not Abraham found faithful in temptation and it was reckoned unto him for righteousness?" (1 Macc 2:51). Judaism mingled things that Paul was careful to keep apart. "Law and works, faith and obedience, obedience and merit, reward and blessing are a unity in the rabbinic theology" (Michel, in loc.). The appeal to Scripture rather than to current teaching is decisive. "Abraham believed God, and it was credited to him as righteousness" (v.3). Nothing whatever is said about his obedience in leaving country and kindred in response to God's call. Faith was required for such a response, and that faith was of the same sort that

Abraham exercised later, but since the incident recounted in Genesis 15 had special bearing on justification, it alone is utilized here.

At the time referred to in the quotation (Gen 15:6) Abraham was in the promised land but had as yet no progeny. Reminding God of this fact, he protested, "a slave born in my house will be my heir" (Gen 15:3). The reference is to Eliezer of Damascus. As revealed by the Nuzi tablets, in the society of Ur of the Chaldees, out of which Abraham had come, a couple could adopt a son to help them in their old age and to see that they were properly buried. In consideration of these services, the one adopted was named the heir. As time went on, Abraham saw no prospect other than this. But God directed him to look up into the heavens and count the stars, promising that his descendants would be as numerous. Abraham accepted this promise, relying on God to fulfill it. This was the basis on which God pronounced him righteous.

The nature of Abraham's faith was essentially the same as that of the NT believer despite the difference in time. (Abraham looked forward to something God would do, whereas the Christian looks back to what God has provided in Christ.) Can we go further and say that the object of faith is the same, implicit in the promise to Abraham, explicit in the gospel? It does seem that we are warranted in concluding that Abraham trusted in a promise that pointed to Christ (John 8:56; Gal 3:16), though at this time this may not have been clear to the patriarch. Much depends on how he understood the promise in Genesis 12:3. Abraham's faith was credited to him "as righteousness," which means that faith itself is not righteousness.

Paul goes on to contrast faith with works (vv.4, 5), noting that work yields wages that must be treated as an obligation for an employer, whereas faith means that the one who exercises it receives a righteous standing simply as a gift (literally, "grace") from God. So grace is pitted against obligation and faith against works (cf. 11:6). It is possible that Paul has borrowed the term "wage" (Gr. *misthos*) from the LXX of Genesis 15:1, where reward or recompense is assured to Abraham.

How far grace goes beyond justice is seen in the statement that God justifies the wicked (or ungodly). Not only does God justify men apart from works but he does so contrary to what they deserve. OT law required the judge to condemn the wicked and justify the righteous (Deut 25:1), but where God is both Judge and Savior the wicked have an opportunity denied to them in human reckoning. The prophetic word anticipated this result through the work of the Servant (Isa 53:5, 6, 11). In saying that God justifies the ungodly, the text is not singling out Abraham as the sinner par excellence but rather is pointing to the type of man who is desperately in need of justification, which actually embraces all (cf. 5:6), including Abraham.

Notes

1 There is a textual problem in this verse. The Gr. infinitive εὑρηκέναι (*heurēkenai*), rendered "discovered " in NIV, is placed after "our forefather" in some MSS, in which case it is naturally taken with κατὰ σάρκα (*kata sarka*), "according to the flesh" or "by his own powers." A more important group of MSS place the infinitive after "shall we say," in which contruction the words *kata sarka* go with "our forefather" to indicate a natural or blood relationship. Then a small group of witnesses, including the important MS B, omit the infinitive. The uncertain position of the infinitive in some witnesses tends to support the omission. A few tr., including the NEB, reflect the omission in their wording.

2. The case of David

4:6–8

> [6]David says the same thing when he speaks of the blessedness of the man to whom God credits righteousness apart from works:
>
> > [7]"Blessed are they whose offenses have been forgiven
> > and whose sins have been covered.
> > [8]Blessed is the man whose sin the Lord will never
> > count against him."

Though the case of David is not strictly parallel to that of Abraham, and though it is treated only briefly, it is clear from the opening word (Gr. *kathaper*) that the general theme remains the same. What strikes one as peculiar is the apparent lack of harmony between what Psalm 32 states and what Paul announces as the bearing of the quotation. Whereas Paul indicates that the quotation has to do with the reckoning of righteousness apart from works, the passage itself contains neither of these terms. Instead, it speaks of offenses that have been forgiven and of sins that have been covered. As we compare v.6 with vv.7, 8, one word stands out as common to both passages. It is the word translated "credit" in v.6 and "count" in v.8 (*logizesthai*). In fact, this word dominates the early part of the chapter, occurring in vv.3, 4, 5, 6, 8, 9, 10, 11.

Paul's training under Gamaliel shows through here, since it is evident that he is utilizing a principle of rabbinic interpretation made famous by Hillel, namely the principle of analogy. This means that in situations where the same word occurs in two passages of Scripture, the sense in one may be carried over to explain the meaning in the other. In the case of Abraham, righteousness was credited to him, apart from works, on the basis of faith. In the case of David. obviously no good work is involved, but on the contrary, sin has been committed. So the far-reaching nature of justification is seen to still greater advantage.

One may add that since David was actually already a justified man, known as the man after God's own heart, in his case we learn the truth that sin in the life of a believer does not cancel justification. God is able to forgive. His gifts are irrevocable (11:29). At the same time, God showed his displeasure regarding David's sin, severely chastening him until the sin had been fully confessed. Even afterward, his sins produced havoc in his family. David suffered the humiliation of the revolt led by Absalom. Yet God did not withdraw his favor and support, as seen by a succession of events: Absalom's setting aside of Ahithophel's counsel, the triumph of David's forces in the battle, the ignominious death of Absalom, and the resurgence of desire on the part of the people for David's return as their king. In contrast to Abraham, David lived under the regimen of the Mosaic law. Though the law is not mentioned, the text says that David "speaks of the blessedness of the man to whom God credits righteousness apart from works" (v.6). There may be a suggestion here that after having sinned, David could not rectify his situation by means of works. He was completely shut up to God's mercy exhibited in the forgiveness of his transgressions.

3. The promise to Abraham—apart from circumcision

4:9–12

> [9]Is this blessing only for the circumcised, or also for the uncircumcised? We have been saying that Abraham's faith was credited to him as righteousness. [10]Under what circumstances was it credited? Was it after he was circumcised, or before?

It was not after, but before! [11]And he received circumcision a sign and seal of the righteousness that he had by faith while he was still uncircumcised. So then, he is the father of all who believe but have not been circumcised, in order that righteousness might be credited to them. [12]And he is also the father of the circumcised who not only are circumcised but who also walk in the footsteps of the faith that our father Abraham had before he was circumcised.

9-12 The issue discussed here is the importance of the time of God's declaration of righteousness on behalf of Abraham in relation to the time of his circumcision. By using the term "blessedness" from the opening of Psalm 32 Paul makes the transition from David back to Abraham. Are the uncircumcised able to share in this blessedness? As Strack and Billerbeck point out, the answer of the synagogue to such a question was that the blessedness was properly confined to the circumcision (*Kommentar zum Neuen Testament aus Talmud und Midrasch*, 3:203). Paul dissents, arguing skillfully that the benefit David enjoyed was enjoyed by Abraham, and Abraham received it when he was still uncircumcised! To all intents and purposes, he was like one of the Gentiles. This opens the door to the extension of the blessedness of justification to the Gentiles. Paul is still using the method of analogy regarding *logizesthai* ("credited"). As Genesis 15:6 had been explained with the aid of Psalm 32:1, 2, now the apostle reverses direction and explains Psalm 32 with the aid of Genesis 15. David, of course, was circumcised, but Abraham was not circumcised at the time of his being credited with righteousness on the basis of faith. According to the record, it was fourteen years later that he received the rite (Gen 17:24-26). Circumcision, then, was really a sign of what he previously had. It was a testimony to justifying faith, not something in which to take any pride (cf. 2:25-29). "We cannot doubt that circumcision was delayed in order to teach the believing Gentiles of future ages that they may claim Abraham as their father, and the righteousness of faith as their inheritance" (J.A. Beet, *A Commentary on St. Paul's Epistle to the Romans* [New York: Thomas Whittaker, 1892[8]]). It could even be said that the Gentile has first claim on the patriarch, who was just like himself when justified. The Jew stands rebuffed for his pride and exclusiveness (cf. Acts 15:11; Gal 2:16). Obviously the apostle is not speaking in v.12 of two groups, Jews and Gentiles, for he has finished speaking of Gentiles in the preceding verse. Here he refers to Jews in two categories—not only as circumcised but, what is more important, as believers who share the faith Abraham had before he was circumcised.

4. The promise to Abraham—apart from the law

4:13-17

[13]It was not through law that Abraham and his offspring received the promise that he should be heir of the world, but through the righteousness that comes by faith. [14]For if those who live by law are heirs, faith has no value and the promise is worthless, [15]because law brings wrath. and where there is no law there is no transgression.

[16]Therefore, the promise comes by faith, so that it may be by grace and may be guaranteed to all Abraham's offspring—not only to those who are of the law but also to those who are of the faith of Abraham. He is the father of us all. [17]As it is written: "I have made you a father of many nations." He is our father in the sight of God, in whom he believed—the God who gives life to the dead and calls things that are not as though they were.

13-17 The thought moves on to the consideration that Abraham's justification was apart from the law or legal considerations. Paul speaks of a promise received by "Abraham and his offspring" that "he should be heir of the world." Nothing so precise can be detected in the text of Genesis. Meyer suggests that the possession of the land of promise, in accordance with God's gift, is here looked on as the foil for a greater inheritance, namely, the messianic kingdom, in which the descendants of Abraham would have a special stake. The objection to this is certainly not that no place for a messianic kingdom can be found in Paul (8:17; 1 Cor 6:2; cf. Matt 19:28), but rather that the subject of the chapter has not changed. Abraham's justification came in connection with the promise of offspring comparable in number to the stars of the heavens. Nothing in the section we are considering suggests the thought of dominion. To be sure, Abraham received a promise that his descendants would possess the gate of their enemies (Gen 22:17) but that concept is not introduced here. Furthermore, "world" lacks the article, so that it is not likely intended to denote the physical world but the multitude of those who will follow Abraham in future generations in terms of his faith. These he can claim as his own. Finally, it is not said that Abraham's offspring will be heirs of the world but that he will be such an heir. This is not favorable to the eschatological interpretation of a millennial kingdom involving the renewed nation of Israel as its core element. The theme is still that vast influence of the man of faith upon succeeding generations and peoples. He will be the father of many nations in the sense that he is the father of their faith, since by that means rather than by some other they will be justified (cf. Gen 12:3; 22:18).

But we must return to Paul's main thrust, that the promise is not conditioned "through law." The thought is not developed in quite the same way as in Galatians 3:17, 18, where it is recognized that the Mosaic law was several hundred years in the future when God was dealing with Abraham, and that the law was not designed to upset the promise or qualify it.

Here, however, the point is made that if inheritance of the promise comes to those "who live by law," then faith is emptied of value and the promise has effectively been put out of operation. As soon as a promise is hedged about with conditional elements, it loses its value. Particularly is this true of the law because of its inflexible character. As Paul puts it, "The law brings wrath." To make the promise conditional on law observance would pit the God of grace against the God of judgment, an intolerable impasse. Where there is no law, there may indeed be sin, but not transgression. In case the promise had been conditioned by law keeping, the human inability to observe the law with complete fidelity would have occasioned disobedience and consequently the operation of wrath, resulting in forfeiture of what was promised. In summary, to introduce law keeping as a condition for receiving the promise would have two disastrous effects. It would put a question mark over the character of God for adding a condition and it would make the realization of the promise impossible for men, since no one has been able fully to keep the law (see vv.14, 15).

The promise, on the other hand, belongs to the realm of faith and grace (v.16). By mentioning faith first, due to its prominence in the whole passage, Paul appears to put grace in a secondary position, but it cannot have been his intent to make grace depend on faith (cf. Eph 2:8). Faith is put forward as a reaffirmation of v.13, after vv.14, 15 have ruled out law. Hence its prominence in the sentence. The only ground for certainty in relation to the promise is grace (as opposed to attempted legal obedience). Probably the element of certainty ("guaranteed") is intended to apply to faith as well as to grace. This is just another way of saying that the ultimate guarantee must be God and his faithfulness.

"Those who are of the law" are not excluded from Abraham's offspring. This means that a person who happened to live during the Mosaic era was not thereby excluded from the blessing of the Abrahamic covenant, provided he had faith. The expression cannot refer to legal obedience without bringing Paul into contradiction with himself. But the blessing of Abraham is also for those who, though not belonging to the Mosaic epoch, yet share the faith of the patriarch. Both groups are in view in the statement "He is father of us all." This is followed by an appeal to the prediction that Abraham would be a father of many nations (Gen 17:5), which could not refer to the twelve tribes of Israel, since they constituted but one nation. Only God could foresee the course of history that was to include the coming of Christ, his finished work, his command to evangelize all nations (Matt 28:9, 20), and the response of faith to the gospel around the world.

God is described by two terms. First, he is one "who gives life to the dead." It is perhaps natural to think of such an expression in terms of resurrection (vv.24, 25), but hardly with reference to receiving Isaac back, as it were, from the dead, when Abraham was ready to offer him to God (a subject pursued in Heb 11:19 but not mentioned here). The thought seems to move rather along the line of making possible the provision of offspring despite the deadness of Abraham and Sarah as producers of offspring (cf. v.19, where the word "dead" occurs twice). This conclusion is favored by the second affirmation in which God is said to be the one who "calls things that are not as though they were." The word "calls" in this case does not mean to describe or designate, but rather "summon," perhaps "call into being." It may be used in this sense for his creative activity (see Isa 48:13, NEB; 2 Baruch 21:4). Isaac was real in the thought and purpose of God before he was begotten.

It is entirely foreign to the context and to all of Paul's teaching to understand him as meaning that God pronounces a man righteous when he really is not. Justification is not a fiction. In the sight of God the justified sinner has a righteous standing that cannot be challenged (8:33, 34).

5. Abraham's faith the standard for every believer

4:18–25

> [18]Against all hope, Abraham in hope believed and so became the father of many nations, just as it had been said to him, "So shall your offspring be." [19]Without weakening in his faith, he faced the fact that his body was as good as dead—since he was about a hundred years old—and that Sarah's womb was also dead. [20]Yet he did not waver through unbelief regarding the promise of God, but was strengthened in his faith and gave glory to God, [21]being fully persuaded that God had power to do what he had promised. [22]This is why "it was credited to him as righteousness." [23]The words "it was credited to him" were written not for him alone, [24]but also for us who believe in him who raised Jesus our Lord from the dead. [25]He was delivered over to death for our sins and was raised to life for our justification.

18–22 The final value of Abraham in respect to justification is that his faith becomes the standard for all believers. "Against all hope," this man believed. In view of his "deadened" condition (and that of Sarah likewise) because of advanced age, the situation seemed past hope. Nevertheless, he believed the promise of God that offspring would be given. "In hope" takes account of the great change that came over his outlook due to the pledge God gave him. After making the original promise (Gen 15:5), God waited until it was physically impossible for this couple to have children. Then he repeated his pledge (Gen 17:5). Abraham's act of faith was essentially the same as on the previous occasion, but meanwhile circumstances had made the fulfillment of the promise impossible apart from supernatural intervention. He was shut up to God and was able to rest his faith there.

He "faced the fact" of his physical condition and that of Sarah and "did not waver through unbelief." The refusal to waver answers to the refusal to weaken in faith. Abraham apparently suffered a momentary hesitancy (Gen 17:17), but it passed and was not held against him. That he really trusted God for the fulfillment of the promise is seen in his readiness to proceed with circumcision for himself and his household before Isaac was conceived (Gen 17:23–27). This act in itself could be construed as giving "glory to God," an expression of trust in the power of the Almighty to make good his promise. Moreover, it was an open testimony to others of his trust in God's faithfulness to his word. If God should fail in this matter, Abraham would be an object of pity by some, of ridicule by others.

As far as Abraham was concerned, he was not taking a chance. He was "fully persuaded" that God's power would match his promise. This man of God was called on to believe in a special divine intervention—not after it occurred, as the Jews were challenged to do concerning the resurrection of Jesus (Acts 2–5), but before. His faith is the more commendable because it was exercised in the face of apparent lack of necessity. Would not Ishmael do as the desired progeny? He had been born to Abraham through Hagar in the interval between the original promise (Gen 15) and its renewal (Gen 17). Abraham was willing to rest in the wisdom as well as in the will of God. Verse 22 probably refers to the original statement of Abraham's justification, emphasizing that his ability to meet the renewed promise of God by unwavering faith was strictly in line with the faith that brought justification at an earlier point (v.3).

23–25 Having dealt with Abraham's situation, the apostle turns finally to applying God's dealings with the patriarch to the readers of the Epistle. This procedure accords with his observation that "everything that was written in the past was written to teach us, so that through endurance and the encouragement of the Scriptures we might have hope" (15:4). There are differences between Abraham's case and the position of the readers. Yet the basic similarity in God's dealings with both is unmistakable. Both believe in God as the one who acts in their behalf; both receive justification. Of course, the mention of the resurrected Jesus (v.24) is an element that could not belong to the OT as history, but the intended parallel with Abraham's experience is fairly evident. The same God who raised Jesus our Lord from the dead quickened the "dead" body of Abraham so as to make parenthood possible.

Death and resurrection were the portion of the Savior (v.25). One can hardly fail to notice the carefully balanced character of this final statement, relating as it does the death of Jesus to our sins and his resurrection to our justification. Beyond question, the statement owes much to Isaiah 53, where in LXX the Servant is pictured as delivered up on account of the sins of the many. Justification appears in the Hebrew text of that chapter (v.11). Moreover, the resurrection, though not stated in so many words, is implied in vv.10, 12. Whether Paul's statement is one he has taken over from Christian tradition (cf. 1 Cor 15:3, 4), as some think, or is entirely his own composition, may be an open question. But at least one can affirm that this passage shows the early tendency to phrase redemptive truth in brief, creedlike formulations.

The chief difficulty for interpretation lies in the preposition "for" that is common to both clauses. In itself our word "for" is ambiguous. It can mean "because of" or "with a view to." So "delivered over to death for our sins" can mean "because our sins were committed" and it was on account of them that Jesus had to die if salvation were to be procured. Similarly, "raised to life for our justification" can mean that Jesus was resurrected because our justification was accomplished in his death (cf. "justified by his blood," 5:9). On the other hand, one can interpret the "for" as meaning that Christ was delivered to death to deal with our sins, to atone for them, and that he was raised in order to achieve our justification. In justice to the Greek text it should be granted that the former alternative is the more natural. The idea of "with a view to" is not readily associated with *dia*, whereas Greek has another preposition (*eis*) that expresses that idea more clearly and is in fact used in the expression "justification that brings life" (literally, "justification with a view to life" (5:18). Furthermore, if one looks for a strict parallel between the passage and the situation of Abraham, he will see that Abraham's justification did not depend on the factor of resurrection, because he believed and was justified before the quickening of his deadened condition. One could reply, of course, that we should not look for complete similarity in the situation of Abraham and that of believers in the Christian era.

It may be helpful to recognize that justification, considered objectively and from the standpoint of God's provision, was indeed accomplished in the death of Christ (5:9) and therefore did not require the resurrection to complete it. Paul does not mention the resurrection in his definitive statement on justification in 3:21–26. Subjectively, however, the resurrection of Christ was essential for the exercise of faith, since his continuance under the power of death would create serious doubts about the efficacy of his sacrifice on the cross. Furthermore, justification is not simply a forensic transaction, important as that aspect is, but involves also a living relationship with God through Jesus Christ (5:18).

Finally, as Murray reminds us (in loc.), the justification to which Paul refers is justification by faith (cf. 5:1) and this applies as definitely to us as to Abraham. To believe in a Christ who died for our sins is only half the gospel. The resurrection cannot be omitted: observe how Paul includes both aspects in 6:3, 4 when showing how the work of Christ provides the foundation for Christian living.

Notes

19 א A B C, among others, have the reading κατενόησεν (*katenoēsen*), meaning "he considered well." Another reading, which puts a negative before this verb, is supported by D G K P Ψ 33, etc. It is a rare situation to have two opposite readings that nevertheless yield much the same sense. The former reading has the stronger attestation.

D. *The Benefits of Justification*

5:1–11

> [1]Therefore, since we have been justified through faith, we have peace with God through our Lord Jesus Christ, [2]through whom we have gained access by faith into this grace in which we now stand. And we rejoice in the hope of the glory of God. [3]Not only so, but we also rejoice in our sufferings, because we know that suffering produces perseverance; [4]perseverance, character; and character, hope. [5]And

hope does not disappoint us, because God has poured out his love into our hearts by the Holy Spirit, whom he has given us.

⁶You see, at just the right time, when we were still powerless, Christ died for the ungodly. ⁷Very rarely will anyone die for a righteous man, though for a good man someone might possibly dare to die. ⁸But God demonstrates his own love for us in this: While we were still sinners, Christ died for us.

⁹Since we have now been justified by his blood, how much more shall we be saved from God's wrath through him! ¹⁰For if, when we were God's enemies, we were reconciled to him through the death of his Son, how much more, having been reconciled, shall we be saved through his life! ¹¹Not only is this so, but we also rejoice in God through our Lord Jesus Christ, through whom we have now received reconciliation.

Here the discussion of justification goes beyond the exposition of what it is in itself, for that has been sufficiently covered. At this point we hear no more of the law or of fancied merit built up through obedience to it. Justification is now viewed in the light of the wealth of blessings it conveys to the child of God. Many indeed are the gifts that lie enfolded in this cardinal truth. It becomes a serious thing, then, to say, as some have done, that justification is not a central teaching with Paul but just an illustration of salvation drawn from the law court, or to call it merely a line of argumentation worked out to save his Gentile converts from the ignominy of being circumcised for their admission to the fellowship of the church. If this general appraisal had any truth in it, we should expect the apostle to make much more sparing use of the term "justify" than he does. Indeed we should look for him to be satisfied with "salvation" terminology.

Some would contend that we are already on the ground of sanctification in this chapter, and in support of this opinion they are able to point to the strong emphasis on experience in vv.2-5. No doubt the elements mentioned there do have an important bearing on Christian life, but the overall emphasis still remains on justification (vv.9, 16) along with reconciliation as seen against the background of enmity occasioned by sin (vv.10, 11). Perhaps even more decisive is usage of prepositions, a small but significant indicator. The emphasis in chapter 5 is on what has been done for the believer *through* Christ and his saving work (5:1, 2, 9, 10, 11, 17, 18, 19, 21; cf. 3:24), whereas in chapter 6 Paul deals with what has happened to the believer together *with* Christ (6:4, 5, 6, 8) and what he enjoys *in* Christ (6:11, 23). Furthermore, it is in chapter 6 (vv.19, 22), not in chapter 5, that sanctification (or holiness) first makes its appearance. Nevertheless, it is true that chapter 5, (especially in vv.12-21) prepares for chapters 6 to 8. In this passage the union of the people of Christ with him, as over against their former union with Adam, furnishes the needed context for the development of the various aspects of sanctification.

1-5 "Therefore" suggests that the whole argument from 3:21 on is the background for what is now set forth. Paul is assuming the reality of justification for himself and his readers ("we have been justified"). This could have been inferred from 4:24, 25, but Paul is careful to emphasize that justification is an assured fact before going on to show what is involved in it. So he includes the part that faith plays also, though this too has been affirmed in 4:24.

Before considering the items that come spilling out of the cornucopia of justification, we must confront a textual problem in v.1. NIV reads, "We have peace with God," but NEB, for example, has "let us continue at peace with God." These two renderings reflect two slightly different forms of the same word "have." (For data regarding the textual support for each, see notes at the end of this section.) The second rendering, the cohortative subjunctive, has the stronger attestation in the manuscripts. However, exhortation seems out of place here, especially since the construction demands that this same hortatory thrust be carried to a point midway through v.3. This is particulary awkward in v.2, because the text says that through Christ we have also gained access—and this is fact, not exhortation. The word "also" (*kai*), which is not indicated in many translations, including NIV, seems clearly to point to something mentioned earlier that we also have through Christ. This decidedly favors the rendering "we have peace."

Again, it is well known that short and long *o* of Greek were often confused in pronunciation during the Hellenistic period. J.H. Moulton writes, "It is indeed quite possible that the apostle's own pronunciation did not distinquish o and ō sufficiently to give Tertius a clear lead, without his making inquiry" (*A Grammar of New Testament Greek* [Edinburgh: T. & T. Clark, 1906]. Vol. I, p. 35). This means that it is precarious to lay too much store by the superior manuscript testimony for the ō reading. Another consideration is pointed out by Field, who notes that "*echomen* may have been changed into *echōmen* to correspond with *kauchōmetha* ('we rejoice'), which was supposed to be subjunctive mood" (p. 155).

The first of the blessings conveyed by justification is "peace." We have encountered the word in the salutation (1:7) and in an eschatological setting (2:10). Here, however, the milieu is the estrangement between God and man because of sin. Peace takes its meaning from the emphasis on divine wrath in the first section of the Epistle. Observe also, in the present chapter, the occurrence of "wrath" (v.9) and "enemies" (v.10). Peace in this setting means harmony with God rather than a subjective state in the consciousness of man.

That the objective meaning is to be adopted in the present passage is put beyond all doubt by the fact that the kind of peace in view is "peace with God." The same expression "with God" is used in John 1:1 to indicate the unity and perfect harmony between the Father and the Son. Since this particular boon is placed first among the benefits of justification, it should be evident how central is the wrath of God to Paul's exposition of the plight of man that God has moved to remedy. Man's plight could be dealt with only through the mediation of our Lord Jesus Christ. Related passages tell the same story. Christ made peace through the blood of his cross (Col 1:20). "He is our peace," writes Paul in Ephesians 2:14, and then he goes on to show how this peace works in two directions, removing the enmity between Jew and Gentile to make them one in the body of Christ and reconciling both in one body to God through the cross. In his lexicon, Bauer remarks that the term "peace" is nearly synonymous with the messianic salvation (cf. Acts 10:36).

The second benefit is "access" (v.2). Here also faith is mentioned as the essential instrumentality, as in justification itself. Since the word rendered "access" can also mean "approach" or "introduction," it is probable that the latter meaning is the more appropriate here, for introduction is fundamental to the access that is gained thereby. We are to think of the Father in his exaltation and glory as the one approached, with the Lord Jesus introducing us as those who belong to him and so to the Father. There is a striking similarity in thought between our passage and Ephesians 2:17, 18, where Paul asserts that Christ came and preached peace to those far away (Gentiles) and to those near (Jews), "for through him we both have access to the Father by one Spirit." Later in that Epistle Paul shows that this access enables one to approach God in prayer with freedom and confidence (Eph 3:12ff.).

The "grace in which we now stand" sums up the privilege of the saints in this present time, enjoying every spiritual blessing in Christ, and the possession of this grace gives warrant for the hope that we shall share the glory of God (v.2). In this prospect believers exult. Grace gives a foothold in the door that one day will swing wide to permit the enjoyment of the glorious presence of the Almighty, a privilege to be enjoyed forevermore. Grace is the only sure basis for the expectation of sharing eternity with God. Worth noting is the close relationship between faith and hope. As with Abraham (4:18), so with the believer in this age, the two virtues have much in common (cf. 1 Peter 1:21; Heb 11:1).

The word "rejoice," which was used to characterize the hope of the Christian for participating in the glory yet to be revealed (v.2), now carries over to another area totally different in nature as well as in time—namely, that of "sufferings." Peace with God does not necessarily bring peace with man. The actual conditions of life, especially for believers in the midst of a hostile society, are not easy or pleasant, but the knowledge of acceptance with God, of grace constantly supplied, and the prospect of future glory enable believers to exult in the face of sufferings. The word "sufferings" is often rendered "tribulations" and emphasizes the element of pressure. As a result, the usual setting for the term is external suffering such as persecution, but it is used occasionally for distress, a natural extension of the application of the word, since external events tend to affect the human spirit.

We do not expect to find a full treatment of the subject of suffering here, since sufferings are viewed simply as one link in a chain of events and interactions designed to show what profit they bring to Christian experience, not what they are in themselves. Elsewhere Paul stresses that they are an extension of the sufferings experienced by Christ in the days of his flesh, rightly to be experienced now by those who make up his body (Phil 3:10). Believers rejoice when by their suffering they can show their love and loyalty to the Savior (Acts 5:41).

Suffering has this value, that it produces "perseverance," or "steadfast endurance." This is a suitable element to go along with tribulation, because it denotes resistance to pressure, literally "a bearing up under it." One does not take the pressure passively by abjectly giving in to it, as much Oriental philosophy counsels its devotees to do. Christ "endured" the cross and thus triumphed over it. Right here lies one of the distinctives of the Christian faith, in that the believer is taught to glory and rejoice in the midst of suffering rather than to sigh and submit to it as a necessary or inevitable evil.

The value of perseverance is that it develops "character." Job sensed its worth, saying in the midst of his troubles, "When he has tried me, I shall come forth as gold" (Job 23:10 RSV). The word rendered "character" indicates tested value. The newborn child of God is precious in his sight, but the tested and proven saint means even more to him because such a one is a living demonstration of the character-developing power of the gospel. When we stand in the presence of God, all material possessions will have been left behind, but all that we have gained by way of spiritual advance will be retained. This progress is a testimony to God, so it rightly has a place in glory.

This helps to explain Paul's statement that character produces "hope." Looking back, we see that hope consummates a series of items beginning with sufferings. But just prior to that Paul has considered hope from the standpoint of another series—faith, peace, access, grace, and then hope of the glory of God. So we are entitled to say that just as our present access gives hope of sharing the divine glory, so with our sufferings. They help to produce character, and approved Christian character finds its ultimate resting place in the presence of God, not in a grave. By the tutelage of suffering the Lord is fitting us for his eternal fellowship.

Next, Paul makes it plain that this hope is not just a pious wish, for it does not put one to shame. It does not disappoint, because it is coupled with the love of God (v.5). Human love may bring disappointment and frustration, but not the love of God. "The Holy Spirit produces in the believer an immediate and overflowing consciousness that he is the object of God's redeeming love, and this is the guarantee that this hope will not disappoint him" (Shedd, in loc.). Subjective desire is supported by an objective divine gift guaranteeing the realization of an eternal fellowship with God.

This passage, then, contains an intimation of the importance of the believer's possession of the Holy Spirit as a certification concerning the future aspects of his salvation. In chapter 8 this is developed more fully. But even in the limited treatment given the Spirit in the present passage we get a glimpse of something that specially characterizes the Spirit. By him God's love is poured out in our hearts. The initial outpouring at Pentecost (Acts 2:33; cf. Ezek 39:29; Joel 2:28; Zech 12:10) is followed by a maintenance of the flow in individuals who receive the Spirit at conversion. The verb "poured out" speaks of the inexhaustible abundance of the supply, being reminiscent of the copious provision for the thirsty children of Israel in the wilderness (Num 20:8, 11). This is particularly impressive in view of Paul's identification of the rock with Christ (1 Cor 10:4). The blessings found in Christ are mediated to the people of God by the Spirit. Looking back over the paragraph, we see that the thought has advanced from faith to hope and from hope to love (the same order as in 1 Cor 13:13).

Notes

1. Support for the subjunctive ἔχωμεν (echōmen, "let us have") among the uncials includes B א A C D E K L, in addition to cursives, versions, and patristic citations. Support for the indicative ἔχομεν (echomen, "we have") is provided by correctors of B א FGP, besides cursives, versions, and patristic citations.

However, the discovery of a vellum fragment of part of Romans in 1950 has altered the situation considerably. It supports the text of B everywhere (through some thirty verses) except at 5:1. The Wyman fragment, designated 0220, is dated by W.H.P. Hatch in the latter part of the third century, whereas B dates from the first third of the fourth century. He writes, "This evidence for echomen is probably pre-Hesychian. Therefore the argument for the indicative is greatly strengthened, and the claim of the subjunctive to be the correct reading is correspondingly weakened" (HTR 45 [1952] 83).

6-8 Having dwelt on the powerful influence of the divine love ministered to the hearts of believers by the Spirit, Paul goes on to explore the depths of that love, finding it in the cross of Christ. The demonstration of God's love in Christ came "at just the right time." This recalls Paul's placing of the incarnation and redeeming work of our Lord in the fullness of time (Gal 4:4). Since the argument of Romans has included the purpose of the law as bringing clear knowledge of sin (3:20) and as working wrath (4:15), the connection with the Galatians material is fairly close. The law had operated for centuries and had served to expose the weakness and inability of man to measure up to the divine standard of righteousness. No further testing was needed. It *was* the right time. One may ask, perhaps, Suppose it be granted that Galatians and Romans have the same emphasis on this point, why then do they not have the same term for "time" (Rom has *kairos* and

Gal *chronos*)? Actually there is no perceptible difference, since the word "fulness" (*plērōma*) in Galatians introduces the very emphasis of *kairos*—time as to its character rather than as to its duration.

"Powerless" is the translation of a word that commonly means "weak" or "sickly," but here it has a somewhat specialized force well expressed by Sanday and Headlam as "incapable of working out any righteousness for ourselves (in loc.)." A still more uncomplimentary description of those who needed the intervention of Christ's death on their behalf is "ungodly." The same term was used in the striking statement of 4:5 that such are the people God justifies.

A third word descriptive of those for whom Christ died is "sinners." The verb "to sin" has been used in 3:23 to summarize the human predicament traced in the opening chapters. We need to see how Paul prepares the way for the impact of this term by contrasting it with both "righteous" and "good." He puts aside for the moment the technical theological force of the word "righteous" in the sense of "justified" and uses it as it is used in ordinary parlance. Likewise, he ignores the fact that in 3:12 he has quoted "There is no one who does good" from Psalm 14:3, and then proceeds to use "good" as we do when recognizing kindness and benevolence in one another. In other words, Paul is illustrating a point from ordinary life. It is a rare thing, he says, to find a person ready to die for an upright man, but conceivably it would be easier to find one willing to die for a good man. Evidently the "good man" stands on a higher plane than the "righteous man."

Lightfoot berates those who profess to see no substantial difference between the two, quoting extensively from the Fathers to show that they are not synonymous. The righteous man is righteous, but nothing more. He lacks feeling for others. He may be so severely just that he is unattractive, if not actually repellent. On the other hand, the good man, while not lacking righteousness, goes beyond the other by being kind and benevolent (*Notes on Epistles of St. Paul* [London: Macmillan, 1895], pp. 286, 287). The interpretation is slightly complicated by the absence of the article with "righteous," whereas "good" has it. This opens the possibility that the reference is not to a good man but to "the good cause," especially the public good (so Leenhardt, in loc.). But the context requires that all three words—righteous, good, and sinners—be treated as personal.

Now Paul is ready to proceed to his point. It was for "sinners" Christ died, for men who were neither "righteous" nor "good." The contrast is between the tremendous worth of the life laid down and the unworthiness of those who stand to benefit from it. Back of the death of Christ for sinners is the love of God (v.8): God loved; Christ died. No attempt is made to deal with the Savior's reaction or motivation. Paul leaves much to Christian awareness of the intimate bond between Father and Son, the whole truth about God being in Christ (2 Cor 5:19) and Christ being motivated by love for the lost (John 15:12, 13). What he puts in the foreground is the love of God, and this Paul underscores by designating it as "his [God's] own love." It is distinctive, unexpected, unheard of (cf. John 3:16).

Four times in these three verses the expression "die for" occurs, and in each instance the preposition is *hyper* (on behalf of), commonly employed by Paul in such contexts. He could have used *anti* in the place of, which would stress the substitutionary aspect of the death of Christ. He probably avoids it, however, because he is desirous of stressing something else as well, in line with the emphasis on the divine love. For this purpose *hyper* is eminently suited; it can express the substitutionary character of the sacrifice of Christ (as papyri usage indicates) plus the additional element of action on behalf of another in line with the loving empathy of God in Christ.

9-11 Whereas the preceding paragraph dealt with the depth of the love of God as seen in the cross, the present section moves on to declare the height of that love, its refusal to stop short of effecting final and everlasting salvation in which the enmity created by sin has been completely overcome.

We are invited to take our stand on the fact of an achieved justification (the terminology is identical with that found in v.1), then turn to face the far-reaching effects of this justification on our future. Lest it be taken lightly, the means of that justification is repeated also—"by his [Christ's] blood." NEB has "by Christ's sacrificial death," and Barrett renders it, "at the cost of his blood." We were reconciled when we were enemies. Surely, then, since God no longer looks on us as enemies subject to his wrath, he will find it possible to maintain the status quo and not suffer us to lapse back into the unreconciled position and, furthermore, will carry us on to the full end of our salvation. The agency of Christ continues to be crucial, only now with this difference, that, whereas our justification was achieved by his death, our preservation is secured by his life. This is a clear reference to his postresurrection life rather than to his life in the days of his flesh. Here Paul conjoins justification and salvation as he did in the theme (1:16, 17).

No doubt, the pivotal word for the right understanding of vv.10, 11 is *echthroi* (enemies), the fourth term Paul has used for those in the unsaved state. (See vv.6-8 for the others.) Is "enemies" used in an active sense to mean those who have enmity toward God (cf. 8:7) or in the passive sense, meaning those who are reckoned as enemies by God? Several reasons dictate that the latter is the intended force of the word. First, that the word is capable of conveying this meaning is evident from 11:28, where the people of Israel are spoken of as enemies in the reckoning of God and yet loved by him, involving the same combination as in the passage we are considering. The enmity in 11:28 is not temperamental but judicial. Second, the mention of "God's wrath" in v.9 points to the conclusion that the *echthroi* are the objects of the wrath. Third, the tenor of the argument leads one to the same conclusion. Paul reasons from the greater to the lesser. If God loved us when we were enemies, now that he has made provision for us at infinite cost, much more will he go on to see us through to the final goal of our salvation. But if the sense is that God loved us and saved us when we were enemies in our attitude toward him, the "much more" loses its point. "He is not arguing that if we have begun to love God we may reckon on his doing so and so for us, but because He has done so much, we may expect Him to do more" (Archibald McCaig in ISBE, 1930, vol. IV, p. 2537a). Fourth, Paul not only states that we have been reconciled (v.10) but that we have *received* the reconciliation (v.11). He avoids saying that we have done anything to effect the reconciliation. God provided it through the death of his Son. The matter is made even clearer, if anything, in the companion statement that God has reconciled us "to himself" (2 Cor 5:18). The appropriate response of the saved community is exultation (cf. vv.2, 3).

E. *The Universal Applicability of Justification*

5:12-21

> [12]Therefore, just as sin entered the world through one man, and death through sin, and in this way death came to all men, because all sinned—[13]for before the law was given, sin was in the world. But sin is not taken into account when there is no law. [14]Nevertheless, death reigned from the time of Adam to the time of Moses, even over those who did not sin by breaking a command, as did Adam, who was a pattern of the one to come.

¹⁵But the gift is not like the trespass. For if the many died by the trespass of the one man, how much more did God's grace and the gift that came by the grace of the one man, Jesus Christ, overflow to the many! ¹⁶Again, the gift of God is not like the result of the one man's sin: The judgment followed one sin and brought condemnation, but the gift followed many trespasses and brought justification. ¹⁷For if, by the trespass of the one man, death reigned through that one man, how much more will those who receive God's abundant provision of grace and of the gift of righteousness reign in life through the one man, Jesus Christ.

¹⁸Consequently, just as the result of one trespass was condemnation for all men, so also the result of one act of righteousness was justification that brings life for all men. ¹⁹For just as through the disobedience of the one man the many were made sinners, so also through the obedience of the one man the many will be made righteous.

²⁰The law was added so that the trespass might increase. But where sin increased, grace increased all the more, ²¹so that, just as sin reigned in death, so also grace might reign through righteousness to bring eternal life through Jesus Christ our Lord.

This difficult portion of the Epistle, packed with close reasoning and theological terminology, stands at the very heart of the development of Paul's thought. He has presented all men as sinners and Christ as the one who has died to redeem them. Now he delves into the question How does it come about that all men—with no exception but Jesus Christ—are in fact sinners? In answer, he goes all the way back to the first man Adam to affirm that what he did has affected the whole of mankind, involving everyone in sin and death. But over this record of disaster and loss he puts the countermeasures taken on behalf of the race by another man, Jesus Christ, of which all are potential beneficiaries.

12 The one man through whom sin entered the world is not immediately named (reserved till v.14). The same procedure is followed with the other man to be considered: he is called a man before he is named (v.15). Except for two nontheological references (Luke 3:38; Jude 14), every mention of Adam in the NT comes from the pen of Paul. In 1 Timothy 2:14 he makes the point that Adam, unlike Eve, was not deceived, but sinned deliberately. In 1 Corinthians 15, as in the Romans passage, he institutes a comparison between the first and the last Adam, but confines the treatment to the issue of death and resurrection, even though sin is dealt with somewhat incidentally (vv.17, 56), whereas in Romans 5 both sin and death are named immediately and are woven into the texture of the argument throughout. In the earlier letter Paul makes the significant statement "For as in Adam all die, so in Christ all will be made alive" (1 Cor 15:22) in line with Romans 5:12. Paul has already referred to the inevitable connection between sin and death in the only previous mention of death in Romans (1:32) exclusive of the death of Christ (5:10). But here in v.12 he pictures sin and death as entering the world through one man, with the result that death permeated the whole of mankind. It was the opening in the dike that led to the inundation, the poison that entered at one point and penetrated every unit of man's corporate life.

If Paul had stopped with the observation that death came to all men because all sinned, we would be left with the impression that all sinned and deserved death because they followed the example of Adam. But subsequent statements in the passage make it abundantly clear that the connection between Adam's sin and death and what has befallen the race is far closer than that. Paul can say that the many died because of "the trespass of the one man" (v.15). Clearly the gist of his teaching is that just as mankind has become involved in sin and death through Adam, it has the remedy of righteousness and life only in Christ.

What, then, is the precise relation of Adam in his fall to those who come after him? Paul does not say, unless he provides the information in the last clause of the verse. NIV uses the word "because," which is certainly the meaning of *eph' hō* in 2 Corinthians 5:4 and probably also in Philippians 3:12. The Vulgate rendering of the Greek is *in quo*, which could be understood as meaning "in which" (i.e., death) or "in whom" (i.e., Adam). The former does not make sense and the latter is so far removed from the antecedent ("man") as to be dubious, though this was Augustine's conclusion.

Now if the correct translation is "because all sinned," why did not Paul go on and say specifically that all sinned in the first man? That he could have done so seems clear from v.19: "For just as through the disobedience of the one man the many were made sinners, so also through the obedience of the one man the many will be made righteous." Was it the sudden breaking off to follow another line of thought (vv.13, 14) that prevented the full statement? Or was it his reluctance to gloss over human responsibility, which he had already established in terms of universal sin and guilt (3:23)? Experience demonstrates that despite the inheritance of a sinful nature from Adam, people are convicted of guilt for the sins resulting from it—the sins they themselves commit. Conscience is a factor in human life and the Holy Spirit does convict of sin (John 16:8). Perhaps, then, as some hold, while the emphasis on original sin is primary in the light of the passage as a whole, there is a hint that personal choice and personal sin are not entirely excluded (cf. "many trespasses" in v.16).

That we could have sinned in Adam may seem strange and unnatural to the mind of Western man. Nevertheless, it is congenial to biblical teaching on the solidarity of mankind. When Adam sinned, the race sinned because the race was in him. To put it boldy, Adam *was* the race. What he did, his descendants, who were still in him, did also. This principle is utilized in Hebrews 7:9, 10, "One might even say that Levi, who collects the tenth, paid the tenth through Abraham, because when Melchizedek met Abraham, Levi was still in the body of his ancestor."

If one is still troubled by the seeming injustice of being born with a sinful nature because of what the father of the race did and being held accountable for the sins that result from that disability, he should weigh carefully the significance of reconciliation as stated by Paul: "... that God was reconciling the world to himself in Christ, *not counting men's sins against them*" (2 Cor 5:19). The sins committed, that owe their original impetus to the sin of the first man, are not reckoned against those who have committed them provided they put their trust in Christ crucified and risen. God takes their sins and gives them his righteousness. Would we not agree that this is more than a fair exchange?

13,14 The dash at the end of v.12 is intended to indicate that the comparison upon which Paul has launched with his "just as" is not carried through. In view of what follows, the complete statement, if given here, would have run something like this: "Just as sin entered the world through one man, and death through sin, and in this way death came to all men, because all sinned, so righteousness entered the world by one man, and life through righteousness." Grammatically, the conclusion is not formally stated at all, although in KJV it is assumed that vv.13–17 are parenthetical, with v.18 stating the conclusion of v.12. As Meyer puts it, in v.18 and following we have recapitulation but not resumption. The necessary conclusion to v.12 has really been stated already in vv.15–17 in various ways. Throughout the passage the thought is so tremendous as to prove intractable from the standpoint of expressing it in orderly sequence. The thought outruns the structural capacity of language.

Judging from the use of "for" at the beginning of v.13, these two verses are intended to support and explicate v.12. The point is made that from Adam to Moses the law was not yet given, so sin was not present in the sense of transgression. Men did not have a charge from God similar to that which Adam had and violated. But the very fact that death was regnant during this period is proof that there was sin to account for it, seeing that death is the consequence of sin. The sin in view was the sin of Adam, which involved all his descendants. Death in this case rather obviously means physical death, which suggests that the same is true in v.12. This agrees with Paul's treatment of the subject of death in 1 Corinthians 15 (see especially v.22).

Adam is described as "a pattern of the one to come." Pattern translates the work *typos*, ordinarily rendered "type." It may seem strange that Adam should be designated as a type of Christ when the two are so dissimilar in themselves and in their effect on mankind. But there is justification for the parallel. "The resemblance, on account of which Adam is regarded as the type of Christ, consists in this, that Adam communicated to those whom he represented what belonged to him, and that Christ also communicated to those whom he represented what belonged to him" (Haldane, in loc.). This amounts to saying that what each did involved others. "The one to come" is to be taken from the perspective of Adam and his time, and has no reference to the second coming of Christ (cf. Matt 11:3). Barrett is of the opinion that since Paul has just mentioned Adam, the word "one" should be thought of in terms of the Adam to come, the last Adam, as Christ is explicitly termed in 1 Corinthians 15:45.

In his book, *Christ and Adam* (Harper, 1956), Karl Barth has advanced a provocative interpretation of Adam as a type of Christ. He has attempted to reverse the order: "Man's essential and original nature is to be found ... not in Adam but in Christ. In Adam we can only find it prefigured. Adam can therefore be interpreted only in the light of Christ and not the other way round" (p. 29). It should be evident, however, that Paul's thought here is not moving in the orbit of man as made in the image of God and therefore in the image of Christ who is the image of God. To import the preexistence of Christ is to introduce an element foreign to Paul's purpose and treatment in this passage. For a careful review of Barth's position and its weaknesses, one may consult Murray, pp. 384–90.

15–17 In this section Christ's effect on men is seen as totally different from that of Adam, and vastly superior. Note the repeated expression "how much more." Any hint of parallelism suggested by "pattern" is replaced by the element of contrast. True, there appears to be similarity in one point, in that the work of Adam and that of Christ relate to the many. It will readily be seen by comparing v.15 with v.12 that "the many" is the same as "all men" ("death came to all men" and "the many died"). The use of "the many" has this advantage, that it underscores the importance of Adam and Christ respectively. What one did, in each case, affected not one but many. The expression goes back to Isaiah 53:11, 12, which underlies our Lord's use in Mark 10:45.

Another notable feature of the passage is the expression "how much more" (vv.15, 17). The force of this seems to be bound up with the recurring use of "grace" and "gift," suggesting that the work of Christ not merely cancelled the effects of Adam's transgression so as to put man back into a state of innocence under a probation such as their progenitor faced, but rather gives to man far more than he lost in Adam, more indeed than Adam ever had. The gift, prompted by grace, includes righteousness (v.17) and life (v.18) which is later defined as eternal life (v.21). Paul makes a further observation to the effect that in Adam's case, a single sin was involved, and that was sufficient to bring condemnation, but in the work of Christ a provision is found for the many acts of sin that have resulted in the lives of his descendants (v.16).

Whereas up to this point Paul's train of thought has been concerned with developing the concept of sin taken over from v.12, now it turns to its companion factor, death, likewise mentioned in v.12, with a view to enlarging upon it (v.17). The point of the "much more" appears to be this—that in Christ not only is the hold of death, established by Adam's sin, effectively broken, but because of Christ's redeeming work the believer is able to look forward to reigning in life through Christ. This, of course, implies participation in the resurrection. Believers will have a share in the Lord's kingdom and glory.

18,19 At this point, as noted above, Paul provides something of a conclusion to v.12, but in such a way as to take account of the intervening material. The opening word, "consequently," shows his intent to summarize. Notice the careful balancing of the clauses. One trespass brought condemnation for all humanity and one act of righteousness brought justification for all. Adam's sin is labeled "trespass," indicating that it was deliberate (cf. "breaking a command" in v.14). The basic meaning of the word rendered "trespass" is to convey the idea of falling aside or going astray. "It refers directly to the disruption of man's relation to God through his fault" (Michaelis in TDNT VI, p. 172).

The reference is clearly to the violation of the divine restriction laid down in Genesis 2:17, with resulting condemnation for the entire human race. His act involved others directly; it did not merely set a bad example. Over against Adam's act, Paul put another of an entirely different character—an act of righteousness. The same Greek word occurs at the end of v.16, where it is rendered "justification." Perhaps "act" is a bit narrow for this context. "Work of righteousness" might be better. In fact, the whole scope of the ministry of our Lord could be in view. He came "to fulfill all righteousness" (Matt 3:15). The word "justification" is set over against "condemnation," but something is added, namely, the observation that justification is more than the antithesis of condemnation, more than the setting aside of an adverse verdict due to sin, more than the imputation of divine righteousness. It is the passport to life, the sharing of the life of God (cf. v.21).

Impressed by the fact that the word "one" is regularly used either of Adam or of Christ in 5:12–21, Leenhardt suggests that consistency demands that in v.18, instead of "one act of righteousness" we should render "one man's act of righteousness" (in loc.). To do this, however, would destroy the balance between this clause and the opening statement, where "one trespass" is inescapably the correct rendering rather than "the trespass of one."

Another term for Adam's failure occurs in v.19, namely, "disobedience." This accents the voluntary character of his sin. Matching it is the obedience of Christ. This concept was highly meaningful for Paul, as we know from Philippians 2:5–11. The interpretation of that passage along the lines of a latent comparison between Adam (unnamed, but in the background) and Christ is most satisfactory. Instead of grasping after equality with God, as Adam had done, the Lord Jesus humbled himself and became obedient even to the point of accepting death on a cross.

The result of Christ's obedience is that "the many will be made righteous." Does this refer to righteous character? Possibly so, if the future tense is definitely eschatological in its thrust, pointing to the consummation in glory, when imputed righteousness will have become righteousness possessed in unblemished fullness. But "will be made righteous" may simply be the equivalent of "will become righteous" in the forensic sense, as in 2 Corinthians 5:21, in which case the future tense need not be thought of as eschatological but as embracing all who in this age are granted justification. Most of these were indeed future to Paul's time. The milieu of thought has not shifted from the forensic.

Does the sweeping language used ("the many" being all men) suggest that all mankind will be brought within the circle of justification, so that none whatever will be lost? Some have thought so. But if the doctrine of universalism were being taught here, Paul would be contradicting himself, for he has already pictured men as perishing because of sin (2:12; cf. 1 Cor 1:18). Furthermore, his entire presentation of salvation has emphasized the fact that justification is granted only on the basis of faith. We must conclude, therefore, that only as "the many" are found in Christ can they qualify as belonging to the righteous.

20,21 At the conclusion of the chapter, Adam as a figure fades from view. Yet his influence is still present in the mention of sin and death. Paul now introduces another factor—the Mosaic law—to show its bearing on the great issues of sin and righteousness. There is scarcely a subject treated by Paul in Romans that does not call for some consideration of the law. The closest affinity to the thought in v.20 is found in 3:20, "Through the law we become conscious of sin." Also, chapter 7 traces the relationship between the law and sin in rather elaborate fashion.

The apostle is not maintaining that the purpose of the giving of the law is exclusively "that the trespass might increase," because he makes room for the law as a revelation of the will of God and therefore a positive benefit (7:12). The law also serves to restrain evil in the world (implied in 6:15; stated in 1 Tim 1:9–11). Paul says the law "was added." Similar language is used in Galatians 3:19, where the law is regarded as something temporary, designed to disclose the transgression aspect of sin and prepare the way for the coming of Christ by demonstrating the dire need for his saving work. This function of the law—viz., to increase transgression—was not recognized in rabbinic Judaism (H.J. Schoeps, *Paul* [Philadelphia: Westminster Press, 1961], p. 174). From the Sermon on the Mount, however, it appears that Jesus sought to apply the law in just this way, to awaken a sense of sin in those who fancied they were keeping the law tolerably well but had underestimated its searching demands and the sinfulness of their own hearts.

Lest someone raise a charge against the Almighty that to make possible an increase in sin is not to his credit, Paul insists that only where sin is seen in its maximum expression can divine grace truly be appreciated. "Grace increased all the more." The apostle waxes almost ecstatic as he revels in the superlative excellence of the divine overruling that makes sin serve a gracious purpose. In only one other passage does he use this verb (*hyperperisseuō*), which expresses "super-increase," and there the theme is not sin but trouble—"in all our troubles my joy knows no bounds" (2 Cor 7:4).

With great effect Paul brings the leading concepts of the passage together in the final statement (v.21). "Sin reigned in death" picks up vv.12, 14; "grace" looks back to vv.15. 17; "reign" reflects vv.14, 17; "righteousness" harks back to v.17 as well as to 1:17 and many other passages; "eternal life" completes and crowns the allusion to "life" in vv.17, 18. Sin and death are virtually personified throughout. Sin poses as absolute monarch, reigning through death as its vicar, but in the end it is exposed as a pretender and is obliged to yield the palm to another whose reign is wholly absolute and totally different, being as much a blessing as the other is a curse.

The treatment of sin, death, and salvation in terms of righteousness is crucial to our understanding of our relation to God. It loudly proclaims that no sinner, whether a mystic aspiring to direct contact with God or a legalist counting on his good works to approve him in God's sight, is able in his own way to find acceptance with God. Because another man, Adam, has intervened between him and the Creator, still another, even Jesus Christ, must be the medium of his return as a sinner to a righteous God. The claim of Jesus of Nazareth resounds through the passage: "I am the way—and the truth and the life. No one comes to the Father except through me" (John 14:6).

Notes

12 Entering the debate about the meaning of ἐφ' ᾧ (eph' hō), Nigel Turner does not attach great importance to the fact that Paul uses (epi) with the dative rather than ἐν (en), the preposition that appears in 1 Cor 15:22. He remarks that "even in classical Greek, and much more so in the New Testament period, the distinctions between the cases with this preposition are difficult to maintain" (*Grammatical Insights into the New Testament* [Edinburgh: T. & T. Clark, 1965], p. 118). He goes on to suggest that man is "under the power of" and "within the jurisdiction of" Adam. He does not deal with the problem of the remoteness of ἐφ' ᾧ (eph' hō) from its alleged antecedent ἀνθρώπου (anthrōpou).

A new departure in the attempted understanding of eph' hō has been made by F.W. Danker, NTS 14 (April 1968) 424–439. He interprets Paul to mean that death passed to all men "on the basis of what law [eph' hō] they committed their sins under." He relies both on the previous teaching about law as involving Jew and Gentile (2:12–16) and on the immediate context in 5:13, 14. He is able to make out a plausible case, but one is left with the uneasy feeling that if scholars have missed this down through the years, the chances that the Roman church caught the meaning are rather slim.

V. Sanctification: The Impartation of Righteousness

Up to this point the letter has answered such questions as these: Why does man need salvation? What has God done to effect it? How can we appropriate it? The answers have come in terms of sin, condemnation, the gift of Christ, faith, and justification. Is there need for anything more? Yes, there is. For the saved man cannot safely be turned over to his own wisdom and his own devices, seeing that he has not yet reached the perfect state. He must still contend with sin and must depend on divine resources. God's plan of salvation does not stop with justification but continues on in sanctification. A diagram may help to clarify the relationship between the two.

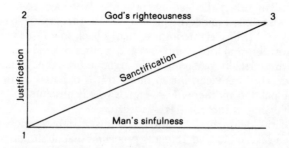

Point 1 marks conversion, or, if we think objectively rather than subjectively, regeneration. It is here that justification takes place. The line from 1 to 2 is not to be thought of as a process but as a change of position effected by God—his declaration of righteousness on behalf of the condemned sinner. Justification by faith means that one is lifted once-for-all to the level of God's righteousness. His standing before God is complete and perfect, because Christ has been made his righteousness (1 Cor 1:30; cf. 2 Cor 5:21). At no time in this life or in the life to come will his status in terms of righteousness be any greater. It will neither diminish nor fade, "for God's gifts and his call are irrevocable" (11:29).

Of course, God is concerned not only with the believer's status but also with his state, his actual condition. No sooner has he justified a person than he begins a process of growth that we know as sanctification. It is represented by the diagonal line between 1 and 3. This is a process, to be sure, but it should be observed that the term "sanctification" is used in Scripture also to express a setting apart that is basic to any progress in the Christian life. Consider the description of the Corinthian believers as (already) "sanctified" (1 Cor 1:2) in seeming contradiction to the unholy state of many of them as evidenced by Paul's exposure of their shortcomings as the letter unfolds. The puzzle is solved by his observation about what happened at their conversion. "You were washed, you were sanctified, you were justified in the name of the Lord Jesus and by the Spirit of our God" (1 Cor 6:11). Mention of their sanctification is actually given priority over their justification, which reverses the expected order. But this is initial or positional sanctification, a setting apart of the sinner to God, which is basic to any improvement in his manner of life (cf. 1 Peter 1:2). This aspect of sanctification cannot be distinguished from justification in respect to time. But sanctification as a process is naturally dependent upon and subsequent to justification.

The significance of point 3 should be noted also. This is the juncture at which the process of sanctification reaches its consummation, when the saint will experience complete sanctification because his sinful nature is left behind and his life is fully conformed to the divine standard as seen in God's Son (8:29). This occurs at death (Heb 12:23) or at the return of Christ in the case of the saints who are alive at that time (1 John 3:2). Then for the first time the believer's actual state in terms of righteousness will conform to the status conferred on him at his justification (Gal 5:5). His standing and his state will be identical.

A. The Believer's Union With Christ in Death and in Resurrection Life

6:1–14

> [1]What shall we say, then? Shall we go on sinning so that grace may increase? [2]By no means! We died to sin; how can we live in it any longer? [3]Or don't you know that all of us who were baptized into Christ Jesus were baptized into his death? [4]We were therefore buried with him through baptism into death in order that, just as Christ was raised from the dead through the glory of the Father, we too may live a new life.
>
> [5]If we have been united with him in his death, we will certainly also be united with him in his resurrection. [6]For we know that our old self was crucified with him so that the body of sin might be rendered powerless, that we should no longer be slaves to sin—[7]because anyone who has died has been freed from sin.
>
> [8]Now if we died with Christ, we believe that we will also live with him. [9]For we know that since Christ was raised from the dead, he cannot die again; death no longer has mastery over him. [10]The death he died, he died to sin once for all; but the life he lives, he lives to God.
>
> [11]In the same way, count yourselves dead to sin but alive to God in Christ Jesus.

¹²Therefore, do not let sin reign in your mortal body so that you obey its evil desires. ¹³Do not offer the parts of your body to sin, as instruments of wickedness, but rather offer yourselves to God, as those who have returned from death to life; and offer the parts of your body to him as instruments of righteousness. ¹⁴For sin shall not be your master, because you are not under law, but under grace.

In this section we will see that Christ passed through certain epochal experiences—namely, death, burial, and resurrection. Viewed from the standpoint of his substitutionary sacrifice for sin, these events do not involve our participation, though our salvation depends on them. Our Lord was alone in enduring the cross, in being buried, and in being raised from the dead. But his redeeming work is not only substitutionary; it is also representative. "One died for all, and therefore all died" (2 Cor 5:14). So Christians are viewed as being identified with Christ in his death, burial, and resurrection. And as truly as he, having borne our sin, is now removed from any claim of sin against him—because he died to sin and rose again—we also by virtue of being joined to him are delivered from any claim of sin to control us. This line of thought is what Paul proceeds to develop in the passage before us. It is evident that God has a plan for dealing with the power of sin as well as with its guilt. The way has been prepared for this emphasis by the presentation of the solidarity between Christ and the redeemed in 5:12–21.

1. *The statement of the fact* (6:1–10)

1–4 It is notable that Paul begins this discussion by raising an objection and answering it. The objection grows out of his presentation of justification, especially the teaching that where sin increased, grace increased all the more (5:20). The query, then, is to this effect: "Are we not able, or even obliged, by the logic of justification, to continue on in sin, now that we are Christians, in order to give divine grace as much opportunity as possible to display itself? The more we sin, the more will God's grace be required to meet the situation, and this will in turn contribute the more to his glory."

The apostle shows his horror at such a suggestion: "By no means!" Other renderings are possible, such as "Away with the notion!" or "Perish the thought!" Paul has already repudiated a similar suggestion in a somewhat different context (3:8). It is probable that in the past, as he taught justification, objections of this sort were raised from time to time by those who feared that his teaching opened the door to libertinism by encouraging indifference to the ethical demands of the law. If so, his answer is not something recently developed, but rather forged out in years of reflection under divine guidance.

His answer is crisp: "We died to sin; how can we live in it any longer?" He does not say that sin is dead to the Christian. Chapter 7 is a sufficient refutation of any such notion. At this point Paul does not explain when or how we died to sin, being content to state the fact and its obvious implication, that to go on sinning is logically impossible. What he does present here is not the impossibility of committing a single sin, but the impossibility of continuing in a life dominated by sin. Death to sin is not something hoped for or resolved upon by the believer; it is something that has already taken place. It is a simple fact basic to the living of the Christian life. The explanation of our death to sin follows immediately (vv.3, 4).

It was accomplished by being "baptized into Christ Jesus." What is being described is a spiritual reality of the deepest import—not a ceremony, not even a sacrament. The metaphor of baptism is clearly used in a relational sense elsewhere, as in the case of the Israelites baptized into Moses by reason of the crossing of the Red Sea (1 Cor 10:2). They became united to him as never before, recognizing his leadership and their dependence on him. Union with Christ means union with him in his death. It is significant that although Jesus emphasized discipleship throughout his ministry, he did not speak of union with himself till he was on the verge of going to the cross (John 14-16). Earlier he spoke of his death under the figure of baptism (Luke 12:50).

Paul uses baptism to illustrate this vital union with Christ in his death (v.4), though baptism does not accomplish it. Apparently, he pictures burial with Christ, however momentarily, in the submergence of the body under the baptismal waters. The importance of burial is that it attests the reality of death (1 Cor 15:3, 4). It expresses with finality the end of the old life governed by relationship with Adam. It also expresses the impossibility of a new life apart from divine action. The God who raised Jesus Christ from the dead has likewise imparted life to those who are his. The expression "to live a new life" is literally "to walk in newness of life," the walk being the evidence of the new type of life granted to the child of God. This is a distinctive type of life realized only by one united to Christ (cf. 2 Cor 5:17), so that Christ is its dynamic. In this connection the question arises, Why should the resurrection of Christ be described as accomplished "through the glory of the Father?" It is because "glory" here has the meaning of power, as in the resurrection of Lazarus (John 11:40).

The latter half of v.4 has a noticeably balanced structure ("just as Christ . . . we too"), recalling the pattern in 5:12, 18, 21. This suggests that the principle of solidarity advanced in 5:12-21 is still thought of as operating here in the significance of baptism. There is no explicit statement that in baptism we were raised with Christ as well as made to share in his death. Resurrection is seen rather as an effect that logically follows from the identification with Christ in his death. However, resurrection is verbally connected with baptism in the parallel passage—Colossians 2:12.

There is a certain awkwardness in the statement that we were buried with Christ through baptism into death, seeing that in human experience burial follows rather than precedes death. However, as Sanday and Headlam point out (in loc.), this awkwardness disappears in the prominence given death in the whole passage. It is not into Christ's *burial* that believers are baptized but into his *death*, because it was there that he dealt with sin.

5-7 In v.5 we encounter a problem concerning resurrection. Is Paul referring to the future bodily resurrection of the saints? Many expositors think so, and they can point to the future tense of the verb ("we will . . . be"). Ordinarily, the future tense relates to something that will happen. Occasionally, however, it indicates what must logically or inevitably occur (cf. Gal 6:5). So if there are other grounds on which to question a future bodily resurrection here, the tense of the verb is not an insuperable obstacle. But a second factor to consider is that Christ's resurrection, mentioned in the previous verse, was indeed a bodily resurrection. This is true enough. But it should be observed that Paul does not say that just as Christ was raised, so we too shall be raised. Instead, he connects the resurrection of Christ with the possibility of a new life for those who are his. And that life belongs to the present time. Furthermore, it is evident from the use of "for" at the beginning of v.6 that what follows is intended to relate closely to the mention of resurrection at the end of v.5. Yet one looks in vain for anything in v.6 that relates to future bodily resurrection. Instead, Paul returns to consider the matter of participation in Christ's death in its bearing on freedom from the bondage of sin. Consequently, one is led to conclude that resurrection in v.5 has to do with spiritual resurrection—raised with Christ—as in Ephesians 2:6; Colossians 2:12, 3:1.

The certainty of our present participation in this new resurrection life is grounded on the truth that "we have been united with him in his death." Paul uses an expression here, translated "united with," that strictly means "grown together," virtually with the force of "fused into one." Clearly this union is not something gradually arrived at through a process of sanctification. Rather it is something established by God that becomes the very basis of sanctification in which the Christ life is expressed through the individuality of the one joined to him.

However, the problem of sin continues to dominate the thought of this section, and Paul returns to this theme by insisting that "our old self was crucified with him" (v.6). While the relation to v.5 is close, the language now becomes sharper and more realistic— e.g., "united with him in his death" becomes "crucified with him" (cf. Gal 2:20). Our spiritual history began at the cross. We were there in the sense that in God's sight we were joined to him who actually suffered on it. The time element should not disturb us, because if we sinned in Adam, it is equally possible to have died to sin with Christ. At this stage of the teaching it is not a question of our personal, conscious participation, but simply of our position as God has arranged it and as he sees it.

But what was it that was crucified? "Our old self " is literally "our old man." The same truth is taught in Colossians 3:9. In Ephesians 4:22, however, the putting off of the old man is a matter of exhortation. In some sense, then, the old man has been crucified; in another sense he may still claim attention. Since "man" has been used of Adam (5:12, 17, 19), it is possible that what has been crucified with Christ is our place in Adam, our position in the old creation, which is under the sway of sin and death. For the Christian, the old is gone; he belongs to the new creation order (2 Cor 5:17).

Yet the old order seeks to dominate the believer, as Ephesians 4:22 implies and experience confirms. Though the seeming inconsistency between that passage and this is not easy to resolve, it may be that in his Epistle to the Ephesians Paul, while presupposing the supplanting of the old Adam, is desirous of exhorting his readers to refuse to live in terms of the old man and instead to live deliberately and consciously in the reality of the new creation. It is necessary to distinguish between the old creation—namely, our inheritance from Adam—and our old nature, or the flesh. The latter still persists in the life of the redeemed and can become a prey to the operation of sin unless countered by the powerful influence of the new life in Christ.

The purpose behind the crucifixion of our old man is that sin should be rendered powerless so far as we are concerned. But the expression "body of sin" is a phrase that needs clarification. It should not be regarded as equivalent to "sinful body," for the body itself is not sinful. Scripture is clear in its teaching that sin arises from the heart, the inner life (Mark 7:21). Should we settle for "sinful self" (NEB)? This is suggestive, since the word *sōma* ("body") sometimes conveys the idea of man in his totality, not simply his physical organism. But this may be going too far in the present passage. The term "body" glances at the fact of crucifixion, which Christ endured in the body. Our body can become the instrument of sin, thus negating the truth of crucifixion with Christ. So "body of sin" seems to mean body insofar as it may become the vehicle of sin. Its previous slavery to the dictates of sin is broken. This annulling of the power of sin is based on a recognized principle—that death settles all claims. Our union with Christ in his death, which was designed to deal with sin once for all, means that we are free from the hold of sin. Its mastery is broken (v.7).

8-10 Union with Christ continues to be the theme in vv.8-10, but attention shifts from its effect on the problem of sin to a consideration of its bearing on the problem of death.

Consequently, resurrection comes into focus. Though there is considerable similarity with the close of v.4, the note of futurity ("we will also live with him") makes it apparent that future bodily resurrection is in view. For a brief time, death, as the executor of sin, held the Savior, but not for long. Since he was not guilty of personal sin, death had no right to hold him indefinitely (Acts 2:24). Likewise, it had no right to recall him to experience death again. Once having been raised from the dead, our Lord is alive for ever and ever (Rev. 1:18).

It was important for Paul to emphasize this truth, for the believer must have full confidence that the captain of his salvation will never again come under the power of sin and death. If he lacks that assurance, the teaching about union with Christ will be of little help to him. "He died to sin once for all." As Meyer puts it, "He submitted Himself to its power in His death, but through that death *He has died to its power*" (in loc.). In his risen life our Lord is set free to resume his face-to-face fellowship with God (John 1:1) and his preoccupation with the consummation of God's eternal purpose. In this respect he presents a pattern for the believer in his expectation of the future and also in his motivation for life in the present time (2 Cor 5:15).

2. *The appeal based on the fact* (6:11-14)

11-14 In the previous section Paul has been imparting information on the subject of union with Christ, and agreeable to this he has three times used the word "know" (vv.3, 6, 9). Now he employs a different key word—"count" or "reckon" (the same term used so often in chapter 4 in connection with righteousness). Reckoning does not create the fact of union with Christ but makes it operative in one's life. The charge to count oneself dead to sin but alive to God in Christ Jesus is in the present tense, indicating a necessity to keep up the process if one is to avoid reactivating the body of sin. Paradoxically, the Christian is dead and alive at the same time, as in Galatians 2:20, dead to sin and self but alive and responsive to God. He is to give no more response to sin than a dead man can give. On the other hand, all the potential that redeemed life affords is to be channeled Godward.

Since Paul seems to lay considerable stress on the importance of this process of counting or reckoning, we should inquire about its value—especially in view of the objection that such a process smacks of attempting to convince oneself of something unrealistic in terms of actual experience and so amounts to self-deception. The justification for the use of this terminology is at least threefold. First, this is a command freighted with apostolic authority. God is speaking through his servant, and what God commands must be efficacious. It must never be treated as frivolous. Second, the command is psychologically sound, for what we think tends to be carried out in action. The thought is father to the act. Third, this process must not be undertaken in a mechanical fashion, as though there were some sort of magic in going through the motions. One must really desire to have freedom from sin and to live responsibly to God. To that end he must avail himself of the means of grace, particularly the diligent use of Scripture and faithfulness in prayer.

This element of willing cooperation receives emphasis in v.12. The implication is that sin has been reigning. The believer must do his part by refusing obedience any longer to sin's enticements. The word "obey" has as its root idea "listening" or "heeding." If the body is kept mortified, it will have no ear for the subtle suggestions of evil. Paul here describes the body as "mortal"—a reminder that despite the glorious asset of being

71

united to Christ, we are still living in a frail instrument subject to the ultimate call of death.

Turning from the body as a whole to its separate members, Paul admonishes his readers not to hand these over to sin (the old master). But this is only half of the Christian's obligation. On the positive side, he is to offer himself (his personality and life-potential) to God with, as a corollary, the separate bodily capacities "as instruments of righteousness." The word "offer," by virtue of its tense, "implies a critical resolve, a *decision* of surrender" (Moule). This passage prepares the way for a similar emphasis in 12:1.

Paul concludes this portion of text with encouragement and an incentive. He promises the Roman Christians that if they will do as he has enjoined, sin will not be their master, and he adds, "because you are not under law, but under grace" (v.14). What is the relevance of this closing observation? Why should law be injected here? Surely because under law sin increases (5:20; cf. 1 Cor 15:56). The inference is that law lords it over its subjects. It condemns and brings them into virtual slavery. It faces them with their guilt and uses that guilt as a manacle to keep them in helpless subjection. But under grace there is liberty to live in accord with a higher principle—the resurrection life of the Lord himself.

It is worthy of attention that Christians are said to be *under* grace. Usually grace indicates a principle of divine operation, a moving out in kindness and love to lift the sinful and unworthy to God. Occasionally it is used of the sphere of the believer's life of privilege (5:2). But here in 6:14 it appears as a disciplinary power, in line with the apostle's effort to show that grace is not license (6:1ff.). Somewhat parallel is the word of Jesus to the weary and burdened, promising rest, but followed up with mention of his yoke (Matt 11:28–30). Related also is Paul's reminder that God's grace has appeared for the salvation of all, *training* us to live sober, upright, and godly lives (see Titus 2:11, 12).

B. *Union With Christ Viewed As Enslavement to Righteousness*

6:15–23

> [15]What then? Shall we sin because we are not under law but under grace? By no means! [16]Don't you know that when you offer yourselves to someone to obey him as slaves, you are slaves to the one whom you obey—whether you are slaves to sin, which leads to death, or to obedience, which leads to righteousness? [17]But thanks be to God that, though you used to be slaves to sin, you wholeheartedly obeyed the form of teaching to which you were committed. [18]You have been set free from sin and have become slaves to righteousness.
>
> [19]I put this in human terms because you are weak in your natural selves. Just as you used to offer the parts of your body in slavery to impurity and to ever-increasing wickedness, so now offer them in slavery to righteousness and to holiness. [20]When you were slaves to sin, you were free from the control of righteousness. [21]What benefit did you reap at that time from the things you are now ashamed of? Those things result in death! [22]But now that you have been set free from sin and have become slaves to God, the benefit you reap leads to holiness, and the result is eternal life. [23]For the wages of sin is death, but the gift of God is eternal life through Christ Jesus our Lord.

15–17 Paul has just affirmed, "You are not under the law." He goes on to show that this does not mean that they are free from the demands of righteousness. It would be strange and contradictory if those who are under grace should evidence a manner of life inferior to the standard held by those who are under law. As a matter of fact, the believer must face the fact that his salvation actually means a change of bondage. As he once served sin, he is now committed to a life of practical righteousness.

At first glance, the opening question seems virtually a repetition of v.1. The difference, however, lies in the tense of the verb. In v.1 the question was "Shall we go on sinning so that grace may increase?" Now the question is "Shall we sin [in any given case, or sin at all] because we are not under law but under grace?" Law is supposed to be a restraining influence. If one moves out from under that umbrella, will he not be exposing himself to the danger of committing sin even more than in his previous situation?

In answer, Paul appeals first of all to a fact familiar to all—namely, that whatever one submits to becomes his master. Jesus had taught this by saying, "Everyone who sins is a slave to sin" (John 8:34). To commit sin, then, puts one into bondage to sin, and the sequel is death (cf. 5:12; 8:13). The other option is a life of obedience resulting in righteousness (cf. 5:19). Paul is happy to acknowledge that his readers have renounced the service of sin and are now wholeheartedly obeying Christian teaching (v.17). Let us take special note of the way he puts the matter, especially because of KJV's mistranslation at this point: "that form of doctrine which was delivered you." In some other context Paul might have expressed himself that way, because he frequently spoke of Christian tradition, that which had been handed down to the church as apostolic teaching. But here the normal order is reversed—"you wholeheartedly obeyed the form of teaching to which you were committed." By virtue of becoming Christians, the believers had obligated themselves to obey what we might call the law of Christ (Gal 6:2). Even though he had not founded the Roman church, Paul was confident that those who had preached the gospel there and taught the converts had reproduced the characteristic teaching that had been standard from the beginning (Acts 2:42). Just as the gospel had certain ingredients (they are the substratum of 6:1-5, namely, Christ's death, burial, and resurrection, as in 1 Cor 15:3, 4), so the teaching relating to the life the believer was expected to live was standard throughout the church (cf. C.H. Dodd, *Gospel and Law* [Cambridge: Cambridge University Press, 1951]). Though the language may vary somewhat, the content is the same from writer to writer. This is the point being made in the use of the word "form."

The teaching of Jesus and the apostles, especially in terms of the demands of discipleship, the ethical requirements of the faith, and the principles that must guide believers in their relations one to the other and to the world became in time so definite and fixed that one could go from one area of the church to another and find the same general pattern. The law was a fixed, definite entity with precepts and prohibitions. Grace has its norms also.

18 The term that most adequately describes the standard Christian instruction is "righteousness." Here Paul arrives at the full answer to the question raised in v.15. To be set free from obligation to serve sin means entrance upon the service of righteousness. There is no middle ground, no place in Christian experience where one is free to set his own standards and go his own way. So it is idle to object that on becoming a believer one is simply exchanging one form of slavery for another. There is no alternative. The psalmist perceived this long ago when he wrote, "O Lord, I am thy servant; I am thy servant, the son of thy handmaid. Thou hast loosed my bonds" (Ps 116:16). Let no one say, however, that the two bondages are on the same plane. The one is rigorous and relentless, leading to death; the other is joyous and satisfying, leading to life and peace. To be free from the bondage to sin is a great boon in itself. But life cannot be lived in a vacuum. Service to righteousness means positive achievement that adds meaning to life.

19,20 Reviewing his own remarks, Paul grants that he has spoken "in human terms" (v.19). This is really a kind of apology (see comments on 3:5) for having described Christian life in terms of servitude to righteousness. "There is not a single Old Testament or Rabbinic text with the phrase 'slaves of righteousness' or anything like it—say, 'slaves of the Law' or 'slaves of good deeds.' The faithful are 'slaves of God'; they could be slaves to no one and nothing else" (David Daube, *The New Testament and Rabbinic Judaism* [London: Athlone Press, 1956], p. 284).

Paul gives as a reason for using the reference to slavery, "because you are weak in your natural selves." The nature of the weakness is not expressed—whether it relates to comprehension, so needing an illustration such as slavery, or whether it refers to moral fiber. At any rate, the weakness of the Roman Christians has called for strong language to drive the point home. The remainder of the verse may be said to favor somewhat the second alternative because the apostle enlarges on his earlier description of their pre-Christian life as slaves of sin, going so far as to speak of their "impurity" and "ever-increasing wickedness" (uncleanness within and lawlessness without). The readiness and zeal with which they once served sin now become the basis for a challenge. Surely the new master is worthy of at least equal loyalty and devotion! That new master is not described in personal terms but in personification—righteousness and holiness. The latter word suggests not so much a state of sanctity as an activity, a progression in the life of sanctification. This is also implied by the parallel with "ever-increasing."

To be a slave of sin, Paul affirms, is to be free from the control of righteousness. Under the circumstances, this is a most undesirable freedom. It would be a misunderstanding to interpret these words as meaning that a sinner has no obligation with respect to righteousness. The intent is simply to maintain that one cannot serve two masters. Each bondage is so rigorous, so exacting, that it demands the whole of one's attention.

21,22 So far is the pre-Christian state from being a desirable one that it yields no benefit. In fact, it leaves behind memories that produce shame (v.21). On the other hand, the Christian state of freedom from the necessity of serving sin and the corresponding commitment to God has produced a harvest of holiness (sanctification). At the end of this process is eternal life (cf. Gal 6:8). Paul is not denying the present possession of eternal life, as the following verse makes plain, but is simply presenting eternal life as the inevitable conclusion of the process of sanctification (see chart at the beginning of the chapter). Jesus similarly taught that eternal life was the sequel to genuine discipleship (Mark 10:29, 30).

23 In a fitting conclusion, Paul puts God (and his mastery) over against sin, gift over against wages, eternal life over against death—crowning it all with the acknowledgment that the mediation of Christ Jesus our Lord accounts for the shift from the one camp to the other. The term "wages" is found mostly in a military context to indicate the pay of the soldier. Something of that background is retained in the present passage. (See notes.)

Looking back over 6:15-23, we see that truth has been taught by means of contrast. Obedience is the one concept common to both sides of the contrast; otherwise, all is different:

```
sin — fruitlessness and shame — death
righteousness — sanctification — life
```

Notes

23 In his study of the word "wages" in this context, H.W. Heidland (TDNT 5:592) finds a threefold connotation: (1) since ὀψώνια (*opsōnia*) means provision for one's living expenses, sin turns out to be a wretched paymaster, promising life but meting out death; (2) since in practice wages are paid not in a lump sum but regularly and periodically, death is not to be regarded merely as the final payment, but as that which already casts its dark shadow over life, a portent of the deeper darkness to come; and (3) inasmuch as *opsōnia* is a legal term, in contrast to χάρισμα (*charisma*, "gift"), we are to see a pitting of law over against grace. "Man has rights only in relation to sin, and these rights become his judgment. When he throws himself on God without claim, salvation comes to him" (ibid.).

C. *Union With Christ Viewed As Deliverance From Law* (7:1–6)

As already observed, sin and death in their correlation have occupied Paul to a great degree from 5:12 on, with an occasional reference to a third element, the law. In chapter 6 he has sought to explain that the believer's crucifixion with Christ has brought freedom from enslavement to sin's dominion. Since the law has served to promote sin (5:20), it is expedient now to show that Christ's death, which involved the death of those who are his, effected release from the law also. At the same time Paul is careful to indicate that this emancipation from the law is in order to permit a new attachment, namely, to the risen Lord and his Spirit, so that from this union might flow a fruitfulness of life unattainable under the law. Since union with Christ has already been shown to be so powerful a factor in its intended result as to warrant the figure of slavery (to righteousness), the way has been made clear to teach deliverance from the law as not opening the door to irresponsible and sinful conduct.

7:1–6

> Do you not know, brothers—for I am speaking to men who know the law—that the law has authority over a man only as long as he lives? [2]For example, by law a married woman is bound to her husband as long as he is alive, but if her husband dies, she is released from the law of marriage. [3]So then, if she marries another man while her husband is still alive, she is called an adulteress. But if her husband dies, she is released from that law and is not an adulteress, even though she marries another man.
> [4]So, my brothers, you also died to the law through the body of Christ, that you might belong to another, to him who was raised from the dead, in order that we might bear fruit to God. [5]For when we were controlled by our sinful nature, the sinful passions aroused by the law were at work in our bodies, so that we bore fruit for death. [6]But now, by dying to what once bound us, we have been released from the law so that we serve in the new way of the Spirit, and not in the old way of the written code.

1 The readers are described as those who know "the law." Some would question this wording, since the definite article is lacking in the original. Could it be that since the recipients of the letter reside at Rome, the seat of legislation and government for the

empire, Paul is referring to secular law? This conclusion is not necessary, since "law" occurs without the article in passages that clearly have to do with the Mosaic legislation (e.g., 5:20). At the same time, it is quite possible that Paul is not interested so much in identifying the law he has in mind as in pointing to its character as law, that which has binding force. The word "man" should not suggest that males only are in view, since this is the broad term used for mankind and here has the force of "person." In this opening statement, where the principle is being laid down that law imposes a lifelong obligation on its subjects, this is the natural word to use. The situation is different in the next verse, where the word for "man" is not the same, since a husband is in view.

Already in this initial statement we have a clue for determining the thought that Paul is about to develop. The law has authority over a person only for his lifetime. Since it has been established that the believer died with Christ, one can anticipate the conclusion—that whatever authority the law continues to exercise over others, for the believer that power has been abrogated. "Only for him who in faith appropriates the righteousness of God in Christ is the law abolished" (W. Gutbrod in TDNT 4:1075). It remains, of course, as an entity that expresses the will of God. The life under grace does not belittle the ethical demands of the law.

2,3 To illustrate the binding character of the law, Paul presents the case of a woman who is married to a husband and remains bound by law in this relationship as long as the husband is living. During this time she is not free to seek another attachment. This may be done only in the event that the husband dies. By design, the status of the wife as subject to the husband is presented by the term *hypandros*, a rather rare word meaning literally "under a husband." This pictures more readily than "married woman" what Paul is seeking to bring out. Particularly in Jewish life this was the actual legal status of the wife, for she could not divorce her husband; divorce was a privilege granted only to the man. If the husband died, she was then released from "the law of marriage" (literally, "the law of the husband"). This may sound as though the husband instituted the marriage law, but this is not the idea intended. Hence, the translators have wisely avoided a literal rendering. NEB has a somewhat fuller wording: "She is discharged from the obligations of the marriage-law."

4-6 The opening word "so" indicates that illustration is now giving way to application. But the reader is apt to be somewhat disturbed in that there is a measure of inconsistency in the way the illustration is applied. Note that in the case under consideration three essential statements are made: a woman is married to a man; the man dies; then the woman is free to be married to another. In the application three statements likewise appear or can be readily inferred: the readers have had a binding relation to the law; they have died to the law; and they are now free to be joined to another, even the risen Lord. A glance at these two triadic propositions shows that the parallel breaks down at the second item, for the law, which is the assumed master or husband in the application, is not represented as dying, since the readers are said to have died to the law. Paul avoids saying that the law died, something that is never affirmed in Scripture, though the law had a certain course to run (Gal 3:19). All he is concerned with is continuing the emphasis already made in chapter 6, that death ends obligation. It was not feasible in the illustration to have the woman die, because then she would not have been available for marriage to another, which is vital to the application in which a new relationship is set up between the believer and Christ. Paul was no doubt aware of a certain incongruity between illustration and application, but counted on the understanding of his readers that he was seeking merely to underscore the truth that death with Christ brought to an end the sway of the law over those who are in him and ushered in a new relationship as superior to the old as Christ is superior to the law.

Death to the law is said to have occurred "through the body of Christ" (v.4). This is a reference to the personal body of the Savior in his crucifixion. Through the same means believers became dead both to the law and to sin. "The body of Christ" should not be interpreted as a reference to the church, since the word has not been used in the corporate, mystical sense so far in the Epistle, and when it is so used (12:4, 5) Paul brings in the human body as an analogy in order to make his meaning clear, as he had done in an earlier letter (1 Cor 12:12, 13).

Death to the law occurred so that believers "might belong to another." To belong to Christ involves participation not only in his death but also in his resurrection. Severance from obligation to serve the law is only part of the truth. We are married, as it were, to the risen Lord, with a view to bearing fruit to God. Perhaps an analogy is intended here—as a marriage produces progeny, so the believer's union with Christ results in spiritual fruit. It should be recalled that in our Lord's teaching the secret of fruit bearing is union with himself (John 15:1ff.), the very truth emphasized in the passage before us. A somewhat different background for fruit bearing is predicated in Galatians 5:22, 23, where the fruit is attributed to the Spirit, in contrast to the output of the flesh and of the law. Since Paul speaks of the Spirit in Romans 7:6, the parallel with Galatians 5 is close. The attribution of fruit to Christ in one instance and to the Spirit in another is not disturbing, because there is much common ground in their relationship to believers (cf. Eph 3:16, 17).

In the pre-Christian state there was fruit of a sort, but it was corrupt and perishable, emanating from the sinful nature and produced by the sinful passions as these were aroused by the law (v.5). The contrast between the two types of fruit is striking (cf. 6:21). The phrase "controlled by our sinful nature" is an attempt to render "in the flesh." Paul has used "flesh" in several senses thus far: (1) the humanity of Jesus Christ (1:3); (2) the physical body (2:28), (3) mankind—"all flesh" (3:20); and (4) moral, or possibly intellectual, weakness (6:19). Now he adds a fifth: the so-called "ethical" meaning of flesh, which is the most common use of the word in his writings and denotes the old sinful nature. It is this sense of the word that pervades chapters 7 and 8, together with a final use in 13:14. Paul did not employ the word "flesh" in this sense when exposing in his earlier chapters the universality of sin. In noting that the passions are aroused by the law, Paul is anticipating his fuller statement in vv.7–13 about the manner in which the law promotes sin.

Release from the law has as its objective a bond service to God "in the new way of the Spirit" in contrast to the old way of the written code (literally "letter"). This contrast is not between a literal mode of interpreting Scripture and one that is free and unfettered. The written code, which has special reference to the law rather than to Scripture in general, has no power to give life and to produce a service acceptable to God. Only a person can beget human life, and only a divine person can impart spiritual life, which is then fostered and nurtured by the Spirit. The word "new" has in it not so much the idea of newness in time as freshness and superiority. This is the only mention of the Spirit in the chapter. It anticipates chapter 8 with its unfolding of the wealth of blessing to be experienced in this relationship.

Notes

6 Although γράμμα (*gramma*, "letter") comes from the same root as γραφή (*graphē*), the word for Scripture, the two are not treated by Paul as equivalents. The very fact that *gramma* is pitted against πνεῦμα (*pneuma*, "Spirit") is revealing. It becomes a surrogate for law in its written form. G. Schrenk notes that "*gramma* is not used when he [Paul] speaks of the positive and lasting significance of Scripture. This positive task is always stated in terms of *graphē*. When the reference is to *gramma*, Paul is always thinking of the legal authority which has been superseded, while *graphē* is linked with the new form of authority determined by the fulfilment in Christ and by His Spirit, the determinative character of the new no longer being what is written and prescribed" (TDNT 1:768).

Considerable affinity can be detected between the presentation here and that in 2 Corinthians 3:6, where the *gramma/pneuma* tension likewise appears. In both passages the concepts of death and life occur; also the verb καταργεῖσθαι (*katargeisthai*) occurs (7:6; 2 Cor 3:7, 11, 13, 14) with the meaning "to be discharged from" in Romans and "to fade or disappear" in the 2 Corinthian passage, except for v.14, where it has the force of "to be taken away." In both passages the subject is the abrogation of the law, though the matter is put somewhat differently in Romans, where believers are said to have been discharged from service to the law. But the thought is essentially the same in both places (see Bernardin Schneider, CBQ 15 [1953] p. 203).

Not all translations allow for mention of the Holy Spirit here. NEB, for example, has "to serve God in a new way, the way of the spirit, in contrast to the old way, the way of a written code" (JB is similar). However, it is probable that we have in 7:6 an anticipation of that fullness of treatment of the Spirit that comes out in chapter 8. Also, the parallelism between Romans 7:6 and 2 Corinthians 3, noted above, favors a reference to the Holy Spirit, since there is no doubt that *pneuma* refers to the Spirit in the latter passage.

D. *The Relationship Between Law and Sin* (7:7–25)

This matter requires clarification if for no other reason than that Paul has flatly stated that the believer has died to sin (6:2) and to the law (7:4). Are these, then, so similar as to be in some sense equated? The explanation has been touched on briefly in 7:5, but Paul now expands it. In essence, the solution of the problem is this: the law cannot be identified with sin, because it is the law that provides awareness of sin (cf. 3:20). Can one say of an X-ray machine that revealed his disease that the machine is diseased because it revealed a diseased condition? That would be utterly illogical.

As Paul has appealed to the experience of his converts to support Christian truth (Gal 3:1–5; 4:1–7), so he now appeals to his own experience (vv.7–13). This personal reference then broadens into a more general picture of the soul-struggle of a person who tries to serve God by obeying the law but finds himself checkmated by the operation of sin within himself (vv.14–25).

The observation that consciousness of sin is produced by the law is sharpened by a specific example. Paul seizes on the tenth commandment, which says, "Do not covet." This is of the highest importance for our understanding of the meaning of law in 7:1–6, the law from which the believer has been released. What the apostle has in mind includes the moral law. While students of Scripture find it convenient at times to distinguish between the ceremonial law and the moral law, Paul regards the law as a unit. To one who may be disturbed by the thought that the divine standard for one's life is abandoned by maintaining release from the law, Paul will reply in due course that no such danger exists (8:4).

7:7–25

> [7]What shall we say, then? Is the law sin? Far from it! Indeed I would not have known what sin was except through the law. For I would not have known what it was to covet if the law had not said, "Do not covet." [8]But sin, seizing the opportunity afforded by the commandment, produced in me every kind of covetous desire. For apart from law, sin is dead. [9]Once I was alive apart from law; but when the commandment came, sin sprang to life [10]and I died. I found that the very commandment that was intended to bring life actually brought death. [11]For sin, seizing the opportunity afforded by the commandment, deceived me, and through the commandment put me to death. [12]So then, the law is holy, and the commandment is holy, righteous and good.
>
> [13]Did that which is good, then, become death to me? By no means! But in order that sin might be recognized as sin, it produced death in me through what was good, so that through the commandment sin might become utterly sinful.
>
> [14]We know that the law is spiritual; but I am unspiritual, sold as a slave to sin. [15]I do not know what I am doing. For what I want to do I do not do, but what I hate I do. [16]And if I do what I do not want to do, I agree that the law is good. [17]As it is, it is no longer I myself who do it, but it is sin living in me. [18]I know that nothing good lives in me, that is, in my sinful nature. For I have the desire to do what is good, but I cannot carry it out. [19]For what I do is not the good I want to do; no, the evil I do not want to do—this I keep on doing. [20]Now if I do what I do not want to do, it is no longer I who do it, but it is sin living in me that does it.
>
> [21]So I find this law at work: When I want to do good, evil is right there with me. [22]For in my inner being I delight in God's law; [23]but I see another law at work in the members of my body, waging war against the law of my mind and making me a prisoner of the law of sin at work within my members. [24]What a wretched man I am! Who will rescue me from this body of death? [25]Thanks be to God—through Jesus Christ our Lord!
>
> So then, I myself in my mind am a slave to God's law, but in my sinful nature a slave to the law of sin.

7 "Sin" is an oft-repeated word in this paragraph. It does not refer here to an act of sin, but to the sin principle, to that mighty force man cannot tame, but which lurks dormant or relatively inactive in a person's life, then is brought to the fore by prohibition and proceeds to rise up and slay its victim, whom it has utterly deceived. Sin, then, has the same meaning here as in 5:12ff. The same conditions of prohibition and desire, leading to a fall, are latent in both passages. But whereas in 5:12ff. sin is further defined as *paraptōma*, which has in it the very word for "fall," here *hamartia* alone is used. This is suggestive, for since the fall of man there is an inability to get back to God. Man is always "falling short," which is the precise meaning of *hamartia*.

The words "for I would not have known" could be translated, "I did not know," giving them a fully historical setting, but the hypothetical construction is no doubt preferable. The subject in hand is the awareness of sin in a personal, existential sense—an awareness created by the law's demands. To come to grips with this the apostle selects an item from the Decalogue, the very last of the Ten Commandments. Is he selecting more or less at random one of the ten for an illustration? Could he have chosen just as readily the prohibition against stealing or bearing false witness? Possibly he saw something basic here, for "to covet" is more precisely "to desire." If one gives rein to wrong desire, it can lead to lying, stealing, killing, and all the other things prohibited in the commandments. The sin indicated here is not so much a craving for this or that wrong thing, but the craving itself (note that Paul does not bother to spell out the particulars of the tenth commandment, such as the possessions or wife of one's neighbor). In analyzing sin, one must go behind the outward act to the inner man, where desire clutches at the imagination and then puts the spurs to the will.

8 In the background is the Genesis story of the temptation and the fall. Eve was faced with a commandment—a prohibition. When desire was stirred through the subtle suggestion of the serpent, a certain rebelliousness came into play that is the very heart of sin—a preference for one's own will over the expressed will of God. The warning "Don't" to a small child may turn out to be a call for action that had not even been contemplated by the child. A sure way to lose blossoms from the garden is to post a sign that says, "Don't pick the flowers." The word "opportunity" in the original is a military term meaning a base of operations. Prohibition furnishes a springboard from which sin is all too ready to take off. The possibilities for seeking satisfaction through giving way to wrong desire are manifold. In the KJV the word for "desire" is rendered "lust" in v.7 and "concupiscence" in v.8. Since both of these renderings are readily associated with sexual desire, they unduly restrict the frame of reference.

"For apart from law, sin is dead." It appears from a comparison of "dead" with "sprang to life" in v.9 that the word "dead" is intended to be taken in a relative sense, namely, quiescent, dormant, inactive. The statement appears to be an axiom, a broad principle. But since the verb "is" does not appear in the original, a possibility exists that "was" should be supplied, making the reference personal to Paul rather than a general statement (so Murray). On the other hand, when some part of the verb "to be" is left for the reader to supply, as here, it is more apt to be a generalization than a specific historical allusion.

9-11 Paul's statement that he was once alive apart from the law should be taken in a relative sense, for there was actually no time in his life before his conversion when he was unrelated to the law. He was the son of a Pharisee (Acts 23:6) and lived in strictest conformity to the regulations of his sect (Acts 26:5). He seems to mean, then, that there was a time when he was living in a state of blissful indifference to the intensely searching demands that the law made on the inner man. He was careless and self-deceived as to his own righteousness. This state is reflected in Philippians 3:6, where he speaks of his preconversion days when he was "faultless" with respect to legalistic righteousness. Paul's struggle before and at the time of his conversion was intellectual rather than moral. He was convinced that Jesus could not be the Messiah, for God had permitted him to die as a criminal. His conversion meant a complete reversal in this matter. "I died" is subjective in its force. He felt within himself the sentence of death, becoming bogged down in hopelessness and despair in contrast to the blithe self-confidence he had had before. It goes without saying that this dying is entirely unrelated to dying with Christ, of which we have been informed in chapter 6. It was not a death to sin but a death because of sin.

The commandment referred to, like the others, "was intended to bring life." That is to say, its design and ideal were to promote observance that would lead to divine blessing and consequent human happiness. "You shall therefore keep my statutes and my ordinances, by doing which a man shall live: I am the Lord" (Lev 18:5 RSV). The practical difficulty, of course, is that sinful man fails to do the will of God as set forth in the commandments.

In v.11 sin is strongly personified, being represented as acting as a person would act.

The language is reminiscent of the fall, with sin taking the place of the tempter and provoking a deception that led to death (the spiritual death that occurred then and there was prophetic of the physical death to follow in due time). The word "deceive" occurs here in a strong form indicating utter deception. Paul uses the same word on two other occasions when speaking of the deception effected by the serpent in relation to Eve (2 Cor 11:3, 1 Tim 2:14; cf. Exod 8:25, LXX). Sin within him led Paul to do the very thing the commandment forbade, thus bringing him under condemnation as a lawbreaker. Recall his statement about the law in 2 Corinthians 3:6—"the letter kills."

> Bornkamm's insight is helpful: What constitutes this deception and death? The deception of sin can only consist in the fact that it falsely promises life to me. This it cannot do by itself, but only with the help of the divine commandment. Deceptively it appropriates the call to life, which actually declares God's law: do that, and you shall live. What it quietly and deceptively conceals from me is simply this, that it has now usurped this call to live, and therefore the encounter with the divine commandment is no longer direct. Sin always stands in between and has fundamentally perverted my relationship to God's commandment. This perversion is both deception and death (Günther Bornkamm, *Early Christian Experience* [New York: Harper & Row, 1969], pp. 91, 92)..

12 It is time for the apostle to give a decisive answer to the question he had raised in v.7: "Is the law sin?" So far from being identifiable with sin, the law is holy, as are the individual commandments it contains. It is possible to understand "the commandment" as a reference to every single precept of the law, but the singular form leads one to think that Paul is casting a backward glance at the tenth commandment. The law is holy because it comes from a holy God and searches out sin. It is righteous in view of the just requirements it lays upon men, righteous also because it forbids and condemns sin. It is good (beneficent) because its aim is life (v.10). The misuse of the law at the hands of sin has not altered its own essential character. Its goodness is reaffirmed in v.13.

13 Having detached the law from any wrongful association with sin, Paul still has the necessity of treating the problem of the law's relation to death, the other great enemy of the race. Continuing to present the case in personal terms, he protests that the responsibility for incurring death must be assigned to sin rather than to the law. Its use of the law to bring death shows how "utterly sinful" sin is. "How evil must that thing be which works the greatest evil through that which is the perfection of righteousness" (Haldane, in loc.). At the same time, the law, which seemed to be victimized by being taken over by sin, emerges as having gained an important objective. It has exposed sin for the evil thing it is.

From this point on to the end of the chapter, the personal emphasis continues, and with increased intensity, as the powerful forces of law and sin are depicted as producing a struggle that ends in a confession of despair relieved only by the awareness that in Jesus Christ there is deliverance. Paul does not shrink from putting himself prominently in this arena of conflict if only his doing so will help others (cf. 1 Cor 4:6).

If his portrayal of the struggle of the soul to observe the law despite the enticement of sin is presented at greater length and with greater intensity than the struggle with the powers of darkness (cf. Eph 6:10ff.), it is not necessarily because the former is intrinsically more important (seeing that the powers are evil also), but because it is so immediately and desperately personal. The other is equally so only in cases of demonic possession.

A shift of emphasis is discernible on moving from vv.7–13 to vv.14–25. In the former section Paul has shown that the fault lay not with the commandment of God but with sin in its use of the commandment. In the latter section he will maintain that the responsible party, ultimately speaking, is not "I" but the sin that dwells within.

14–20 At the outset Paul wants it understood that he is not depreciating the law, for it is "spiritual"—that is, emanating from God (vv.22, 25) who is Spirit (John 4:24). Of course, it is true also that the law as a part of Scripture is the product of the Holy Spirit, who inspired the writers. But that aspect is not prominent here. The law is a reflection of the character of God. Godly people recognize this fact ("we know").

"But I am unspiritual." What a stark contrast! The word "unspiritual" is literally "fleshly," what I am in myself. I am not subject to the law and therefore I am in rebellion against God, since the law is from him. (The problems as to whether Paul speaks individually or universally here and whether as a saved or an unsaved man will be dealt with at the close of the chapter.) Here he moves on to a second description more wretched than the first: "sold as a slave to sin." This strikes the keynote of what follows, down to the anguished cry, "Who will rescue me . . . ?" (v.24). The slavery extends to the totality of his being. It numbs and blinds him, for he confesses that he does not know what he is doing (v.15). It is a graphic picture of many an action carried out by a slave, going through certain motions under the authority and direction of a master. If there appears to be obedience, it is really not a matter of volition, but something almost mechanical. Paul's figure of slavery is cogent here, since he is forced to carry out what he does not want to do, what he really hates, whereas what he would like to do never seems to materialize (v.15).

The failure to do what he desires to do is not to be attributed to a wrong attitude toward the law, since he concurs in the verdict that the law is praiseworthy. It inculcates the right kind of conduct, the things that are beneficent in their results (v.16). If the failure does not come from a wrong attitude toward the law, such as indifference or defiance, then the doing of things contrary to the law must be traced to the power of sin working within him (v.17). Paul is not attempting to escape responsibility, but rather putting his finger on the real culprit—indwelling sin. The invader has managed to secure more than a foothold; he roams the place, considering it his home. In putting the matter like this, Paul has moved from a consideration of outward acts to an emphasis on the unwanted tenancy of sin. With this alien master in control, no matter how strongly he wants to do the good, he finds himself checkmated. He cannot carry it out (v.18). Verse 19 is a virtual repetition of v.15 and the same is true of v.20 in relation to v.17.

Since Paul was a Jew, it is natural to inquire if there was anything in his Jewish inheritance he may have been drawing upon to depict the struggle against sin. A strong case can be made, simply on the basis of similarity, for the conclusion that Paul was indeed dependent on rabbinic teaching at this point so far as the formal framework of his presentation is concerned (W.D. Davies, *Paul and Rabbinic Judaism* [London: SPCK, 1948], pp. 20–27). The Rabbis taught that within man there are two impulses, both attributable to God. One is evil (usually understood as present from birth but inactive during the early years); the other good, making itself felt at the time a Jewish lad at thirteen became a "son of the law." Thereafter the two impulses contend for mastery within the person. The rabbinic remedy suggested for this situation was a devoted study and application of the law. At this point, however, Paul's presentation differs radically from the rabbinic view, for he stoutly maintains that the law, despite its divine origin and intrinsic excellence, cannot counteract the power of sin.

21-25 "So I find this law at work." The language clearly indicates a purpose to summarize what has gone before. So far, the law under discussion is the law of Moses, but here a specialized meaning—that of principle (cf. 3:27; 8:2)—is intended. This usage makes it necessary, when speaking once more of the (Mosaic) law, to call it "God's law" (v.22) for the purpose of differentiation. In Paul's inner being the divine law is welcome and brings delight, but that which manifests itself in the bodily members (what may be called the outward man) is the law (principle, or perhaps authority) of sin. It is a state of war and he finds himself a captive (cf. the earlier figure of a slave in v.14) to the imperious operation of sin. The agony of this unhappy condition comes out in the cry "What a wretched man I am!" It is a powerful and moving cry, recalling the words of Isaiah when he became aware of his sin (Isa 6:5). Since Paul is unable to help himself he must look elsewhere. In this verse and the next one the "I" is clearly the man himself, which warns us against trying to analyze the "I" at earlier points in the chapter in schizophrenic terms. "The source of Paul's wretchedness is clear. It is not a 'divided self,' but the fact that the last hope of mankind, religion, has proved to be a broken reed. Through sin, it is no longer a comfort but an accusation. Man needs not a law but deliverance" (Barrett).

In line with this, the apostle does not say, "What will rescue me?" but "Who ... ?" There is deliverance, provided by God through Jesus Christ. The appeal from self to the Lord Jesus is meaningless if the latter has the same problem as the tormented suppliant. Jesus' sinlessness and triumph over evil are assumed. Further, "if Christ is my Deliverer, it is implied that '*I myself*' without Christ cannot get beyond the state of distraction and self-contradiction already described in vv.14-23" (Gifford, in loc.).

The final statement of the chapter is another summary. Coming as it does after the cry of thanksgiving for deliverance through Christ, it seems strange that there should be a reversion to the state of tension described earlier. Because of this, some students have ventured the opinion that this part of the verse has somehow been misplaced in the course of the transmission of the text. In his translation Moffatt actually puts it after v.23, despite the fact that there is no manuscript authority for this. As Gifford points out, the reason for the expression "I myself" in the concluding verse is to establish a contrast with "Jesus Christ" in the same verse (in loc.). How then shall we account for the strange order? Apparently Paul felt the desirability of stating once more the essence of the struggle he had depicted in order to prepare the reader to appreciate the more the grand exposition of the deliverance in terms of Christ and the Spirit in the following chapter.

Before moving on to that portion, we must return to the overall problems of interpretation in chapter 7. First of all, is Paul giving a truly autobiographical sketch, or is the "I" a vehicle to present man in his extremity, a means to universalize the experience treated here? It is difficult to decide. The first person ("I") was occasionally used in antiquity as a rhetorical device for expressing something applicable to others. It was so used somewhat by the Rabbis (W.G. Kümmel, *Römer 7 und die Bekehrung des Paulus* [Leipzig: J.C. Hinrich, 1929], pp. 128-131). That Paul could think and write in this fashion is apparent from Romans 3:7. Romans 7, however, is unique in its extent. Perhaps the personal and the universal are intended to mingle here. It has even been suggested that the "I" is a projection of Adam, the man who had so much to do with sin and death.

The more strenuously debated issue is the question of interpretation of the material itself, especially vv.14-25. Are we to regard the state pictured here as that of the unsaved man or of the Christian? The case for the unsaved condition is as follows: (1) It was the prevailing view among the Greek Fathers of the early church. (2) Such expressions as "sold as a slave to sin" and "unspiritual" seem more fitting as a description of the unsaved than of the genuine believer. Donald M. Davies writes, "The main message of chapter six is that in Christ a man is free from sin. How then could Paul, describing a situation of tension in his Christian experience, say that he was sold under sin? Where then is the freedom from sin which he insists on in the previous chapter?" (Int 7 [1953] 159). (3) If the "now" of 8:1 means what it seems to mean, Paul is passing from a consideration of the unsaved to the saved condition. (4) The absence of the Holy Spirit from the discussion and even of Christ (until the very close) is hard to understand if a redeemed experience is under review.

The other interpretation, in contrast, holds that a Christian is being depicted, despite his wretchedness. (1) This was the conclusion of Augustine and of the Reformed interpreters. (2) Appeal is made to the change from the use of the past tense in vv.7–13 to the use of the present tense in vv.14–25. This is understandable if the former section relates to Paul's pre-Christian experience and the rest of the chapter to his postconversion experience. (3) The author's description of his pre-Christian life in Philippians 3:6 as a blameless condition in terms of the law does not jibe with the passage before us. Paul counted this faultlessness as one of the things that could be listed as gain. Both pictures cannot readily apply to the same period. It has been replied that he is speaking in Philippians of his standing with men and not, as in Romans 7, of his relation to God. However, Paul was not a devious person, but transparent. Would he represent himself as possessing what he recounts in Philippians in a merely manward frame of reference if everything within him protested against it as a hollow unreality? (4) The progress of thought in Romans needs to be taken into consideration. Paul has passed beyond his description of the unsaved state and is now giving attention to sanctification and its problems; so the theme is really relevant only to believers. (5) That conflict of the sort described here can and does characterize the Christian life is apparent elsewhere in Paul, especially in Galatians 5:17. (6) The power of self-diagnosis at the penetrating level found here (see vv.22, 23) is beyond the capacity of the natural man. Advocates of the other view suggest that the explanation here is that Paul is writing as a Christian who naturally has gained in perception, and this colors his presentation. (7) A person desiring holiness of life, as pictured here, could only be a believer, for the unsaved person does not long for God but is hostile toward him. (8) The close of the chapter, in terms of the text as it stands and without attempted rearrangement, acknowledges the deliverance in Christ, yet goes on to state the very problem sketched in vv.14–24 as though it continues to be a problem for one who knows the Lord.

The wide difference between these two views puts the general reader in a dilemma. Which view is correct? Which has the better of the argument?

Another and more satisfying approach is possible—namely, that the experience pictured here is not wholly autobiographical but is deliberately presented in such a way as to demonstrate what would indeed be the situation if one who is faced with the demands of the law and the power of sin in his life were to attempt to solve his problem independently of the power of Christ and the enablement of the Spirit. This viewpoint has been well expressed by William Manson:

> It is in this way, I think, that we grasp the actual character of Romans VII. It is an unreal, in the sense of non-historical, a hypothetical situation which is called up before us. It corresponds to no actual phase either of Jewish-Christian or of Pauline-Christian existence, for in neither of these situations can we suppose the soul's darkness to have been unrelieved by some ray of heavenly grace. St. Paul has set the stage for an enquiry dictated by a purely argumentative necessity. *What is life under the law according to the logic of its nature?* St. Paul presents the case from the standpoint of Christianity,

but a Christianity not present in all its terms. We are contemplating an abstraction developed by dialectic, not the actual situation either of the regenerate or of the unregenerate man, but only the hypothetical condition of a Christian under Law (*Jesus and the Christian* [Grand Rapids: Eerdmans, 1967], p. 159).

A parallel use of methodology may be detected in Ecclesiastes. The writer knows God but purposely and deliberately views life from the standpoint of the natural man in order to expose it as vanity, empty of lasting value.

Romans 7 performs a service by calling into question certain popular notions that lack biblical foundation: that the soul's struggle is essentially against specific sins or habits (Paul talks here not of sins but of sin); that human nature is essentially good (cf. v.18); that sanctification is by means of the law; that if one will only determine to do the right, he will be able to do it. These are some of the misconceptions that must be removed, and they might not have been removed had the apostle proceeded directly from chapter 6 to chapter 8. Without chapter 7 we would not be able to appreciate to the full the truths presented in chapter 8.

Notes

18 The final clause of the sentence ends in οὐ (*ou*, "not") unaccompanied by a verb. Some MSS add "find"; others, "know." NIV accurately conveys the sense.

E. *The Blessings of Life in the Spirit* (8:1–39)

It is altogether too narrow a view to see in this portion simply the antidote to the wretched state pictured in chapter 7. Actually the chapter gathers up various strands of thought from the entire discussion of both justification and sanctification and ties them together with the crowning knot of glorification. Like chapter 5, it presents the blessings of the justified life, grounded in the removal of condemnation. Like chapter 6, it stresses freedom from the bondage of sin and ultimately from the bondage of death. Like chapter 7, it deals with the problem of the flesh, finding the solution in the liberating and productive ministry of the Spirit. The chapter begins with instruction, rises to consolation, and culminates in jubilation. This is high and holy ground indeed for the Christian pilgrim to tread.

1. *Liberation by the Spirit from the law of sin and death*

8:1–11

> ¹Therefore, there is now no condemnation for those who are in Christ Jesus, ²because through Christ Jesus the law of the Spirit of life set me free from the law of sin and death. ³For what the law was powerless to do in that it was weakened by our sinful nature, God did by sending his own Son in the likeness of sinful man to be a sin offering. And so he condemned sin in sinful man, ⁴in order that the righteous requirements of the law might be fully met in us, who do not live according to our sinful nature but according to the Spirit.
> ⁵Those who live according to their sinful nature have their minds set on what that nature desires; but those who live in accordance with the Spirit have their minds

set on what the Spirit desires. [6]The mind of sinful man is death, but the mind controlled by the Spirit is life and peace, [7]because the sinful mind is hostile to God. It does not submit to God's law, nor can it do so. [8]Those controlled by their sinful nature cannot please God.

[9]You, however, are controlled not by your sinful nature but by the Spirit, if the Spirit of God lives in you. And if anyone does not have the Spirit of Christ, he does not belong to Christ. [10]But if Christ is in you, your body is dead because of sin, yet your spirit is alive because of righteousness. [11]And if the Spirit of him who raised Jesus from the dead is living in you, he who raised Christ from the dead will also give life to your mortal bodies through his Spirit, who lives in you.

1,2 The reader is hardly prepared by the contents of chapter 7 for the glorious pronouncement that there is no condemnation at all for those who are in Christ Jesus, and he finds it hard to associate the "therefore" with anything in the immediately preceding context. The connection must be sought in the entire sweep of the thought as developed from chapter 3 on. The natural antithesis to condemnation is justification. It can be replied, of course, that Paul has already covered this truth and would not be likely to revert to it here. However, this is such a basic truth that Paul brings it even into his discussion of the Christian life (8:33, 34; cf. 8:10). Justification is the basis and starting point for sanctification. One must be assured of acceptance with God before he can grow in grace and conformity to Christ. At the same time, one must grant that the construction of vv.2-4 carries us beyond the thought of freedom from condemnation in the sense of guilt. What is developed is the application of the redeeming work of Christ by the Spirit to the believer's life in such a way that the dominion of sin is broken and the reign of godliness assured. The noun "condemnation" has its counterpart in the verb "condemned" (v.3), which is followed immediately, not by a statement about the standing of the believer, but by one concerning his manner of life (v.4). Consequently, there is both a forensic and a practical force in "no condemnation."

Verse 2 immediately picks up this practical, dynamic aspect by concentrating on the freedom from the imperious rule of sin and death, a freedom now available to the believer through the operation of the Spirit. The word "law" is used figuratively here (cf. 7:21, 23). Clearly it would be impossible for Paul to refer to the law of Moses as "the law of sin and death," even though it provokes sin (7:7, 8) and produces death (7:9-11; 2 Cor 3:6, 7). The law in itself is holy (7:12). In the present passage, therefore, "law" is used to indicate the certainty and regularity of operation that characterizes sin (which leads to death) on the one hand and the Spirit on the other. Whereas the word "law" emphasizes regularity, "life" emphasizes both supernaturalness and spontaneity. Hence the superiority of the Spirit's operation over that of sin.

The NIV differs from the familiar wording "the Spirit of life in Christ Jesus" by stating that "through Christ Jesus the law of the Spirit of life set me free." The former wording points to the Spirit as the life-giver (cf. 2 Cor 3:6) but only as mediating that which is in Christ (Col 3:4). Yet the construction is somewhat cumbersome, a disadvantage not shared by the other wording. Either is possible syntactically. Paul has already noted the enslaving power of sin and the freedom from it achieved by Christ (6:18, 22). This truth was anticipated in the teaching of Jesus (John 8:34-36).

3,4 But how was this freedom gained (v.3)? The opening statement about the powerlessness of the law because of the weakness of the sinful nature to which its commands are addressed is an obvious reminder of the major thrust of chapter 7. The law makes demands, and it condemns when those demands are not met, but it cannot overcome sin. This inability of the law required the personal action of God in Christ. He sent "his own Son." The mission could not be entrusted to anyone else or anyone less than his Son. While the preexistence of the Son is not formally taught here, it is implied, as it frequently is in the Gospel of John where the sending of the Son is mentioned (e.g., 3:17; 7:33; 17:18; 20:21). When vv.2, 3 are taken together, they bear a close resemblance to Galatians 4:4–6, where Father, Son, and Spirit are pictured as involved in the mission of Christ.

The Son was sent "in the likeness of sinful man" ("man" is literally "flesh"). Observe with what care the incarnation is stated. Paul does not say "in sinful flesh," lest the Son's sinlessness be compromised, nor "in the likeness of flesh," which would convey a docetic idea and thereby deny the reality of the humanity of our Lord, making it only an appearance of corporeality. As it stands, the terminology is in full agreement with Philippians 2:7: "being made in human likeness."

So much for Christ's person. What about his work? "To be a sin offering" is the purpose of his coming. The proper translation here is a matter of some controversy. Certainly, "sin offering" is a possible rendering (as in 2 Cor 5:21), but this may be more than Paul intends to say, since he does not surround the expression with sacrificial language. And if it were his intent to stress expiation, a more natural expression would have been "*as* a sin offering." If we translate literally, "for sin," then we are adopting the view that Paul is simply stating that the mission of Christ was to deal effectively with sin, making possible among his people the type of life presented in the following verse. This does not exclude expiation but goes beyond it. Certainly it would be wrong to interpret the passage merely as a reference to the perfection of Christ's life as a rebuke to sin in humanity. This would only tantalize and frustrate those who supposedly were the beneficiaries of his mission.

"So he condemned sin in sinful man." It should be noted again that, in the Greek, "sinful man" is simply "flesh." It is possible that "in the flesh" is intended to be correlated with "through the flesh" at the beginning of the verse, in which case the NIV translation is justified. However, since "flesh" can be used of Christ apart from any sinful connotation (e.g., Col 1:22), it is also possible to refer the phrase to the Savior rather than to sinful humanity (TDNT 7:133). The viewpoint is well expressed by John Murray:

> In that same nature which in all others was dominated and directed by sin, God condemned sin and overthrew its power. Jesus not only blotted out sin's guilt and brought us nigh to God. He also vanquished sin as power and set us free from its enslaving dominion. And this could not have been done except in the "flesh." The battle was joined and the triumph secured in that same flesh which in us is the seat and agent of sin. (in loc.)

This brings the teaching in line with 6:5–11. The words "for sin" create a difficulty for those (e.g., Godet) who see the condemnation of sin as accomplished (according to this passage) simply in the spotless life of the Son. Rather, the entire Christ-event is intended.

The purpose of the incarnation, so far as the believer's life is concerned, is stated in v.4 in such a way as to indicate that the apostle has not allowed the agonizing struggle of chapter 7 to fade from view. There the law was pictured as faultless in itself, a revelation of a holy God, but agonizingly elusive for the man who tries to keep it in his own strength. The self-satisfied man will minimize the law's demands by magnifying his own achievement, whereas the conscientious man will end up in despair. In God's plan, however, the law is to be honored not simply in lip service or in desire but in reality. Its righteous requirement is to be fully met. This can be done only by living according to the Spirit rather than according to the flesh, i.e., the sinful nature of man (cf. "Spirit of life" in v.2). Divine aid is needed to meet the divine requirement.

Paul makes no attempt to particularize the divine requirement but later on he significantly depicts love as the fulfillment of the law (13:10). That love is the primary item in the fruit of the Spirit (Gal 5:22) is surely no happenstance. Observe the balance in this passage between the divine and human elements in Christian life. Paul recognizes that the believer has a life to live; he is not a robot, but a person accountable for his redeemed life as a stewardship. At the same time Paul pictures the requirement of the law as fulfilled (passive) *in* the believer, not *by* him, as though to remind him that the redeemed person does not possess spiritual power he can control and utilize on his own. Rather, the Spirit is always channeling that power and never releases it to those he dwells in for them to use independently of him. The power resides in the Spirit, not in the one he indwells.

It would be a mistake to ground the Christian "walk" solely on the enabling ministry of the Spirit. The close connection with v.3 demands that we include the saving work of Christ. In a previous passage Paul has observed that identification with the Savior in his death and resurrection has this very objective, that "we too may live [Gr., 'walk'] a new life" (6:4).

5-8 At this point Paul launches upon a fairly extended statement contrasting the terms "flesh" and "Spirit," which he has used in v.4. Both terms are difficult because they can have more than one meaning. For example, "flesh" can be used of ordinary physical life shared by believer and unbeliever alike (cf. 2 Cor 10:3). But usually in Paul the ethical force of the word, referring to human nature as corrupted and weakened by sin, is dominant. Because the variety of expressions about the flesh may be confusing, some explanation is necessary. To be in the flesh, as the word is used here (v.8), is to be in the unregenerate state. To be (*ontes*, v.5) according to the flesh is to have the flesh as the regulating principle of one's life. To walk (*peripatousin*, v.4) according to the flesh is to carry out in conduct those things dictated by the flesh.

Less complicated is the use of "Spirit," but even here there is some question as to whether the word used in contrast to "flesh" may not properly be considered as referring to the (redeemed) human spirit. This much is clear, that in the passage under consideration *pneuma* does not mean "spirit" simply as an element in the constitution of man. (It has this meaning in 1 Cor 5:3.) The problem is to determine whether *pneuma* in this passage means the divine life-principle (the new nature communicated to the believer) or whether it should be understood to mean the Spirit of God.

The presence or absence of the definite article does not decide the question, since a reference to the Holy Spirit, considered as a proper name, would not require the article. Neither does the contrast (flesh versus spirit) necessitate a reference to the new nature on the ground that if flesh has a human reference, the same must be true of spirit, for the context of Galatians 5:16, 17, where the two terms are in evident contrast, requires that this be understood as a reference to the Holy Spirit.

Two considerations strongly favor the view that this is a reference to the Holy Spirit. One is the fact that the chapter has begun with an obvious allusion to the divine Spirit (v.2), so that unless there is clear indication to the contrary, one should expect this to be the intended meaning of *pneuma* in the verses that follow. The other is the likelihood that in stating the ground of Christian victory over sin the apostle would assign the basis of that victory to the highest source rather than to a lower, intermediate factor. "'The Spirit' here regarded as the regulating principle (*kata*) cannot be man's own spirit however renewed and sanctified, but the Divine power itself which renews and sanctifies, i.e., the indwelling Spirit of God" (Gifford, in loc.). The decision on the meaning of *pneuma* in v.10 is more difficult and will be deferred until we come to that verse.

The statements made about the flesh or man's sinful nature in vv.5–8 are to be understood as referring to the unregenerate man, judging by the care with which Paul excludes his readers in v.9. This is not sufficient ground, however, for claiming that the Christian has nothing to do with the flesh. The warning of 8:12ff. would be meaningless if that were the case. But for the moment Paul wishes to expose the flesh in its stark reality as being totally alien to God and his holy purposes. He makes the point that there is a correspondence between a man's essential being and what interests him. The fleshly are occupied with fleshly things, whereas those who possess the Spirit and are controlled by him are concerned with the things of the Spirit. Paul had already taught (1 Cor 2:14) that the fleshly man does not welcome the things of the Spirit. They are foolishness to him. He neither comprehends them nor desires to do so. His mind-set is otherwise. This expression ("to set the mind on") denotes far more than a mental process. It includes not only concentration of thought but also desire (cf. Phil 2:5ff.; Col 3:2).

The same root word appears again (v.6), only in the noun form: "The mind of sinful man is death." Because he is unsaved, this man is cut off from God, and this amounts to death in the sense of separation from God. The spiritual man, on the contrary, enjoys life from God (cf. v.2) and the peace such life affords (cf. 14:17). The dead state of the natural man, both present and future, is traced to the inveterate opposition to God that characterizes "flesh." This hostility manifests itself in the natural man's attitude toward the law of God. The fact that it is God's law does not move him or soften him. He refuses to obey it and thereby puts himself into the position of a rebel against God, since the law is an expression of God's will.

Note the sharp contrast to the response of the believer to the law (v.4). There is a contrast too with the "I" in chapter 7, where there is at least a desire to fulfill the law's demands, even if doing this is grossly deficient. Sinful man (generically understood) is plagued by a double limitation; he neither submits to God's law nor is able to do so (cf. a similar twofold limitation of the natural man respecting spiritual knowledge as stated in 1 Cor 2:14). He neither can nor will receive the things of the Spirit. In summary, Paul has named four characteristics of sinful man: hostility toward God, insubordination to his law, failure to please God, and death. It is no wonder that when Jesus spoke to Nicodemus of the flesh, he went on to declare, "You must be born again" (John 3:7).

9–11 Turning now to his readers, Paul reminds them of the basic difference between themselves and those he has been describing, those who have nothing more than sinful human nature. As believers, they have, in the Spirit, an antidote for the flesh. Furthermore, the Spirit of God "lives" in them. They are his dwelling-place. The "if" is not intended to raise doubt, as though to suggest that some of Paul's readers might have to be excluded. The "if" in this type of construction presupposes the truth of the statement. Previously (v.2) the Spirit has been called the Spirit of life because of his regenerating and renewing power; here he is set forth as the Spirit of God and as the Spirit of Christ, indicating that he carries out the purposes of God and applies the fruits of Christ's redemptive mission to the lives of believers (cf. "the Spirit of his [God's] Son" in Gal 4:6).

No one who lacks the Spirit belongs to Christ. Everyone who trusts Christ has the

Spirit (Eph 1:13). The title "Spirit of Christ" is justified and made meaningful by the deliberate way in which Paul says essentially the same thing about both the Spirit and Christ in relation to the believer: the Spirit lives in you (v.9) and Christ is in you (v.10). The presence and fullness of Christ are realized in the life of the Christian by means of the indwelling Spirit (Eph 3:16, 17). Clearly, the notion that "the Spirit of Christ" is a reference to our Lord's disposition, his kindness, etc., is entirely wide of the mark.

Paul's observation (v.10) about those in whom Christ lives—"your body is dead because of sin, yet your spirit is alive because of righteousness"—has proved difficult for interpreters. Translation is to some extent interpretation, and NIV stands in line with most leading modern translations in making "spirit" refer to the spirit of the Christian rather than to the Spirit of Christ. On the other hand, able commentators in increasing numbers (e.g., Michel, Barth, Barrett, Murray, and Leenhardt) are coming to a different conclusion. Two factors seem decisive. One is the unlikelihood that in a passage that has consistently referred to *pneuma* in terms of the Spirit of God, the word would be given a different frame of reference in this one instance. To be sure, the use of "body" over against "spirit" might seem to be sufficient ground for assuming that Paul is talking about two contrasting elements of the human constitution. But whereas such a sharp contrast is congenial to Greek thought, it is alien to the Hebraic concept of life that characterizes both Testaments. In fact, it has been recognized that in Paul's usage, "body" usually means the totality of one's being, "man as a whole, not a part which may be detached from the true I" (TDNT 7:1064). Can we really suppose that when he speaks of "this body of death" (7:24) he has reference merely to the physical organism? In the passage before us he is asserting that sin necessitated our dying with Christ and that even so we must expect physical death in the future. The second reason for choosing the rendering "Spirit" over "spirit" is found in the last clause, where the *pneuma* is said to be alive because of righteousness. Actually Paul says more than this, for he does not use "alive" but "life." This is more than can be properly said of the human spirit. It has been said, however, of the Spirit at the beginning of the chapter (v.2).

So the best conclusion is that *pneuma* refers to the Holy Spirit. The very fact that the first part of the following verse refers to the living presence of the Spirit in the believer seems to indicate that Paul is repeating what he sought to say at the end of v.10 in order to build on it for a further observation—namely, that the same Spirit will provide resurrection life in due season. The close of v.10 teaches that the Spirit who is life in himself brings life to the person he indwells only because that person has already been granted God's righteousness (justification). So the presence of the Spirit in the redeemed life is at once the evidence of salvation bestowed and the earnest of that final phase of salvation that belongs to the future (v.11). In this passage righteousness cannot be understood in any other light than as imputed righteousness (cf. 1 Cor 1:30).

In v.11 the Spirit is given yet another title: "the Spirit of him who raised Jesus from the dead." The reference is, of course, to God (cf. 4:24). Paul is not asserting, as some claim, that the Spirit raised Jesus from the dead. The title is simply a specialized variation of the Spirit of God. His future work on behalf of the saints will be to "give life" to their mortal (i.e., subject-to-death) bodies. This accords with Paul's description of the glorified bodies of believers as "spiritual" (1 Cor 15:44). "The Spirit is both the instrumental cause of the resurrection-act and the permanent substratum of the resurrection-life" (G. Vos, *The Pauline Eschatology* [Princeton, 1930], p. 169). The life bestowed by the Spirit in that coming day is beyond the power of death or any other agency to vitiate or destroy. It is the very life of God, blessedly spiritual and indestructibly eternal.

Notes

1 In v.1 KJV has a longer wording than NIV, concluding the verse with "who walk not after the flesh, but after the Spirit." This addition is not warranted, being absent from the leading MSS; clearly it has been introduced by scribal zeal from the end of v.4.

2 A decision must be made between two readings: "me" or "you"—με (me) or σε (se). "You" has the stronger MS support, and for this reason a number of versions follow this reading. On the other hand, there are two factors that warrant retaining "me." For one thing, it is the logical term for Paul to have used, in agreement with the personal thrust of ch. 7. Also, the close of the preceding word in the Gr. text ("set free") has in it the letters se, so that a copyist could easily have transcribed se for me by visual error. If this is what happened, it must have occurred early in the transmission of the text, since σε (se) appears in many of our early and most reliable MSS. A mistake of this kind was more easily made in the earlier copies because for several centuries the text was written without any space between the words.

5 The argument of Lenski (*The Interpretation of St. Paul's Epistle to the Romans* [Columbus: Wartburg Press, 1945], p. 503) that "the decisive point is the fact that the Spirit is not a norm (κατά, *kata*) as are flesh and spirit," is not convincing, for the same preposition is used with the Spirit elsewhere (Gal 4:29) as well as with God (8:27) and with Christ (15:5).

2. Additional ministries of the Spirit

8:12–27

12Therefore, brothers, we have an obligation—but it is not to our sinful nature, to live according to it. 13For if you live according to the sinful nature, you will die; but if by the Spirit you put to death the misdeeds of the body, you will live.

14Those who are led by the Spirit of God are sons of God. 15For you did not receive a spirit that makes you a slave again to fear, but you received the Spirit who makes you cry, "*Abba*, Father." 16The Spirit himself testifies with our spirit that we are God's children. 17Now if we are children, then we are heirs—heirs of God and co-heirs with Christ, if indeed we share in his sufferings in order that we may also share in his glory.

18I consider that our present sufferings are not worth comparing with the glory that will be revealed in us. 19The creation waits in eager expectation for the sons of God to be revealed. 20For the creation was subjected to frustration, not by its own choice, but by the will of the one who subjected it, in hope 21that the creation itself will be liberated from its bondage to decay and brought into the glorious freedom of the children of God.

22We know that the whole creation has been groaning as in the pains of childbirth right up to the present time. 23Not only so, but we ourselves, who have the firstfruits of the Spirit, groan inwardly as we wait eagerly for our adoption as sons, the redemption of our bodies. 24For in this hope we were saved. But hope that is seen is no hope at all. Who hopes for what he already has? 25But if we hope for what we do not yet have, we wait for it patiently.

26In the same way, the Spirit helps us in our weakness. We do not know how we ought to pray, but the Spirit himself intercedes for us with groans that words cannot express. 27And he who searches our hearts knows the mind of the Spirit, because the Spirit intercedes for the saints in accordance with God's will.

12,13 The apostle turns now from instruction to exhortation, from what God has done through Christ and the Spirit to what the believer is expected to do by way of response. But even with a strong emphasis on human responsibility, we see behind the human effort that which can be accomplished only "by the Spirit." The special ministry described here is *mortification*. It is the message of 6:11–14 all over again except for the reminder that no one can hope to deal effectively with the sinful nature simply by determination alone. The Holy Spirit is needed, and he is the Spirit of power.

"Obligation" is the keynote. Only the negative side is stated; the positive side—that we are debtors to the Spirit—must be inferred. If we do not have an obligation to live in terms of the sinful nature, the conclusion must be that our obligation is to live and serve God in terms of the Spirit. It is tremendously important to grasp the import of v.12, because it teaches beyond all question that the believer still has the sinful nature within himself, despite having been crucified with Christ. The flesh has not been eradicated. But we are obliged not "to live according to it." There is really no option, for the flesh is linked to death as life is linked to the Spirit. Sanctification is not a luxury but a necessity. As Bishop Handley Moule stated, "It is not an ambition; it is a duty" (in loc.). Life in accordance with the flesh is doomed to suffer death (cf. v.6). The solicitations of the fleshly nature are constant; hence the necessity of continually putting to death (that is the force of the verb) the deeds of the body. Here "body" is equivalent to "the flesh" as in 6:6. Though this may seem to give a negative emphasis to the life of sanctification, it should be emphasized that this is only part of the divine plan. The positive is just as important—the putting on of the Lord Jesus in such complete preoccupation with him and his will that the believer does not make provision for the flesh (cf. 13:14). Yet since the Spirit is the Spirit of life, he cannot do otherwise than oppose the flesh and its desires, the things that lead inevitably to death.

14–17 The Spirit's ministry set forth in these verses may be thought of as his *attestation*, in which he confirms for the believer the reality of his position as a son of God based on adoption into the heavenly family. Though this ministry is mentioned after that of mortification, it is basic to it, because to be successful in contending against the flesh one must be assured that he has been claimed by God and equipped with his infinite resources. Later (v.23) Paul will move on to set forth another aspect of adoption that belongs to the future, identified with redemption in its ultimate realization.

The relation of the Spirit to the sons of God is presented as being much like that of a shepherd to his sheep. They are "led" by him as their guide and protector. In Galatians 3:24 the law is pictured as having a responsibility to "lead" men to Christ. Once this goal is achieved, the law must hand over the guiding role to the Spirit, who guides into the truth (John 16:13) and, as in the present passage, into holiness. Unlike sin, which may at first only gently seduce, then deceitfully begin to drive as a hard taskmaster, the Spirit relies on persuasion rather than force. In fact, Paul goes to some pains to avoid misunderstanding on this very point, assuring us that the Spirit's leadership does not involve a new bondage that is no improvement over the old in which fear ruled the life (probably a fear of the consequences of sin and a fear of death, as in Heb 2:15). The new title given to the Spirit, namely, "the Spirit who makes you sons" (literally, "Spirit of adoption"), emphasizes the vast gulf between slavery and family relationship. By the Spirit believers cry, "*Abba*, Father." The two terms are equivalents, the first being the Aramaic word Jesus used in prayer (Mark 14:36). Paul's use of the Aramaic alongside the Greek both here and in Galatians 4:6, a closely related passage, may well indicate that the tradition concerning the prayer life of Jesus filtered down through the church even before Mark wrote his Gospel. J. Jeremias notes that in permitting the Twelve to use the Lord's

Prayer, Jesus "authorizes his disciples to follow him in saying *Abba*. He gives them this address as the token of their discipleship" (*The Central Message of the New Testament* [New York: Scribner's, 1965], p. 28). The "cry" refers to calling on God in prayer.

The important term "adoption" bears a relationship to justification in that it is declarative and forensic (inasmuch as it is a legal term). Adoption bestows an objective standing, as justification does; like justification, it is a pronouncement that is not repeated. It has permanent validity. Like justification, adoption rests on the loving purpose and grace of God (Eph 1:5). Though the term is used of Israel in relation to God (9:4; cf. Hos 11:1), it is doubtful that adoption was practiced in OT days. Much more likely is the conclusion that Paul was drawing on the background of Roman law both here and in Galatians 4:5. The readers of both Epistles would be familiar with adoption in their own society (Francis Lyall, "Roman Law in the Writings of Paul—Adoption," JBL 88 [Dec. 1969] 458–66).

Paul's readers are called sons (v.15) and children (v.16), without any appreciable distinction. Both are family terms. "Children" emphasizes family relationship based on regeneration, while "sons" stresses legal standing. (This is not according to the usage of the apostle John, since John uses "children" for believers and reserves "son" for the Son of God.)

Here (v.16), as in Galatians 4:6, the Spirit is represented as bearing witness together with the redeemed spirit in man to the reality of membership in the family of heaven, that is, to the actuality of salvation through Christ. Hebrew law prescribed that at the mouth of two or three witnesses every matter was to be established (Deut 17:6; cf. Matt 18:16). Similarly, there are two witnesses to one's salvation, the person himself in his inmost being and the Holy Spirit, who confirms the believer's realization that he has indeed been made God's child through faith in Christ. Because this witness takes place in the heart (Gal 4:6), it is not a witness others receive, though it may be the basis for testifying to others about the reality of salvation. It may be aided by Scripture (John 20:31; 1 John 5:13) but is not dependent on the written word. It is a secret inner witness (see Bernard Ramm, *The Witness of the Spirit* [Grand Rapids: Eerdmans, 1959]).

A comparison of vv.15 and 16 will bring out an important truth concerning the assurance of salvation. All too often a believer may come to the point of doubting his salvation because his sanctification has proceeded so slowly and so lamely. The Spirit, however, does not base his assuring testimony on progress or the lack of it in the Christian life. He does not lead us to cry, "I am God's child." Rather, he leads us to call upon God as Father, to look away from ourselves to him who established the relationship.

A final truth about adoption is that it involves an inheritance (v.17). In line with current legal provisions that enabled even a slave, once adopted, to inherit his master's possessions, Paul teaches that the Christian follows a similar course: a slave (to sin), a child, then an heir (vv.15–17; cf. Gal 4:6, 7). How unexpected and how breathtaking is the gracious provision of God! The marvel increases with the news that we are co-heirs with Christ. Sharing his sufferings may be looked at as simply the cost of discipleship. Yet it has a brighter aspect, because it is the prelude to partaking with him of the coming glory (cf. 1 Peter 4:13).

18–25 Before passing to the final ministry of the Spirit (vv.26, 27) Paul lingers over the concept of future glory in relation to present suffering. His presentation may be seen as an expansion of what he had already written to the Corinthians (2 Cor 4:17). Weighed in the scales of true and lasting values, the sufferings endured in this life are light indeed, compared with the splendor of the life to come—a life undisturbed by anything hostile or hurtful. Scripture does not tell us much of *what* that glory will be, but it assures us *that* it will be. The glory will be revealed "in us." Another rendering, adopted by several versions, has "to us," which is the more usual force of the construction used here. Possibly the idea is that the glory will be manifested or made available to us, becoming our possession.

Instead of considering the future simply from the standpoint of the redeemed, Paul enlarges the perspective to include the whole creation, which is here personified as longing for the time when the sons of God will enjoy the consummation because the creation's own deliverance from the frustration imposed on it by the fall cannot come until that time. This accords with the superior place given man in the creation (Gen 1:26–28; Ps 8:5–8). "Eager expectation" is a picturesque term describing a person leaning forward out of intense interest and desire. Most of its occurrences relate to the Christian's attitude toward the Lord's coming (e.g., Gal 5:5; Phil 3:20; Heb 9:28). The personification is continued by the use of "frustration," which, as Sanday and Headlam note, "is appropriately used of the *disappointing* character of present existence, which nowhere reaches the perfection of which it is capable" (in loc.).

The one who subjected the creation is not named. Some early Fathers assumed that Adam is in view. Others (e.g., Godet) incline to the notion that Satan is meant. But by far the most natural interpretation is that which postulates God as the one who did the subjecting. The personification is sustained, with the creation being pictured as not willingly enduring the subjection yet having hope for something better, i.e., liberation from its "bondage to decay." The creation longs to share the glorious freedom of the children of God. Shedd remarks, "The restoration of material nature is a condition similar, in its own lower sphere, to the restoration of man's spiritual nature, in its higher sphere. St. Paul here teaches, not the annihilation of this visible world, but its transformation" (in loc.). The apostle is concerned with the creation only as it relates to man. How gracious of God to retain for believers the habitat they have long been accustomed to, only so changed and beautified as to harmonize with their own glorified state.

From v.22 it appears at first sight that "the whole creation" includes man. But v.23 alters this impression, for it sets the entire creation over against the whole body of the redeemed ("we ourselves") and therefore does not include in it the people of God. The groaning of the creation looks back to its subjection to frustration (v.20), whereas the pangs of childbirth anticipate the age of renewal. In other words, the same sufferings are at once a result and a prophecy. Christ spoke of the renewing of the world and called it a "rebirth" (*palingenesia*, Matt 19:28).

Paul makes a parallel between the saints and the material creation. In at least two respects their situation is the same—groaning (cf. 2 Cor 5:2) and eagerly awaiting the new age (v.23). Perhaps a third element of comparison is intended: "the redemption of our bodies," answering to the transformation of the earth. But in one respect no parallel can be made. Only the people of God have "the firstfruits of the Spirit."

The concept of firstfruits (v.23) is prominent in the OT, where, according to the law, Israelites were expected to bring the first-ripe elements of grain, fruit, etc., to the Lord as an offering (Exod 23:19; Neh 10:35). By this observance of worship the offerer acknowledged that all produce was the provision of God and was really his. Implicit also in the ritual was the assurance from the divine side that the general harvest to be enjoyed by the offerer would providentially follow. As applied to our passage, the concept may appear to be somewhat out of place, for if the Spirit is truly a person, how can any more of him be given in the future than has been given at conversion? Clearly, this is not the line of thought intended. On the contrary, we are to understand that the gift of the Spirit to the believer at the inception of Christian life is God's pledge of the completion of the process of salvation, which is here stated as "adoption as sons, the redemption of our bodies." Recall that previously Paul has described the finished product as the spiritual body (1 Cor 15:44). The future bodily resurrection of believers will be the full harvest of redemption. Our bodies will be like that of the glorified Lord (Phil 3:20, 21).

In this connection we encounter adoption for the second time (cf. v.15). The saints already have an adoption: they are acknowledged as God's children. They are sealed by the Spirit for the day of redemption (Eph 1:13, 14; 4:30). Then will take place the second and final adoption. Between the two, there stretches the course of sanctification; but only at the final adoption will the child of God be fully conformed to the likeness of God's Son (v.29; cf. 1 John 3:2). As the physical body is admirably suited to life in this world, the promised spiritual body will be seen to be wonderfully congruent with the realm of light and freedom and limitless movement. But most important of all, it will be like the body of him who has provided redemption from sin and death. This is the Spirit's work of *glorification.*

In keeping with the eager waiting of those who long for their complete salvation (v.23) is the emphasis on hope (vv.24, 25). The connection between hope and suffering should not be overlooked either (cf. 5:4). NIV's "in this hope" is correct, suggesting that from the very moment of the reception of the gospel one must look forward to the final phase set forth in v.23. KJV's "we are saved by hope" unnecessarily makes hope encroach on the sphere of grace (Eph 2:8). The translation of JB, "For we must be content to hope that we shall be saved," is both inaccurate (Paul says we *have* been saved) and unfortunate, suggesting that one cannot in this life be sure of his salvation. The Christian pilgrim is on the road to glory, assured that the promises of the word and the spiritual energy provided for his "walk" are not illusory. As he sees the dark tunnel of death ahead of him, he is confident that beyond it the road leads on to his destination, though it remains unseen. Simply because an element of our salvation—the redemption of the body—is held in reserve, we have a legitimate exercise of hope. If all were ours now, there would be no place for it. Since the object of our hope is not yet realized, "we wait for it patiently." Whether to translate *di' hypomonēs* "patiently" or "with endurance" or "with fortitude" is a difficult decision. If God's promise is chiefly in view (cf. Abraham in 4:18), then "patiently" is appropriate, but if the hardships and sufferings that remain to be faced are in view (note the emphasis on suffering in the context), then the more usual force of the word as "endurance" should be preferred. One can understand the reason for the combined rendering sometimes chosen here, namely, "we wait with patient endurance."

26,27 At length Paul arrives at the final ministry of the Spirit mentioned in this chapter, his work of *intercession.* "In the same way" seems to link this ministry with hope. Both help to sustain the believer amid the burdens and disappointments of life. It is uncertain whether the weakness spoken of here is a general expression for the Christian's limitations while still in the flesh, or whether it is intended to point to his weakness in the specific area of prayer. We know that the apostle had long before discovered his weakness and along with it the compensating factor of the power of God (2 Cor 12:9, 10). The broader interpretation of weakness may well be correct here. Paul may be saying that we do not know how to pray so as to get help for our many-sided weakness. The word "how" could suggest that we do not know the art of prayer—how to phrase our petitions properly. But this is not the Greek word commonly used for "how." Even the wording "what we should pray for" is questionable, since "for" has no equivalent in the original text. So we come by elimination to the more literal wording "what we should pray," that is, the content of our prayers rather than simply the topics. Do we know our real needs as God sees them, and do we know the needs of others? Going deeper, do we know the will of God respecting these things? In the last analysis, it is that that will determine how our prayers will be answered.

Standing over against this severe limitation is the gladdening information that "the Spirit helps us." This word for help occurs in the NT in only one other passage (Luke 10:40). Martha had more than she could handle in the preparation of the meal and asked the Lord to bid her sister Mary come to her aid. We can paraphrase the request like this: "Tell her to help me by taking hold of her end of the task." This picture is useful, because it helps solve a rather vexing problem—viz., that we fail to find in the remainder of this passage any statement about *our* praying. Everything that is said relates to the activity of the Spirit on our behalf, culminating in the declaration that he intercedes "for the saints." Added to this is the fact that when we refer to intercessory prayer, we mean prayer for others rather than for ourselves. On the other hand, the word picture in "help" cannot lightly be dismissed. Furthermore, a previous mention of prayer and communion with God makes it a joint activity of the Spirit and the children of God (vv.15, 16). Since "our hearts" (v.27) suggests immediate personal involvement as well as the residence and operation of the Spirit, the best conclusion seems to be that prayer activity on the part of the believer goes on in the background, though overshadowed by the part played by the Spirit of God. Elsewhere (Eph 6:18) this is called praying in the Spirit.

Verse 27 is needed to clarify something referred to in v.26, i.e., the inexpressible groanings. How can such prayer, if it be called prayer at all, be answered? Are not such prayers unintelligible? Not for God! He is no stranger to the intent of the Spirit. He knows what the inexpressible meaning is, because the petitions the Spirit voices are strictly in accord with the will of God. Barth observes that God "makes himself our advocate with himself, that he utters for us that ineffable groaning, so that he will surely hear what we ourselves could not have told him, so that he will accept what he himself has to offer" (*A Shorter Commentary on Romans,* p. 102). It is a mistake to associate the inexpressible groanings with glossolalia. As Leenhardt notes, the passage is intended to include all Christians, whereas speaking in tongues is a special charismatic gift not possessed by all. In addition, tongues are not mentioned elsewhere in connection with intercession.

Notes

24 A twofold problem is encountered here. Some good authorities, including ℵ and A, read ὑπομένει (*hypomenei,* "endures") instead of ἐλπίζει (*elpizei,* "hopes"). Also the reading τίς (*tis,* "who") faces several competing readings. NIV follows τίς ... ἐλπίζει (*tis ... elpizei,* "who hopes").

3. *The security and permanence of the life of the redeemed* (8:28–39)

God's provision for his own is spelled out in exalted and fervent language—reaching back into the past to include his eternal purpose and its implementation in the love and sacrifice of Christ, moving into the present to proclaim God's keeping power, and sweeping down the years to defy any power to separate the saint from the abiding love of God in Christ.

8:28–39

28And we know that in all things God works for the good of those who love him, who have been called according to his purpose. 29For those God foreknew he also predestined to be conformed to the likeness of his Son, that he might be the firstborn among many brothers. 30And those he predestined, he also called; those he called, he also justified; those he justified, he also glorified.

31What, then, shall we say in response to this? If God is for us, who can be against us? 32He who did not spare his own Son, but gave him up for us all—how will he not also, along with him, graciously give us all things? 33Who will bring any charge against those whom God has chosen? It is God who justifies. 34Who is he that condemns? Christ Jesus, who died—more than that, who was raised to life—is at the right hand of God and is also interceding for us. 35Who shall separate us from the love of Christ? Shall trouble or hardship or persecution or famine or nakedness or danger or sword? 36As it is written:

"For your sake we face death all the day long;
    we are considered as sheep to be slaughtered."

37No, in all these things we are more than conquerors through him who loved us. 38For I am convinced that neither death nor life, neither angels nor demons, neither the present, nor the future, nor any powers, 39neither height nor depth, nor anything else in all creation, will be able to separate us from the love of God that is in Christ Jesus our Lord.

28–30 Verse 28 has problems of text, of connection with the context, and of interpretation. As to the text, some manuscripts make "all things" the subject; others include God as the subject (see note). The problem is not crucial, since even without God being named, there could be no thought in Paul's mind that all things by themselves worked for the good of believers. The entire chapter protests against any such impersonal notion. As to the context, the thought may be connected with the foregoing after this fashion— that we now have a broad, general statement after a more specific one relating to the work of the Spirit as intercessor. So, for example, NEB reads, "And in everything, as we know, he cooperates for good with those who love God." The difficulty with this lies in the remainder of the sentence, where "purpose" must then be referred to the Spirit, whereas elsewhere this is regularly the function of God.

We must also try to settle the meaning of "all things." It is unlikely that the items in vv.29, 30 are intended to provide the content of the "all things," which is deliberately general and suggests especially those things that, while themselves adverse, are turned to good account by the sovereign operation of God on our behalf. This line of thought agrees with 5:3–5 as well as with the mention of sufferings and opposition in the present chapter. The "good" is not defined, but should be sought in the intended conformity to God's Son. The beneficiaries are those who on the human side love God and on the divine side are called according to God's purpose. Paul seldom refers to love for God on the part of the saints (1 Cor 2:9; 8:3). Nor does he introduce it here as the ground for the benefit he has been describing, for it is not meritorious but simply a response to the divine love and grace. The "called" are not those who are merely invited to respond to the proclamation of the gospel; they are called according to God's (electing) purpose. This calling is further explained in terms of foreknowledge and predestination (v.29).

The former term does not indicate advance awareness or knowledge of someone; it refers to God's choice, his electing decision. This is rendered crystal clear in 1 Peter 1:20. God's calling is not a haphazard thing, nor is it something cold and formal. It is filled with the warmth of love, as in the Hebrew word "to know" (Gen 18:19; Amos 3:2). Though foreknowledge is not mentioned in Deuteronomy 7:6–8, that passage illumines the concept. The antecedent character of God's choice precludes any possibility of human merit as entering into the decision (cf. Eph 1:4). Observe also that we are called according to purpose, not according to foreknowledge, hence foreknowledge must be included in the electing purpose.

If "predestined" stood by itself without any amplification, one might conclude that all that is involved is an action by God whereby one is chosen to salvation. But the remainder of the sentence indicates otherwise, pointing to much more than deliverance from sin and death. The background is adoption, but now presented not as in v.15 (where it is related to the Father and the Spirit) but as related to the Son. Paul presents two aspects of this conformity. By a sharing in the sufferings of Christ (Phil 3:10) that is based on having the mind of Christ (Phil 2:5–8), the believer is gradually being made into his likeness. This is the essence of sanctification. Its second and final aspect is conformity of the body to that of the risen Lord, to be realized at the resurrection (Phil 3:21), which is the culmination of a growth in likeness to Christ based on the Spirit's work in the believer (2 Cor 3:18).

From these passages we learn that fellowship with Christ in his sufferings is the prelude to sharing with him in his glory. God sent his Son in our likeness (v.3) that we might eventually be like him. This makes understandable and legitimate the use of "brothers" as a description of believers in relation to the Son. The likeness will be complete except for the fact that glorified humanity never, of course, becomes deity.

Verse 30 states the various steps involved in the realization of the divine purpose: the call (cf. v.28), justification, and glorification. The marvel is that the final item is stated as though it had already occurred. This led Denney to declare (in loc.) that this is "the most daring verse in the Bible." One is reminded of the so-called prophetic perfect used occasionally in the OT, as for example, in Isaiah 53, where the work of the Servant of Jehovah is spoken of as though his sacrifice had already been made.

Why is sanctification not mentioned in this verse? It is probably left out deliberately because sanctification is the one area in which human cooperation is essential. There is no appeal anywhere to be called or justified or glorified, but there are numerous appeals to cooperate with God in the realization of the life of holiness.

31–36 From this point on to the end of the chapter Paul expounds the impregnable position of the believer. The key lies in the sentence "If God is for us, who can be against us?" (v.31). God has not given empty promises. He has acted, and what he has done in Christ and by the Spirit constitutes all the proof we need that the glorification will be ours in due season. This is precisely the point of v.32. God's activity has cost him dearly—he did not spare "his own Son." In the background is the readiness of Abraham to give up his son Isaac (Gen 22). But whereas a substitute was found for Isaac and he was restored to his father without dying, no other than God's own Son could take away the world's sin and provide reconciliation. So Jesus had to endure the cross. In all of this God was with him (2 Cor 5:19). Moreover, the Son was not an unwilling victim pressed into sacrificial service. "God gave him up" expresses the Father's participation, but the same verb is used of the Son's involvement (Gal 2:20). With the cross before us as the mighty demonstration of God's grace in giving his dearest to help the neediest, it

98

naturally follows that the same gracious spirit will not withhold anything from those who are his. Such is the assurance given us in 2 Peter 1:3 that everything we need for life and godliness has been given.

Paul does not deny that the Christian faces foes and hardships. Yet his challenging question stands: "If God is for us, who can be against us?" Amplifying it, he proceeds to ask a series of questions, and provides answers to them. First, "Who will bring any charge against those whom God has chosen?" (v.33) No one can successfully press charges, no matter how hard he may try. Satan is busy doing just that (Rev 12:10), no doubt pointing out the discrepancy between the profession of believers and their "walk," but he gets nowhere with his pretended zeal for righteousness. Ultimately, as David also perceived (Ps 51:4), all sin is committed against God, no matter how much it affects others. Logically, therefore, God is the only one in position to bring charges against us. This, Paul is saying, God refuses to do, because he is for us, not against us.

The second question, "Who is he that condemns?" (v.34), finds its answer in Christ. He will never renounce the efficacy of his own work on our behalf. Paul packs four aspects of that work into one great sentence (v.34b). (1) Christ died and thereby secured the removal of sin's guilt; (2) he was raised to life and is able to bestow life on those who trust him for their salvation (John 11:25; 14:19); (3) he was exalted to God's right hand, with all power given to him both in heaven, so as to represent us there, and on earth, where he is more than a match for our adversaries; (4) and he intercedes for us at the throne of grace, whatever our need may be (Heb 4:4–16; 7:25).

A third question is "Who shall separate us from the love of Christ?" (v.35). Can there conceivably be a contradiction between Christ's love for his own and his allowing suffering to overtake them? Should the saints question whether Christ's love has grown cold? Severance from his love is no more thinkable than that the Father ceased to love his Son when he allowed him to endure the agonies of the cross, apparently forsaken. Christ predicted trouble for his people who are left in the world, but told them to be of good cheer because he had overcome the world (John 16:33). The quotation from Psalm 44:22 (v.36) reminds believers that suffering has always been the lot of the godly, and therefore their own situation is not peculiar. Whereas the people of God in the OT were often perplexed about the reason for their trials, the saints of NT times can trace their sufferings back to identification with Christ and rejoice that they are counted worthy to suffer for his name (cf. Acts 5:41).

37–39 Here Paul bursts into a magnificent piece of eloquence. This passage, like 1 Corinthians 3:21–23, is notable for largeness of conception and majesty of expression: "No, in all these things we are more than conquerors through him who loved us" (v.37).

Some have found "more than conquerors" puzzling. It could mean that believers turn their enemies into helpers as indicated in 5:3–5. But this is rather conjectural. Bauer affirms that the verb *hypernikaō* used here is a heightened form of "conquer" and suggests the translation "We are winning a most glorious victory." Bauernfeind (TDNT 4:945) renders it, "We win the supreme victory through him who loved us."

By saying "loved us," Paul does not intend to restrict Christ's love to the past, but rather he is emphasizing the historic demonstration of this love that gives assurance of its continuing under all circumstances. Death cannot separate the believer from that love (cf. Phil 1:21; 2 Cor 5:8). Neither can life, with all its allurements and dangers and trials.

Surprisingly, Paul includes angels here (v.38). Since he uses other terms for hostile supernatural powers, the angels should be understood as good ones. Perhaps the meaning is that no angel of this sort would seek to come between Christ's love and the object of that love. Demons are evil spirits such as those often mentioned in the Gospels. Being agents and underlings of the devil, they would delight to separate Christians from Christ, but they cannot do so. Time is equally powerless to do this, whether it be the present with its temptations and sufferings or the future with its uncertainties. "Powers" probably has reference to hostile spiritual intelligences who, though conquered by Christ (Eph 1:21), are nevertheless permitted to carry on spiritual warfare against the saints of God (Eph 6:12).

Nor can space come between us and the love of Christ (v.39). If there are other possibilities, Paul is sure they are all equally impotent. For he declares that there is nothing in all creation that can drive a wedge between the love of the Savior and his redeemed people. After all, the creation itself is his handiwork and cannot thwart the will of the Creator. God is love, and that love has been manifested in the redemption of man.

S. Angus translates "neither height nor depth" as "neither the ascension of the stars nor their declinations," considering that Paul has in mind the fatalism of astral religion (*The Religious Quests of the Graeco-Roman World* [New York: Scribners, 1929], p. 254).

Notes

28 The KJV rendering "all things work together for good" is based on the text attested by ℵ C D G and the great bulk of MSS and many quotations from the Fathers. The rendering "in all things God works for the good" is supported by P[46] A B, among others. It is probable that the second form of the text came into being at an early date to clarify the meaning by tracing this activity definitely to God. Otherwise it is hard to explain how "God" could have dropped out of the majority of witnesses to the text.

VI. The Problem of Israel: God's Righteousness Vindicated (9:1–11:36)

This section contains "unfinished business." Although Paul has insisted on the priority of the Jew (1:16) and has noted in part his advantages (3:1ff.), he has also been obliged to expose the Jews' failure and guilt, despite their being the chosen people of God. Those who have been under divine tutelage for centuries in preparation for the coming of the Messiah have failed to receive him. Has the purpose of God been frustrated? What does the future hold for this people? The problem faced here was underscored in Paul's own ministry. He had been faithful in going to the Jew first, but in place after place he had been rebuffed by Jewish unbelief. In Rome itself his strenuous effort to win a favorable verdict for the Lord Jesus Christ was to prove largely unsuccessful (Acts 28). Was his earlier statement about the power of the gospel (1:16) too hasty, too optimistic? Or were his own labors among his people inadequate? Paul could not subscribe to either conclusion. He had to face the problem from the standpoint of God's purposes and ways.

Jew and Gentile are distinguished in the first three chapters and are still distinguished, as the circumcised and the uncircumcised, in chapter 4. In chapters 5 to 8 the Jew/Gentile tension drops out of sight, only to be renewed in chapters 9 to 11 and brought under searching examination. Notable is the shift in terminology. Although "Jew" occurs twice in this section, Paul prefers "Israel," using it ten times here and nowhere else in the letter. The reason for the change will be noted later.

In line with the nature of the problem Paul is dealing with, he frequently mentions God in chapters 9 to 11 (twenty-six times). References to Christ are limited (seven times), and the Holy Spirit has no place except in 9:1.

For all its distinctiveness, this section does not lose continuity with the foregoing material. "Salvation" (cf. 1:16) and "save" are prominent. "Righteousness" (cf. 1:17) is found nine times; "believe" (cf. 1:16), eight times; and "faith," six times.

Not only is there a connection with the theme of the letter, but also a tie-in with the close of chapter 8; for election, which is treated on an individual basis in 8:28–30, 33, is now viewed from the national perspective of Israel. Adoption is an element common to both portions (8:15; 9:4), as is also the concept of "call" or "calling" (8:28–30; 5 times in ch. 9).

Another feature is the liberal use of OT quotations, partly to emphasize the sovereignty of God and his covenant faithfulness and partly to substantiate the apostle's exposure of Israel's failure. Unfaithfulness to God in OT times has its parallel in rejection of his Son in recent times. Israel according to the flesh has not materially changed.

A survey of the movement of thought in these chapters warrants the conclusion that Paul, who has written so penetratingly on the justification of sinners, now turns to write on the justification (vindication) of God himself (cf. 3:3, 4). He reminds us that the Almighty is free and sovereign in what he does (ch. 9). Then he turns the discussion to the Jews' mistake in trying to establish their own righteousness before God in terms of meritorious obedience to law instead of responding to the gospel of Christ by faith. They have not lacked opportunity to hear (ch. 10). So God did not set Israel aside arbitrarily. This matches the great section on condemnation at the beginning of the Epistle.

In chapter 11 Paul introduces further considerations. One is that Israel's rejection was not complete, for there was a believing remnant in Paul's day. This answers to the treatment on justification in chapters 3 to 5. Also, the rejection is not final, for a mass conversion of Israel will occur, answering roughly to the glorious future pictured in chapter 8. In addition, Paul weaves in the observation that during the time Israel is set aside God continues his work of grace by saving a host of Gentiles. In the end, God is found faithful to his covenant promises in spite of the unfaithfulness of Israel. Moreover, he has turned to good account the failure of the Jew by bringing in the Gentiles during the period of Israel's hardening. This grand achievement embracing both Jew and Gentile leads Paul to conclude with a worshipful note of praise for this unfathomable divine wisdom. It is a testimony to the divine mercy (11:32) which, along with God's righteousness, provides the insight needed to appreciate his ways.

A. Paul's Sorrow Over Israel's Condition

9:1–5

> I speak the truth in Christ—I am not lying, my conscience confirms it in the Holy Spirit—²I have great sorrow and unceasing anguish in my heart. ³For I could wish that I myself were cursed and cut off from Christ for the sake of my brothers, those of my own race, ⁴the people of Israel. Theirs is the adoption as sons; theirs the divine glory, the covenants, the receiving of the law, the temple worship and the promises. ⁵Theirs are the patriarchs, and from them is traced the human ancestry of Christ, who is God over all, forever praised! Amen.

1–3 The apostle begins on a personal note, expressing his concern for his own people.

His soul is burdened over their condition, as were the prophets of old. Since he has left Judaism behind, this sorrow might be interpreted as somewhat less than sincere. Hence the solemn introduction in which he summons two witnesses—his union with Christ who is the truth (cf. Eph 4:21) and his conscience as aided by the Holy Spirit (cf. 8:16). As though that were not enough, he declares himself ready to accept severance from Christ (cf. 8:39) if that would avail to bring his countrymen into the fold of the Savior (cf. Exod 32:32). The phrase "I could wish" (v.3) faithfully brings out the idiomatic construction used here for stating an impossible wish. Paul could not actually become anathema from Christ (chapter 8 proclaims the impossibility of that). Yet if it were possible, he would gladly make the sacrifice. This readiness takes on poignancy in light of the fact that Paul had suffered the loss of all things in order to gain Christ (Phil 3:8). So he would be facing a double loss.

Paul's longing for the salvation of his people comes out in the way he speaks of them—"my brothers." To avoid misunderstanding, he has to qualify this by noting that the bond is one of "race" rather than of a common faith in Christ. But more than a blood relationship is involved, because he goes on to cite the spiritual heritage of his people that he shares with those of them who have not become Christians. This use of "brothers" appears elsewhere (e.g., Acts 2:29; 3:17; 22:1; 28:17).

4,5 It is notable that the apostle avoids the term "Jews" in v.4, for ordinarily that would stress merely the racial, political, and ritualistic aspects of his nation, unless qualified in some way, as in 2:29, where the description of the true Jew is equivalent to "Israelite." By referring to his countrymen as "the people of Israel," he is emphasizing that they are the covenant people of God, different from every other people on earth. This distinctiveness explains Paul's avoidance of the term "Israel" when speaking of the church (TDNT 3:387). Such is the case even in Galatians 6:16 (Richardson, pp. 74–84).

It is only when the distinctives of Israel are spelled out that the full implication of the word can be appreciated. Probably Paul has in mind his implied promise to enlarge on the advantages of his people (3:2). In the forefront in v.4 he puts "the adoption as sons." The Greek word *hyiothesia* ("adoption as sons"—used also in 8:15) does not occur in LXX, but the idea is certainly present, especially in Deuteronomy 14:1, 2 (cf. Exod 4:22; Hos 11:1). "Paul uses the word, as though to say that even the status of Israel was not something necessary and inherent, but the result of an act of graciousness on the part of God" (IDB 1:48b). This explains Israel's enjoyment of "the divine glory" or "the splendour of the divine presence" (NEB), that which was symbolized by the pillar of cloud that settled over the sanctuary in the wilderness and filled the temple at its dedication.

"The covenants" could be the arrangements God entered into with Abraham, with the nation of Israel at Sinai, and with David. On the other hand, the reference could be to the covenant made with Abraham (Gen 15), then renewed with Isaac (Gen 17), and with Jacob (Gen 28). There is rather good manuscript evidence for "covenant" rather than "covenants," but this reading can hardly be original, for it would most naturally suggest the Mosaic covenant (2 Cor 3:6, 14), which would render the next item, the reception of the law, quite unnecessary. The word "covenant" used here implies divine initiative rather than a mutual agreement between equals.

"The receiving [literally, 'giving'] of the law" refers, of course, to what was communicated through Moses to the children of Israel at Sinai. In Paul's time the nation tended to look upon this as its most prized possession (2:17), the most precious portion of the OT. A closely related item is "the temple worship," since the sacrificial cultus maintained by the priests is meant, and all this was prescribed in the law. "The promises" have a close relationship to the covenants (cf. Eph 2:12) and represent various aspects of the messianic salvation promised in the OT.

The importance of "the patriarchs" (v.5) can be seen in 11:28. They are the men to whom the promises were given prior to the giving of the law. God is pleased to announce himself as the God of Abraham, Isaac, and Jacob (Exod 3:15).

"From them is traced the human ancestry of Christ" (v.5). By "them" we are probably to understand the people of Israel (v.4) rather than the patriarchs. Account is taken of the intervening generations prior to the advent of the Messiah (cf. the genealogies in Matthew and Luke). A subtle distinction is to be noted between "theirs" and "from them." Israel cannot lay claim to Christ in the same way she can claim the patriarchs, even though he entered the human family through the Israelitish gate (cf. 1:3). Christ is much more than the patriarchs. Only in his earthly origin does he belong to the one nation. Because of his heavenly origin and mission he cannot be claimed exclusively by any segment of the race, seeing he is "God over all."

But is "God over all" the correct translation? On the ground that elsewhere Paul avoids such a stark identification, despite his high Christology, some scholars reject the traditional rendering, preferring something on the order of NEB: "May God, supreme above all, be blessed for ever." This involves taking the closing portion of the verse as a doxology and referring it to God (the Father).

Several considerations favor the traditional wording, which refers "God" to Christ: (1) Christ's relationship to Israel on the human side has been stated in such a way as to call for a complementary statement on the divine side. This is provided by the usual translation but not by the other rendering. (2) "Who" can properly be coupled only with the foregoing subject (Christ). If another subject (God) is being introduced, there is no reason at all for the "who." (3) A doxology to God can hardly be intended, since in doxologies the word "blessed" is regularly placed before the one who is praised. Here it comes after. (4) A doxology to God would be singularly out of place in a passage marked by sorrow over Israel's failure to recognize in Christ her crowning spiritual blessing. (5) The definite article, "the," is not linked in the text with "God," but with the foregoing words (literally, "the one being over all"), so Paul is not trying to displace God with Christ, but is doing what John does in saying that the Word was God (John 1:1), that is, has the rank of God. In any case, this is really implied in recognizing him as "over all" (it is very awkward, with NEB, to refer this to God in distinction from Christ).

Looking back over vv.1–5, one is bound to conclude from the combination of Paul's sorrow and the extended enumeration of Israel's privileges that the subject of his nation's spiritual condition must have constantly weighed on him. His statement of the advantages of Israel anticipates the fuller discussion of her election and serves to accent the element of tragedy in her current state. A double purpose is served by the culminating statement concerning the Messiah: it not only underscores the blindness of Israel but is also calculated to keep believing Gentiles from gloating over Israel's fall (11:20), seeing that Israel has been the channel by which God gave Christ to the world.

Notes

5 An alternative wording has been favored by a few scholars, arrived at by emendation of the text (reading ὧν ὁ, *hōn ho*, instead of ὁ ὢν, *ho ōn*) and yielding the following: "whose is the God

over all, blessed for ever." This would make Israel's possession of the true God her climactic blessing, and it would be a fitting close to the paragraph. However, this conjecture lacks any MS authority.

Those who wish an exhaustive and scholarly study of the punctuation and interpretation of Romans 9:5, should see B.M. Metzger's article "The Punctuation of Rom. 9:5" in *Christ and Spirit in the New Testament*, ed. by B. Lindars and S.S. Smalley (Cambridge: Cambridge University Press, 1973), pp. 95–112.

B. *God's Choice of Israel Based on Election, Not on Natural Generation or Works of Merit*

9:6–13

> [6]It is not as though God's word had failed. For not all who are descended from Israel are Israel. [7]Nor because they are his descendants are they all Abraham's children. On the contrary, "Through Isaac shall your offspring come." [8]In other words, it is not the natural children who are God's children, but it is the children of the promise who are regarded as Abraham's offspring. [9]For this was how the promise was stated: "At the appointed time I will return, and Sarah shall have a son."
>
> [10]Not only that, but Rebecca's children had one and the same father, our ancestor Isaac. [11]Yet, before the twins were born or had done anything good or bad—in order that God's purpose in election might stand: [12]not by works but by him who calls—she was told, "The older will serve the younger." [13]Just as it is written: "Jacob I loved, but Esau I hated."

6–9 At once the atmosphere of tragedy is qualified by Paul's forthright denial that the course of events has taken God by surprise. If there is failure, it must be attributed to men, not to God. By "God's word" (v.6) we are to understand "the declared purpose of God" (Sanday and Headlam). This certainly involves the element of promise (cf. vv.8, 9). God's saving purpose does not include all who belong to Israel in the biological sense. This distinction is similar to that drawn concerning the use of the term "Jew" (2:28, 29). Though unnamed, Ishmael is apparently in view, in contrast to Isaac, when a contrast is made between merely being a descendant of Abraham in a physical sense and enjoying God's call to spiritual destiny—belonging to the godly line of descent that would culminate in the Messiah himself (Gal 3:16). It was not true of Isaac that he was born in due course, by natural processes, and that God then acknowledged him for the reason that he belonged to Abraham. Such was the case with Ishmael insofar as it provided a ground for bestowing on him material blessings (Gen 17:20; 21:13). Isaac was unique in that he was the child who was promised. God's purpose was centered in him before he was born. It was God, in fact, not man, who set the time of his birth. Apart from divine enablement to the parents, Isaac would never have been born, for Abraham was impotent and Sarah was no longer able to bear children.

10–13 "Not only that" (v.10). Something more needs to be said, for it could be pointed out that the nation of Israel looked back to its origin in Isaac rather than in Ishmael or the sons of Abraham by Keturah. After all, it was only natural that the son of Sarah should be chosen rather than the son of Hagar the bondwoman. So Paul feels impelled to cite the case of the twin brothers, both of them sons of Isaac and Rebecca, with nothing in the least lacking regarding their parentage. According to ordinary human expectation, they should stand on equal terms before God in his dealings with them. But it was not so. Natural generation from Isaac, the promised seed of Abraham, did not assure them of the same place in the divine economy. God made a distinction between them before they were born—before their characters had been shaped or any deeds had been performed that might form a basis for evaluation. The freedom and sovereignty of God were thus safeguarded. He deliberately disturbed the normal pattern of the culture into which the children were born by decreeing that the elder should serve the younger.

In this connection, by quoting Malachi 1:2, 3, Paul lifts the discussion from what might appear to be a purely personal one to the plane of corporate, national life. God's love for Jacob and hatred for Esau ought not to be construed as temperamental. Malachi is appealing to the course of history as fulfilling the purpose of God declared long before. Hatred in the ordinary sense will not fit the situation, since God bestowed many blessings on Esau and his descendants. The "hatred" is simply a way of saying that Esau was not the object of God's electing purpose (cf. the use of hate in Luke 14:26, where discipleship is stated to involve "hatred" for one's own family and one's own life; they are simply put out of consideration when one takes on himself the responsibility of following Christ). The value of the account of the two brothers is to make clear that in election God does not wait until individuals or nations are developed and then make a choice on the basis of character or achievement. If he did so, this would make a mockery of the concept of election, because it would locate the basis in man rather than in God and his purpose. God's love for Jacob, then, must be coupled with election rather than explained by some worthiness found in him (cf. Deut 7:6–8).

C. God's Freedom to Act in His Own Sovereign Right

9:14–29

14What then shall we say? Is God unjust? Not at all! 15For he says to Moses,

"I will have mercy on whom I have mercy,
and I will have compassion on whom I
have compassion."

16It does not, therefore, depend on man's desire or effort, but on God's mercy. 17For the Scripture says to Pharaoh: "I raised you up for this very purpose, that I might display my power in you and that my name might be proclaimed in all the earth." 18Therefore God has mercy on whom he wants to have mercy, and he hardens whom he wants to harden.

19One of you will say to me: "Then why does God still blame us? For who resists his will?" 20But who are you, O man, to talk back to God? "Shall what is formed say to him who formed it, 'Why did you make me like this?' " 21Does not the potter have the right to make out of the same lump of clay some pottery for noble purposes and some for common use?

22What if God, choosing to show his wrath and make his power known, bore with great patience the objects of his wrath—prepared for destruction? 23What if he did this to make the riches of his glory known to the objects of his mercy, whom he prepared in advance for glory—24even us, whom he also called, not only from the Jews but also from the Gentiles? 25As he says in Hosea:

"I will call them 'my people' who are not my people:
and I will call her 'my loved one' who
is not my loved one,"

26and,

105

"It will happen that in the very place where
    it was said to them,
  'You are not my people,'
they will be called 'sons of the living God.' "

[27]Isaiah cries out concerning Israel: "Though the number of the Israelites should be like the sand by the sea, only the remnant will be saved. [28]For the Lord will carry out his sentence on earth with speed and finality." [29]It is just as Isaiah said previously:

"Unless the Lord All-powerful had left us
    descendants,
we should have become like Sodom,
and would have been like Gomorrah."

14–18 God's dealings with Jacob and Esau might be challenged as arbitrary, on the ground that Esau was the object of injustice. To demonstrate that this is not God's character, Paul goes further into the history of Israel, focusing on the golden calf incident at Sinai. There the people sinned grievously. If God had acted simply in justice, he could have blotted out his people. Instead, he recalled Moses to the mount and for a second time gave him the tables of commandments, yet not until he had proclaimed to his servant Moses, "I will have mercy on whom I will have mercy" (Exod 33:19). That mercy was seen in sparing a sinful nation. And lest that mercy be construed as depending on man's "desire" or "effort," Paul denies any such qualification (v.16). Mercy, like grace, stands over against human worth and effort whenever salvation is concerned. It is free, because God is not bound to show mercy to any.

The thought moves from Moses to Pharaoh, the king of Egypt at the time of the Exodus—from the leader of Israel to its oppressor (v.17). The Scripture is represented as speaking, a vivid reminder that it is God's word. "I raised you up" is not strictly a reference to Pharaoh's emergence in history, but to God's providence in sparing him up to that time. Pharaoh deserved death for his oppression and insolence, but his life would not be taken during the series of plagues, so that the full extent of his hardness of heart might be evident and the glory of God in the deliverance of his people enhanced (cf. Josh 9:9). The fame of this Pharaoh actually depended on the mercy of God in sparing him. God can be glorified through those who oppose him as well as through those who trust and serve him. The wrath of man can contribute to the praise and glory of God (Ps 76:10).

Paul concludes the Pharaoh episode with this observation: "Therefore God has mercy on whom he wants to have mercy, and he hardens whom he wants to harden" (v.18). He does not so much as bother to indicate that Pharaoh hardened his own heart, an evidence of unbelief and rebellion, because he is emphasizing the freedom of God's action in all cases. The hardening of Pharaoh's heart can profitably be related to the principle laid down in Romans 1, that God's method of dealing with those who reject the revelation of himself in nature and history (and in Pharaoh's case also in miracles) is to abandon them to still greater excess of sin and its consequences.

19–26 Paul, continuing the review of God's sovereign activity, presents another problem. If God acts unilaterally, according to his own will and purpose, does this not remove all basis for judgment, since man is not in a position to resist the divine will? Why, then, should man be blamed? In reply, Paul first points out the inappropriateness of the creature talking back to God (v.20) as though he had sufficient wisdom to judge the Almighty. The illustration of the potter and the clay (v.21) shows how ridiculous this is.

Two of Israel's prophets had made the same point (Isa 29:16; Jer. 18:6). Some interpreters have concluded that Paul has in mind the creation. While it is true that Genesis 2:7 contains the word "formed" which is the same root word as "potter," it is clear that Paul envisions the clay as a "given," and the real problem is what the potter does with the clay, namely, fashioning one type of vessel or another. The apostle is insisting on the right of the potter to make whatever type of vessel he chooses. Those made for "noble purposes" are valuable for their beauty and decorative function, while those made for "common use" are not admired, though they are actually more essential to the household than the other ones. Pharaoh was useful in fulfilling God's purpose. Apart from this, he would not even have appeared on the pages of sacred history.

In v.22 the crucial problem is to interpret correctly the expression "prepared for destruction." Is Paul teaching a double predestination? This is improbable, because he avoids involving God in this case, whereas he *is* involved in showing mercy to the objects of his mercy (v.23). Furthermore, God's patience in bearing with the objects of his wrath suggests a readiness to receive such on condition of repentance (cf. 2:3, 4; 2 Peter 3:9). So "prepared for destruction" designates a ripeness of sinfulness that points to judgment unless there is a turning to God, yet God is not made responsible for the sinful condition. The preparation for destruction is the work of man, who allows himself to deteriorate in spite of knowledge and conscience.

Presumably, and in view of what follows, when Paul speaks of "the objects of his [God's] wrath" (v.22), he has in mind those in Israel who have remained obdurate in opposing the gospel, yet are still the objects of the divine longsuffering. In contrast to them are "the objects of his mercy" (v.23) in whom God wills to show the riches of his glory (in contrast to his wrath). These, whom he has prepared for glory, include both Jews and Gentiles (v.24), in line with the previous teaching (1:16; 2:10, 11; 3:22) and with the prophetic announcement. The same God who declared to Israel through Amos: "You only have I known of all of the families of the earth" (Amos 3:2) declared through Hosea his freedom to call others to be his people (v.25). In all strictness, this passage from Hosea 2:23 refers to the reversal in Israel's status from being called "not my people" (Hos 1:9) to being restored, but in both Romans 9:25 and 1 Peter 2:10 the application is apparently broadened to include Gentiles, as Romans 2:24 intimates. Gentiles, who are not actually a people but only masses of humanity, are called by the grace of God to a distinctive role—that of being the people of God. This was happening in Paul's day.

The second quotation is from Hosea 1:10, omitting the first half of the verse, which refers to the prophesied increase in the number of the people of Israel. Here also the background is the Lo-ammi prophecy of Hosea 1:9, which is now seen to be revoked when Israel will once again be called "sons of the living God. " Since Peter uses the Hosea 2:23 passage as applying to Gentiles, Paul's intimation of a similar application is the more understandable. It is just possible that he does not intend the second passage (Hos 1:10) to apply to Gentiles (though this is by no means certain), in which case by the sequence of the passages he may be giving a hint of something developed in chapter 11—namely, the influx of Gentiles during Israel's temporary rejection, to be followed by the turning of Israel to the Lord in great numbers (11:25-27).

27-29 As Paul has used Scripture to show that it teaches God's purpose to extend his mercy to Gentiles, so now he uses Scripture again to make clear that the election of Israel does not preclude her reduction through chastening judgments, yet in the sparing of the remnant his mercy and faithfulness are to be seen. Both passages are from Isaiah. The former anticipates the depletion of the nation by reason of the Assyrian invasion under Sennacherib, described from God's viewpoint as "the rod of my anger, the staff of my fury" (Isa 10:5). Without softening his decree and without delay, God will permit the judgment to fall. Jacob, now numerous, will be reduced to a remnant (Isa 10:22). Thus far, judgment is emphasized, but the remainder of the sentence underscores the divine mercy—"the remnant will be saved." The Hebrew text has "... will return" (i.e., after deportation). Paul, however, sees the promise of a greater deliverance, for he says, "will be saved." Even as he wrote, there was a remnant of Israel to be found in the church. In view of the nation's rejection of Jesus as Israel's Messiah, Messianic Jews should be grateful for the minority of Jews who have embraced the gospel of Christ. In 11:5 Paul returns to this theme. If God's judgment had been unsparing, the nation would have become as truly wiped out as Sodom and Gomorrah (v.29). But the divine judgment is tempered by unfailing mercy, of which the remnant is the eloquent proof. This dual theme of the kindness and severity of God comes into focus again at 11:22.

D. *Israel's Failure to Attain Righteousness Due to Reliance on Works Rather Than Faith*

9:30–10:21

30What then shall we say? That the Gentiles, who did not pursue righteousness, have obtained it, a righteousness that is by faith; 31but Israel, who pursued a law of righteousness, has not attained it. 32Why not? Because they pursued it not by faith but as if it were by works. They stumbled over the "stumbling stone." 33As it is written:

"See, I lay in Zion a stone that causes
        men to stumble
    and a rock that makes them fall,
and the one who trusts in him will never
        be put to shame."

10:1 Brothers, my heart's desire and prayer to God for the Israelites is that they may be saved. 2For I can testify about them that they are zealous for God, but their zeal is not based on knowledge. 3Since they disregarded the righteousness that comes from God and sought to establish their own, they did not submit to God's righteousness. 4Christ is the end of the law so that there may be righteousness for everyone who believes.

5Moses describes in this way the righteousness that is by the law: "The man who does these things will live by them." 6But the righteousness that is by faith says: "Do not say in your heart, 'Who will ascend into heaven?' " (that is, to bring Christ down), 7or " 'Who will descend into the deep?' " (that is, to bring Christ up from the dead). 8But what does it say?

"The word is near you;
    it is in your mouth and in your heart";

that is, the word of faith we are proclaiming: 9that if you confess with your mouth, "Jesus is Lord," and believe in your heart that God raised him from the dead, you will be saved. 10For it is with your heart that you believe and are justified, and it is with your mouth that you confess and are saved. 11As the Scripture says, "He who believes in him will not be put to shame." 12For there is no difference between Jew and Gentile—the same Lord is Lord of all and richly blesses all who call on him, 13for, "Everyone who calls on the name of the Lord will be saved."

14How, then, can they call on the one they have not believed in? And how can they believe in the one of whom they have not heard? And how can they hear without someone preaching to them? 15And how can they preach unless they are sent? As it is written, "How beautiful are the feet of those who bring good news!"

¹⁶But not all the Israelites responded to the good news. For Isaiah says, "Lord, who has believed our message?" ¹⁷Consequently, faith comes from hearing the message, and the message is heard through the word of Christ. ¹⁸But I ask, did they not hear? Of course they did:

"Their voice has gone out into all the earth,
their words to the ends of the world."

¹⁹Again I ask, did Israel not understand? First, Moses says,

"I will make you envious by means of those
who are not a nation;
I will make you angry by a nation that
has no understanding."

²⁰Then Isaiah boldly says,

"I was found by those who did not seek me;
I revealed myself to those who did not
ask for me."

²¹But concerning Israel he says, "All day long I have held out my hands to a disobedient and obstinate people."

9:30–33 Here Paul introduces a contrast between Gentiles and Israel, emphasizing that what has come to the former by the exercise of faith has been denied the latter by their insistence on seeking righteousness on the basis of works.

There is no blanket inclusion of all Gentiles; only those are included who meet the description laid down here—that of not pursuing righteousness in the manner followed by the children of Israel. So far as the construction of the sentence (v.31) is concerned, it follows the pattern of 2:14 in the way Gentiles are referred to, despite the difference in theme. The figure of a foot race is introduced, as indicated by "pursue" and "obtained." The paradox is sharp, picturing Gentiles who are unconcerned about acquiring righteousness actually getting the prize, even though not competing in the race with the Jews. The prize is justification by faith. It is a pitiful picture of the nation of Israel struggling intensely to perfect their religious life and coming up empty-handed. Hodge puts the matter well: "The Gentiles, sunk in carelessness and sin, have attained the favor of God, while the Jews, to whom religion was a business, have utterly failed" (in loc.). It would be a mistake to suppose that Paul is putting a premium on carelessness regarding moral and spiritual considerations. Gentile success is attributed to their avoidance of the false approach of the Jew and their willingness to receive righteousness as a gift. Hardly a passage in the NT is stronger than this one in its exposure of the futility of works as a means of justification.

Verse 31 presents a difficulty. NIV reads, "But Israel, who pursued a law of righteousness, has not attained it." What is the "it"? The Greek has the word "law" in this verse. Yet the reader naturally looks for a repetition of the word "righteousness." Perhaps we can translate, "has not attained to such a law" (namely, the law of righteousness in the sense of righteousness gained by means of the law). Ragnar Bring suggests, "Paul means that they did not attain the kind of righteousness that the law speaks of " (ST 25 [1971] 46). They confusedly identified their own works, in which they took pride, with the absolute standard the law requires. Their whole effort was not grounded in faith but in works designed to gain acceptance (v.32).

"They stumbled over the stumbling stone" (v.32). Doubtless, the analogy of the race continues to influence Paul's thought. Absorbed in their own efforts, the Israelites did not recognize in Christ the stone of their prophetic Scripture, the sure foundation for their faith and life, and fell headlong over him. By failing to receive him, they denied also their own election of which he was the fulfillment and crown. The passage Paul quotes is a combination of Isaiah 8:14 and 28:16. From it we glean that the Lord himself, provided as a foundation stone, was actually to become for Israel a stumbling stone. This became especially true with respect to his cross (1 Cor 1:23). The misdirection of Israel's thinking became painfully clear in that the preaching of the cross, the event that was at once the quintessence of her sin and the sole hope of her salvation, left her defiant in her self-righteousness.

The chapter division does not mark a break in the thought, for the key words, such as "righteousness," "law," and "faith," continue to appear, especially in the beginning of the chapter.

10:1–4 Paul has spoken pointedly about Israel's failure, but not censoriously. He feels for his countrymen. He knows their plight because their condition was his own condition prior to his conversion. His desire for their salvation is reflected in his going to the Jews first (Acts 13:46; 18:5, 6; cf. Rom 1:16) but also in praying to God on their behalf. His preaching may be earnest, but it alone cannot convert. God must move in their hearts.

Paradoxically, it is Israel's zeal for God that constitutes their greatest barrier (v.2). The apostle knows whereof he speaks, for his zeal on behalf of Judaism had been notorious (Acts 22:3; Gal 1:14). That very zeal so preoccupied him that he felt bound to consider Jesus and his followers as traitors to the faith of his fathers. But he persecuted in ignorance (1 Tim 1:13). So here he diagnoses the zeal of Israel as lacking in "knowledge." His people have ignored "the righteousness that comes from God" (cf. 1:17). In trying to establish their own righteous standing before God, they have refused submission to God's righteousness. By looking forward to v.4, where the law is mentioned, we see that this attempt of Israel to achieve a standing in righteousness was related to finding satisfaction in their imagined success in meeting the demands of the law of Moses. Paul is able to analyze their trouble in expert fashion, for he has been over the same route in his spiritual pilgrimage. It was a great day for him when he gave up his cherished righteousness, based on service to the law, in exchange for the righteousness that comes from God and depends on faith (Phil 3:9).

Israel's covenant relation to God and reliance on law keeping do not add up to salvation (John 14:6; Acts 4:12). For this reason Paul points to Christ and his righteousness as Israel's great need (v.4). The proof that Israel was out of line with respect to the will of God, to the extent of rebelling against him, lies in the fact that when he sent his Son as the bringer of a salvation in full accord with the divine righteousness, the nation rejected him. The same kind of revolution in thinking that was necessary for Paul is required for his people.

Considerable debate has centered on the interpretation of v.4, especially on the intended meaning of the word translated "end." Just as in English we speak of "the end of the matter" and use the expression "to the end that"—the one expression meaning conclusion or termination, and the other purpose—the same dual possibility lies in the Greek word *telos.* The second meaning has some plausibility here, because the statement "Christ is the end of the law" (NIV; also KJV, RSV), rather than "Christ brought to an end the law," fits in with the teaching of Paul about the law as the child-leader to bring men to Christ (Gal 3:24). Favorable to the first meaning (Christ brought to an end the law) is the fact that the law had a certain course to run (Luke 16:16; Gal 3:19, 23) in the economy of God. Both concepts seem to fit rather well in our passage. However, the decisive factor that favors "termination" rather than "purpose" as the main idea is the contrast in 9:30ff. between the law and God's righteousness. Though the law is righteous in its requirements, it fails as an instrument of justification (cf. 8:3, 4). Paul's contention regarding the Jew (v.3) is not the incompleteness of his position, which needed the coming of Christ to perfect it, but the absolute wrong of that position, because it entailed an effort to establish righteousness by human effort rather than by acceptance of a divine gift. This consideration makes improbable the view that "end" is used in the sense of fulfillment, as though the thought were aligned with Matthew 5:17.

Paul adds a certain qualification to the statement about Christ as the end of the law for righteousness. He is that "for everyone who believes." This seems to suggest that the law is still applicable to those who do not believe. "Those who have not yet passed from the being-in-the-Law to the being-in-Christ, and those who allow themselves to be misled into exchanging the being-in-Christ for the being-under-the-Law, are under the Law and are made to feel its power" (A. Schweitzer, *The Mysticism of Paul the Apostle* [New York: Henry Holt and Company, 1931], p. 189).

5–13 The thread of the discourse is a continuation of the emphasis on "everyone who believes." This is developed in two ways: first, by showing that the principle of faith is amply set forth in the OT, in fact, in the pages of Moses, and then by expressly indicating, in line with 1:16, that "everyone" includes the Gentile as well as the Jew.

5–8 Paul deals first with the negative side of the attainment of righteousness. He does this by citing a passage from Moses (Lev 18:5) that calls for obedience and performance of the will of God as contained in his statutes and ordinances. The one who complies will live. Paul adds "by it" (So RSV, NEB, et al.; NIV—"by them"), which apparently refers back to the word "righteousness" earlier in v.5 (see Note). Fortunately for our understanding, this passage had already been cited in Galatians 3:12, "The law is not based on faith; on the contrary, 'The man who does these things will live by them.'" In both letters the emphasis falls on *doing* if one expects to live, the very thing insisted on earlier in Romans 2:13. The dark side of the picture is that a curse rests on the one who fails to meet the law's demands. The upshot of the matter is that the course being pursued by Israel, the attempt to gain righteousness for themselves by law keeping (v.3) cannot bring life because of man's weakness and imperfection. It can only lead to self-deception and pride.

Next Paul addresses himself to the positive approach, for which purpose he makes use of another passage from Moses (Deut 30:11–14), this one designed to describe "the righteousness that is by faith." At first sight, the selection of this portion seems inappropriate, since neither "righteousness" nor "faith" can be found here, and there is heavy emphasis on doing, as in Leviticus 18:5. But the context helps us, for the passage presupposes a heart attitude of loving obedience (Deut 30:6–10) rather than a legalistic attempt to attain righteousness. The whole burden of the passage is to discourage the idea that the doing of God's will means to aspire after something that is too difficult and out of reach. Actually, if the life is attuned to God, his will is as near as the mouth and heart (the mouth as the organ to repeat the word of God and turn it back to him in prayer and praise, the heart as the source of desire to please him).

Paul makes his own application of the reference to heaven (v.6) in order to emphasize aspects of the gospel. There is no need to try to ascend to heaven to gain spiritual knowledge or acceptance, for Christ has come from heaven to proclaim and effect salvation for the world. He has come within human reach by his incarnation. In v.7 Paul substitutes "the deep" (abyss) for "the sea" in the Deuteronomy passage, changing the figure from one of distance to one of depth, which makes the contrast with heaven sharper. This affords opportunity to think of Christ as going down into death as a prelude to resurrection. Apparently lost to us by death, he has been returned to us by resurrection. This means that our grasp of the righteousness of God, with his Son as the object of our faith, is not difficult. We have had no part in bringing about the Lord's resurrection any more than in effecting his incarnation. All has been of God. Our part is to believe. There is no place in Christianity, as in some religions, for meritorious pilgrimages. The saving message lies at hand, waiting to be received.

9-13 Building on the Deuteronomy passage, especially its use of "mouth" and "heart," Paul goes on to speak directly of the Christian gospel as to its content and its availability to Jew and Gentile alike.

9,10 "The word of faith" or gospel message is something to confess as well as to believe (cf. 2 Cor 4:13, 14). "Confess" (ὁμολογέω, homologeō) when used of sin means to say the same thing about it that God says; when used in the creedal sense, as here in v.9, it means to say the same thing that other believers say regarding their faith. This was done within the Christian group especially by new converts in connection with their baptism; when it was done "before men" (Matt 10:32) it had an evangelizing function. The oddity that in our passage confession is given prior mention over believing is simply due to Paul's preservation of the order given in Deuteronomy 30:14, which he had just quoted, where "mouth" is mentioned before "heart." The influence of the OT passage is likewise evident in that, whereas it provided a point of contact for citing the resurrection of our Lord (vv.7, 9), there was nothing to provide a basis for mention of the saving death of Christ (contrast 1 Cor 15:3, 4). The concentration on the resurrection is understandable also when it is recognized that the creedal statement before us pertains to the person of Christ rather than to his redeeming work. "Jesus is Lord" was the earliest declaration of faith fashioned by the church (Acts 2:36; 1 Cor 12:3). This great truth was recognized first by God in raising his Son from the dead—an act then acknowledged by the church and one day to be acknowledged by all (Phil 2:11).

It was natural for the church to have a fundamental confession of this sort, since at the beginning it was Jewish/Christian in its composition and therefore had in its background the example of confession in Israel, "The Lord our God is one Lord" (Deut 6:4). The incarnation necessitated the enlargement of the confession to include the Lord Christ. "For us there is but one God, the Father, from whom all things came and for whom we live; and there is but one Lord, Jesus Christ, through whom all things came and through whom we live" (1 Cor 8:6).

Paul's statement in vv.9, 10 is misunderstood when it is made to support the claim that one cannot be saved unless he makes Jesus the Lord of his life by a personal commitment. Such a commitment is most important; however, in this passage, Paul is speaking of the objective lordship of Christ, which is the very cornerstone for faith, something without which no one could be saved. Intimately connected as it was with the resurrection, which in turn validated the saving death, it proclaimed something that was true no matter whether or not a single soul believed it and built his life on it.

11-13 Scripture indicates how faith can be transforming for one's life, replacing fear and hesitation with bold confidence that rests on the sure promises of God. For this purpose Paul uses Isaiah 28:16 (cf. the close of 9:33). This belief and its blessing is open to Jew and Gentile alike. Whatever "difference" there may be in the two groups in some respects, there is no difference when it comes to the need for Christ and the availability of his salvation (cf. 3:22). The source of their spiritual life is found in "the same Lord," whose blessings are richly bestowed upon them without partiality. The all-embracing blessing is salvation. In support of this, Paul cites Joel 2:32. Peter used the same passage in his Pentecost sermon to indicate to his Jewish audience that the door of salvation was open to them all, despite their shared guilt in rejecting the one whom God had sent (Acts 2:21). This calling on the Lord is the echoing within the human heart of the call of God according to his gracious purpose (8:28–30). The prayer promises of Scripture are restricted to the people of God, with one notable exception—namely, that God will hear the cry of any who call upon him for salvation. When v.13 is compared with v.9, it becomes evident that the Lord of Joel 2:32 is being identified with the Lord Jesus Christ. This poses a problem for those who refuse to ascribe full deity to the Savior.

14,15 Now the apostle turns from the responsibility of the seeker after salvation to emphasize the role that believers are intended to have in God's plan for reaching the lost. Calling on the Lord is meaningless apart from some assurance that he is worthy of confidence and trust, that he has something to offer that guilty sinners need. Calling on him and trust in him are two sides of the same coin. The verse suggests that calling on the Lord continues to be a mark of the believer, not simply the first step in the direction of establishing relationship to him (cf. 1 Cor 1:2). Paul proceeds to the second consideration in his closely reasoned argument, and it is this—that faith depends on knowledge. One must hear the gospel before he can be expected either to receive it or reject it. The choice of words is suggestive. To "hear" the message was the one vehicle open to people in that day. The NT had not yet been written so as to be available to the reader, though a few churches had received letters from Paul. There was no visual depiction of the Savior and his mission. The message had to be communicated by word of mouth to the hearing of others. This was as true in the days of the apostles as in the time of the prophets. A glance at the concordance reveals the consistent prevalence of hearing throughout Bible times.

The third step is the necessity that there be someone to proclaim the message. "How shall they hear without a preacher?" (v.14, KJV) is somewhat misleading as a translation, suggesting that the one who communicates the gospel must hold the office of clergyman. This is not the intent. "Someone preaching" (NIV) accurately reflects the original text. We are saved to serve, and the paramount element in that service is to bear witness to the saving power of Christ.

"And how can they preach except they be sent?" (v.15) rounds out this series of questions. No answers are given, for the logic is so airtight that no one could properly question the essential role of each step in the process. To be "sent" suggests at least two things: that one operates under a higher authority and that his message does not originate with himself but is given him by the sending authority. The prophets were men who were sent in these two respects. So was the Lord Jesus (John 3:34; 7:16). So is the Christian in his witness-bearing capacity. The apostles received their commission from the risen Lord as he in turn had been sent by the Father (John 20:21). In addressing the Roman church, Paul was careful to state at the very beginning that he was called and set apart for the ministering of the gospel (1:1).

Is the apostolate alone in view here as representing Christ and his gospel? This is unlikely, judging from what Paul says later about the widespread proclamation of the gospel to the Jews (vv.17, 18). The task was too big for a handful of men. In this connection, see Acts 8:4; 11:19. It is not clear from vv.14, 15 whether the sending that is in view here is intended to include the sending out of missionaries by a sponsoring group of believers, as in Acts 13:3. But even if this is not included, it is obviously an integral part of the entire process of the communication of the gospel. In the case of the church at Antioch, the divine and the human aspects of the sending were closely bound together (Acts 13:2, 3).

Once again (v.15) Paul corroborates his words by the sayings of the prophets, this time by the word of Isaiah (52:7) heralding the favor of the Lord to the city of Jerusalem that had lain desolate during the Babylonian captivity. The tidings are good; the proclamation is one of peace. Paul changes the wording somewhat—the single announcer in Isaiah becomes a company in line with the "they" in his own depiction of gospel messengers in the same verse. If the message to returning Israel in the former day was good news, how much more the promise of eternal salvation in God's Son!

16–18 But here an element of tragedy enters. The good news of physical restoration may have been welcome to Israel, but the spiritual salvation God promised to provide through his Servant and did provide in the fullness of time has met with unbelief. What a change of atmosphere from Paul's quotation of Isaiah 52:7 (v.15) to his quotation of 53:1 (v.16)! The prophet foresaw a repudiation of the message about salvation through a suffering Servant. History has sustained prophecy (1 Cor 1:23).

Paul sums up by saying (v.17) that faith depends on hearing the message, that is, hearing it with understanding and acceptance. "And the message is heard through the word of Christ" (v.17). This could mean either the word about Christ or the word proclaimed by Christ. The former sense is somewhat favored by the fact that in Isaiah 53, which may still be in Paul's thought, the Servant is not a proclaimer but a suffering Redeemer. On the other hand, the second possibility cannot be ruled out. Barrett, for example, says, "Christ must be heard either in his own person, or in the person of his preachers, through whom his own word (v.17) is spoken; otherwise faith in him is impossible" (in loc.).

18,19 In his indictment of Israel, Paul is prepared to investigate any possibility that would offer an excuse for the nation's failure. Could it be, he asks, that they did not hear (the gospel)? He is writing more than twenty-five years after Pentecost. Not only in Palestine but also out in the dispersion, where he himself has been especially active, the message has been heralded. But instead of appealing to this activity, of which the Book of Acts testifies, he is content to cite Scripture, that Israel may stand condemned by the testimony of God rather than by that of man. In making use of Psalm 19:4 (v.18), he does not say that this passage has been fulfilled, for he is aware that the heavens bear a different kind of testimony than the Word of God. But he sees a parallel between the diffusion of light and darkness every day and night, of which no one can be ignorant who has eyes to see, and the widespread proclamation of the gospel in the areas where Jews made their home. This was essentially the Mediterranean basin, where Paul and his helpers had been laboring for some years. His countrymen could not claim lack of opportunity to hear the gospel (cf. Acts 17:6; 21:28).

There remains the possibility, however, that in spite of hearing the message, Israel has not understood it (v.19). So in all fairness this should be considered, for if it were true, it would be a mitigating factor in their situation. But the very form of the question in the original contains an implicit denial that Israel's failure results from lack of understanding. At Pentecost Peter spoke of the ignorance of his countrymen as explaining the crucifixion. But as time went on, fewer and fewer Jews in proportion to the total population of the nation responded to the gospel. A hardened attitude set in. The precedent of the Jews who did respond to the gospel, instead of moving their fellow-Jews, only embittered them. Then, as the gospel spread abroad and was received by Gentiles in ever greater numbers, this served to antagonize them still further.

It is over against this situation that Paul quotes Deuteronomy 32:21b, a part of Moses' song to Israel in which he chides the congregation for perversity and (in Deut 32:21a, not quoted here) voices the complaint of God that the people had provoked him to jealousy by their idolatry. This in turn prompts God to resort to something that is calculated to make Israel jealous. It will be done through "a nation that has no understanding." This is to be understood of Gentile response to God and his Word in such a way as to surpass the response of Israel. Exactly such a situation had developed by the time Paul wrote, so the quotation is apt and telling in its effect. Those who lacked special revelation and the moral and religious training God provided for Israel have proved more responsive than the chosen people.

20,21 The quotation from Isaiah 65:1 is clearly intended to support what has been declared in the previous passage (Deut 32:21), as is evident from the "then" in v.20, which answers to "first" in v.19. Paul sees in the Isaiah passage an anticipation of what has come to pass in his day. The thought is somewhat similar to the implication in 9:30, that the pagan world, occupied with its own pursuits, was in the main, not seeking after God. If there was a religious interest, cults and superstitions abounded to which one could turn.

In the following quotation from Isaiah (65:2) the paradoxical situation regarding Israel is set forth. God is the one who is seeking, reaching out to his people continually with a plea that Israel return to him in loving obedience, only to be rebuffed. So we may draw the conclusion that the spiritual condition of Israel does not come from a lack of opportunity to hear the gospel or a lack of understanding of its content, but must be traced to a stubborn and rebellious spirit such as cropped up in the days of Moses and the days of the prophets. It is the more grievous now because God has spoken his final word in his Son and has been rebuffed by those who should have been the most ready to respond.

Notes

5 MSS vary considerably in the wording of the quotation from Lev 18:5. Those that read "shall live in [or by] them" (αὐτοῖς, autois) doubtless have been influenced by LXX and by Paul's wording in Gal 3:12, where he follows LXX because "in them" fits the context ("all things written in the book of the law"). But here in Rom 10:5 Paul substitutes "in it" (ἐν αὐτῇ, en autē) (i.e., "in the righteousness that is by the law") because this is his own expression at the beginning of the verse. This sort of liberty in handling OT quotations is not uncommon.

17 "The word of God" is the reading of TR, but "the word of Christ" clearly has superior attestation (ℵ* B C D*, et al.)

E. *Israel Not Entirely Rejected; There Is a Remnant of Believers* (11:1-10)

Thus far, Paul has treated the problem of Israel from two standpoints. In chapter 9 he has emphasized the sovereignty of God in choosing this people for himself in a special sense. In chapter 10 he has dealt with Israel's failure to respond to God's righteousness, ending with the verdict that she is "a disobedient and obstinate people" (10:21). These two presentations involve a serious tension. Will Israel's sin and stubbornness defeat the purpose of God, or will God find a way to deal effectively with the situation so as to safeguard his purpose? To this question Paul now turns. His answer will dip into Israel's past, encompass her present, and reveal her future.

11:1-10

¹I ask then, Did God reject his people? By no means! I am an Israelite myself, a descendant of Abraham, from the tribe of Benjamin. ²God did not reject his people, whom he foreknew. Don't you know what the Scripture says in the passage about Elijah—how he appealed to God against Israel: ³"Lord, they have killed your prophets and torn down your altars; I am the only one left, and they are trying to kill me"? ⁴And what was God's answer to him? "I have reserved for myself seven thousand who have not bowed the knee to Baal." ⁵So too, at the present time there is a remnant chosen by grace. ⁶And if by grace, then it is no longer by works; if it were, grace would no longer be grace.

⁷What then? What Israel sought so earnestly it did not obtain, but the elect did. The others became hardened, ⁸as it is written:

"God gave them a spirit of stupor,
    eyes so that they could not see
    and ears so that they could not hear,
to this very day."

⁹And David says:

"May their table become a snare and a trap,
    a stumbling block and a retribution for them.
¹⁰"May their eyes be darkened so that they
        cannot see,
    and their backs be bent forever."

1-6 Preparation for this section has been made—especially in 9:27-29, where the teaching of the OT concerning the remnant is summarized by quotations from Isaiah. That teaching involved both judgment and mercy—judgment on the nation as a whole for its infidelity and wickedness, and mercy on those who are permitted to escape the judgment and form the nucleus for a fresh start under the blessing of God.

The opening question, "Did God reject his people?" (based on Ps 94:14) requires that we keep in mind what was made clear early in the discussion—that "not all who are descended from Israel are Israel" (9:6). The loss of the bulk of the nation that proved disobedient (both in OT days and at the opening of the gospel period) should not be interpreted as rejection of "his people." The remnant is in view, as the ensuing paragraph demonstrates.

Why is it that Paul, in repudiating the suggestion that God has rejected his people, injects himself into the discussion as an Israelite, descended from Abraham, and belonging to the tribe of Benjamin (cf. Phil 3:5)? Some understand this as intended not for proof but only as assurance that in view of his background Paul can be expected to handle the subject with fairness to Israel rather than with prejudice. Perhaps the position of this personal note, placed before the OT illustration, favors this view somewhat. But it is also possible to hold that Paul, sensing his prominence in the purpose of God, is willing to risk the charge of lack of modesty by citing himself as evidence sufficient to refute the charge that God had rejected Israel. Barrett gives the sense as follows: "I myself am both a Jew and a Christian; this proves that Christian Jews may exist" (in loc.).

For God to reject his people would require repudiation of his deliberate, unilateral choice of Israel (for the meaning of "foreknew," see commentary on 8:29). The inference is that God could not do such a thing (v.2). But instead of dealing in abstractions, Paul turns to the OT for confirmation, to the time of Elijah. If ever there was a period of flagrant apostasy, it was during the reign of Ahab, when his queen Jezebel promoted Baal worship in the court and throughout the land. The situation was so bad that Elijah, in his loneliness, cried to God against the killing of prophets and destruction of altars. He even went so far as to assert that he was the only one left and that he was being hunted down so as to complete the destruction of God's servants (1 Kings 19:10). He knew that other prophets had escaped through the action of Obadiah (1 Kings 18:13), but they were in hiding. Elijah had stood alone on Mt. Carmel and later fled alone to the desert— an object of pursuit. It is just possible that Paul, likewise persecuted by his own countrymen, felt a special kinship with Elijah, and this may help to account for his mention of himself in v.1.

The really important thing is the contrast between the assertion of Elijah—"I am the only one left"—and God's reply: "I have reserved for myself seven thousand who have not bowed the knee to Baal" (v.4). If in that dark hour such a goodly company of the faithful existed, this is sufficient evidence that God does not permit his own at any time to approach the vanishing point. The sparing of the remnant is inseparably related to the choice of the remnant. The very fact of God's choice excludes the possibility of his desertion of his own. In the Greek, God's "answer" is literally his "oracle" (*chrēmatismos*), indicating both its revelatory character and its intrinsic importance (it was given to Elijah at Horeb, the mount of God, the place where God had appeared to Moses to affirm his preservation of Israel in her affliction and his purpose to deliver her from bondage in Egypt; cf. Exod 3; 1 Kings 19).

Since Paul sees a parallel between the days of Elijah and his own time, the inference can be drawn that when he wrote, the vast majority of Israel had resisted the gospel, and that therefore, despite their claim of loyalty to God and the law, they had failed to move forward in terms of the climactic revelation in his Son. Those who had turned to Christ were only a remnant (v.5).

But the matter of numbers is not crucial. What is more important is the reminder that irrespective of its size, it is "chosen by grace." This means that the character of the remnant is also not important, as though the choosing depended on the quality of its constituency. "The remnant has its origin, not in the quality of those saved, but in the saving action of God" (Herntrich in TDNT 4:203). Notice how this is brought out in the quotation "I have reserved *for myself* seven thousand" (v.4). It is also evident, though not expressed, that the existence of the church, far from being contrary to the will of God, as the leaders of Judaism supposed, is actually the present channel of the operation of his grace. Having mentioned grace at the end of v.5, the apostle cannot pass by the opportunity to contrast grace with works (v.6). They are mutually exclusive as a means of establishing relationship to God (cf. Eph 2:8, 9).

7-10 Here is set forth in the case of Israel according to the flesh the tragic consequences of persisting in the pattern of "works." Once again Paul cannot overlook Israel's "earnestly" seeking to get from God what they prized. There is a clear connection with 10:3, which refers to the effort of Israel to attain righteousness in God's sight by their method rather than his. The elect obtained righteousness because they did not go about it the wrong way but depended on divine grace. While this was true in the past, Paul is apparently thinking mainly of the present situation (cf. v.5). In distinction from the elect, Israel as a whole has become hardened. The comparison between present and past, already made on the favorable side between the current remnant according to the election of grace and the 7,000 in Elijah's time, is now projected to cover the dark aspects of the situation.

The failure of the bulk of Israel to attain divine righteousness and their being hardened instead, is in line with OT history. By the device of quoting, Paul throws the weight of Scripture behind his presentation and by so doing avoids having to speak on his own as bluntly and severely as the Word of God has done. In the first quotation, he weaves together two passages (Deut 29:4 and Isa 29:10) so as to provide illustration from two periods. In Deuteronomy, it is the testimony of the eyes that is stressed; the people have seen the wonders of the Exodus time and the miracles of the nation's preservation in the wilderness, but from these experiences they did not derive a heart of loving trust in God. In Isaiah, the background is the faithful testimony of the prophets. Yet the people shut their ears to the voice of God through these spokesmen. As a consequence, God sent them a spirit of stupor. The verb (*katanussōmai*) from which the word "stupor" comes means "to prick." At first sight, this appears to give a wrong idea, but the thought is as follows: "The torpor seems the result of too much sensation, dulled by the incitement into apathy" (A.T. Robertson, *Word Pictures in the New Testament*. Richard R. Smith, Inc., 1931, 4:393). From our observation of the setting of the quotations, it is clear that God did not give his people deaf ears to mock them any more than he gave them blind eyes to taunt them. What was involved was a judicial punishment for failure to use God-given faculties to perceive his manifested power and to glorify him. See John 12:39, 40.

Before leaving v.7, something should be said on the word rendered "hardened," especially since it is not the same as the term used in 9:18. Liddon (in loc.) has a note on this distinction:

> The *pōrōsis* of v.7, though describing the same moral fact as the *to sklērynesthai* of 9:18, is perhaps stronger in its import. The metaphor implies not merely the stiffening of the existing soul and character, but the outgrowth of a new feature, which obscures while it hardens, by an outer coating of mental habit. *Pōrōsis* differs from *sklērynesthai* by the idea of a *new outgrowth* of mental obduracy. *Pōros*, the tufa-stone, is especially used of a callus or substance exuding from fractured bones and joining their extremities as it hardens: hence *pōroō* to petrify, form a bony substance, and so metaphorically, to harden. . . . This *pōrōsis* produced permanent bluntness and insensibility in the intelligence.

David's word of imprecation follows in vv.9, 10, taken from Psalm 69:22, 23. He suffers reproach and torment from his enemies, who are also viewed as the enemies of the Lord. Apparently their feasts are times for special outbreaks of blasphemy. David prays that the Lord will make their table their snare so as to entrap them. Then comes the prayer for the darkening of the eyes that have looked with complacency and even glee at the sufferings of the one whom God has permitted to be smitten. John 15:25 and other NT passages indicate that Psalm 69 was treated as messianic, so that its use here makes the application to Paul's own day the more obvious and meaningful.

One problem arises in connection with the final word of the quotation. "Forever" renders *dia pantos*, which in Greek usage may occasionally mean forever but which more commonly means "continually." This latter sense has the advantage of fitting in with the following context, where Israel's obduracy and rejection is not treated as lasting indefinitely, certainly not eternally, but as giving way to a great ingathering of repentant Israel (see article by C.E.B. Cranfield in SE 2:546–50). The bending of the back, as Paul would be likely to apply it, suggests bondage to the law (cf. Acts 15:10).

Notes

6 The additional words, "But if it be of works, then is it no more grace: otherwise work is no more work," made familiar by KJV, lack sufficient MS authority to be included in the text.

F. Israel's Temporary Rejection and the Salvation of Gentiles

11:11–24

11Again I ask, Did they stumble so as to fall beyond recovery? Not at all! Rather, because of their transgression, salvation has come to the Gentiles to make Israel envious. 12But if their transgression means riches for the world, and their loss means riches for the Gentiles, how much greater riches will their fullness bring!

13I am talking to you Gentiles. Inasmuch as I am the apostle to the Gentiles, I make much of my ministry 14in the hope that I may somehow arouse my own people to envy and save some of them. 15For if their rejection is the reconciliation of the world, what will their acceptance be, but life from the dead? 16If the part of the dough offered as firstfruits is holy, then the whole batch is holy; if the root is holy, so are the branches.

17If some of the branches have been broken off, and you, though a wild olive shoot, have been grafted in among the others and now share in the nourishing sap from the olive root, 18do not boast over those branches. If you do, consider this: You do not support the root, but the root supports you. 19You will say then, "Branches were broken off so that I could be grafted in." 20Granted. But they were broken off because of unbelief, and you stand by faith. Do not be arrogant, but be afraid. 21For if God did not spare the natural branches, he will not spare you either.

22Consider therefore the kindness and sternness of God: sternness to those who fell, but kindness to you, provided that you continue in his kindness. Otherwise, you also will be cut off. 23And if they do not persist in unbelief, they will be grafted in, for God is able to graft them in again. 24After all, if you were cut out of an olive tree that is wild by nature, and contrary to nature were grafted into a cultivated olive tree, how much more readily will these, the natural branches, be grafted into their own olive tree?

Having dealt with the remnant, Paul returns to a consideration of Israel as a whole, insisting that her rejection is not final and that during the period when the nation continues to resist the divine plan centered in the Messiah, God is active in bringing salvation to the Gentiles. The figure of the olive tree emphasizes that Gentile salvation is dependent on Israel's covenant relationship to God. Gentiles have to be grafted into the olive tree. The purpose of Gentile influx into the church is not merely to magnify the grace of God toward outsiders, but to evoke envy on the part of Israel as a factor in leading to her ultimate return to God as a people. This in turn prepares the way for the climax in 11:25–27.

11,12 A dark picture of Israel has been painted both from the OT and from present observation. This leads naturally to an inquiry. What is the result of this hardening? Is it a hopeless situation? Now that the people have eyes that do not see, are they doomed to stumble so as to fall and rise no more? "Not at all." The stumbling is admitted; an irreparable fall is not. This is a broad hint of the future salvation of Israel that Paul goes on to affirm. Those who stumbled are "the others" of v.7, not included in the believing remnant. The language recalls the indirect reference to the Messiah in 9:32, 33 as the stumbling stone.

God is bringing good out of apparent evil. Israel's stumbling has opened the way for Gentile salvation on such a scale as to make Israel envious (cf. Acts 13:42–47). That envy, though it may involve bitterness, will ultimately contribute to drawing the nation to her Messiah. The longer the process goes on, the more unbearable the pressure on Israel becomes. Her transgression "means riches for the world"; i.e., the nations in contrast to Israel, as the following statement—"means riches for the Gentiles" (v.12)—makes clear.

A word should be said about "loss." The Greek term *hēttēma* seems to involve the idea of defeat, both here and in 1 Corinthians 6:7. It is basically a military figure. An army loses the battle because of heavy casualties. The logic of the verse compels us to take it in this sense, that as surely as Israel's defeat (identified with her stumbling) has brought the riches of God's grace to the Gentiles on a large scale, the conversion of Israel to her Messiah (v.26) will bring even greater blessing to the world. The word "fullness" refers to the conversion, meaning the full complement in contrast to the remnant. It will mark an end to the state of hardening that now characterizes the nation.

13–16 This paragraph follows naturally from the preceding, because Paul now applies to his own position and ministry the truth he has stated. He wants the Gentiles in the Roman church to catch the full import of what he is saying. They have looked on him as "the apostle to the Gentiles" ("an apostle" is the strict rendering of the Gr.). Very well, but they must not suppose that he has lost sight of the need of witnessing to Israel. He is returning to the idea of emulation set forth in v.11, meaning that his work among Gentiles is regarded not simply as an end in itself but as a means of reaching his countrymen. "The Gentiles are not saved merely for their own sake, but for the sake of God's election of Israel. How unshakable is the faithfulness of God to the nation he has chosen!" (James Daane, *The Freedom of God* [Grand Rapids: Eerdmans, 1973], p. 145). "However strange it may sound, the way to the salvation of Israel is by the mission to the Gentiles" (Munck, *Paul and the Salvation of Mankind*, p. 301). This involves the envy/emulation idea already stated in v.11. Paul hopes thereby to "save some of them"— that is, fellow Israelites (cf. 1 Cor 9:22). He knows that only Christ can save, but he himself can be the instrument. The word "some" is important. It is a clear indication that he does not expect his efforts to bring about the eschatological turning of the nation to the crucified, risen Son of God, when "all Israel will be saved" (cf. v.26). This belongs to the indefinite future. There is warmth in Paul's reference to Israel as "my own people." If God could turn *him* around, this proud Jew who bitterly set himself against Jesus as the Christ, surely through him as God's instrument others can be won. These others are the firstfruits who contain in themselves the promise of the ultimate harvest of a nation of believers (cf. v.16).

There is some difficulty in ascertaining the meaning of "life from the dead" (v.15). In order to retain the balance of the sentence, it seems necessary to understand this expression as pertaining to the world (cf. the structure of v.12). Life from the dead could refer to literal resurrection, though it is strangely general for such an explicit event, but it is perhaps better to see in it the promise of a worldwide quickening and deepening of spiritual life when Israel is restored to divine fellowship. She becomes a tonic to the nations that are to be saved.

There is no great difficulty in understanding the relation between "the dough offered as firstfruits" and "the whole batch" (v.16). The word "firstfruits" is the key, referring to the remnant of Israel, whereas "the whole batch" has in view the nation as converted. Both are holy in the primary sense of the word—separated, consecrated to God. The grain taken from the fields as the firstfruits was prepared and worked into dough, then baked into a cake for an offering (Num 15:18-21). The difficulty in interpretation lies in the final statement: "if the root is holy, so are the branches." We have observed that the parallelism in vv.12, 15 points the way to proper assignment of the component parts used there. One would suppose that the same thing should apply here, meaning that the root is the remnant and the branches the rejuvenated Israelites of the future. There is, however, an obvious awkwardness in this interpretation, since presently Paul uses "root" in reference to the historic Israel, especially of its patriarchal foundation (vv.17ff.). So it is prudent to assume that the close of v.16 looks forward rather than backward. As to the meaning, it is sufficient to quote Godet: "Their [Israel's] future restoration is in conformity with the holy character impressed on them from the first; it is therefore not only possible, but morally necessary" (2:244).

17-24 Here Paul continues to use the figures of root and branches, enlarging on the theme so as to set forth the allegory of the olive tree. Actually, there are two trees, the cultivated olive and the wild olive. Israel is the cultivated olive, the Gentiles the wild olive. The breaking off of some of the branches of the former and the grafting in of the branches of the latter represent the present partial rejection of Israel and the corresponding reception of the Gentiles. From this presentation two lessons are drawn. The first is a warning to the Gentile Christians who may be in danger of repeating the sin of the Jew—boasting of their privileged position (vv.18-21). Even more important is the point that if God, by cutting off the branches of the natural olive, has made room for Gentile believers, how much easier will it be for him to restore the natural branches to their place in the cultivated olive (vv.23, 24)! So the groundwork is laid for the next stage in the argument. God is not only able to do this; he will do it (vv.25-27).

By stating that only some of the branches have been broken off (v.17), Paul inserts a reminder of the fact that Israel's rejection is not complete (cf. v.5). The "others" are the Jewish Christians who rub shoulders with Gentile believers in the church. Both depend on the "olive root," the patriarchal base established by God's covenant (cf. 4:11, 12). Here we may consider with profit what the apostle says in Ephesians 2:11-22. The Gentiles, once aliens and foreigners, are now fellow citizens with God's people and members of God's household. The two are made one in Christ.

"Do not boast over those branches" (v.18). They are the broken-off branches mentioned in vv.17, 19. The temptation to boast must have been considerable, a kind of anti-Semitism that magnified the sin of the nation Israel in rejecting the Lord Jesus and saw in Jewish persecution of the church a sure token of an irreparable rift between the nation and her God. But Israel's plight is not to be traced to a change of attitude on the part of God toward her. It is due simply to her unbelief, a condition noted earlier (3:3). The reason Gentile believers have a standing with God is that they have responded to the gospel in faith, the very thing that Israel has failed to do. Paul treats the Gentile element in the church as a unit, addressing it as "you" (singular—Gr. *su*). This should not be understood on an individual basis as though Paul were questioning their personal salvation. The matter in hand is the current Gentile prominence in the church made possible by the rejection of the gospel on the part of the nation of Israel as a whole. Let Gentile Christians beware. Their predominance in the Christian community may not last!

Kindness and sternness (v.22) are aspects of the divine nature, the latter experienced by Israel in her present condition, the former being the portion of Gentile believers. But the positions can be reversed, and if this occurs, it will not be due to any fickleness in God, but to the nature of the human response. Gentiles can become objects of God's sternness and Israel can just as easily become the object of his kindness. Once her unbelief is put away, God is prepared to graft her branches in again (v.23).

Paul's concluding observation (v.24) has a double value. It helps to explain the curious circumstance that his illustration of the olive tree does not follow the pattern of grafting ordinarily found in the ancient Mediterranean world but is in fact the reverse of it. Paul seems to be granting that his allegory is "contrary to nature." William M. Ramsay, making use of the research of Professor Theobald Fischer, observed:

> As regards Palestine, but no other Mediterranean country, he [Fischer] points out that the process which St. Paul had in view is still in use in exceptional circumstances at the present day. He mentions that it is customary to reinvigorate an olive-tree which is ceasing to bear fruit, by grafting it with a shoot of the Wild-Olive, so that the sap of the tree ennobles this wild shoot and the tree now again begins to bear fruit.... The cutting away of the old branches was required to admit air and light to the graft, as well as to prevent the vitality of the tree from being too widely diffused over a large number of branches (*Pauline and Other Studies* [London: Hodder and Stoughton, 1906], pp. 223–224).

A more specific matter in which the illustration runs counter to horticulture is the expectation that the natural branches, though broken off, will in fact be grafted in again. Paul's argument is that if the hard thing, the thing contrary to nature—i.e., the grafting of wild branches into the cultivated olive—has been accomplished, one should not find it difficult to believe that God will restore the broken-off branches of the cultivated olive to their former position. "The future restoration of the Jews is *in itself* a more probable event than had been the introduction of the Gentiles into the Church of God" (Liddon, in loc.). Since in tree culture this would be impossible because of the deadness of the branches after they were removed, Paul is indeed talking "contrary to nature." But he rests his case not on nature but on God's being "able" to do it. With God nothing is impossible. Inevitably, the branches that will be grafted in are not identical with those that were broken off, but they are the same in two respects, their Israelitish heritage and the attitude of unbelief they have maintained in the past. They represent a continuum with the Israel of Paul's day. It should also be noted that the grafting in again of Israel is not intended to suggest that this involves a supplanting of the Gentiles, but only that both Jew and Gentile share together the blessings of God's grace in Christ.

G. *Israel's Future Salvation* (11:25–32)

This is the crowning feature of the discussion, the outcome everything in the three chapters has been pointing to. The same mercy that has overtaken the Gentiles who were formerly disobedient will finally overtake the now disobedient Israel.

11:25-32

> [25]I do not want you to be ignorant of this mystery, brothers, so that you may not be conceited: Israel has experienced a hardening in part until the full number of the Gentiles has come in. [26]And so all Israel will be saved, as it is written:

> "The deliverer will come from Zion;
>   he will turn godlessness away from Jacob.
> [27]And this is my covenant with them
>   when I take away their sins."

> [28]As far as the gospel is concerned, they are enemies on your account; but as far as election is concerned, they are loved on account of the patriarchs, [29]for God's gifts and his call are irrevocable. [30]Just as you who were at one time disobedient to God have now received mercy as a result of their disobedience, [31]so they too, as a result of God's mercy to you, have now become disobedient in order that they too may now receive mercy. [32]For God has bound all men over to disobedience so that he may have mercy on them all.

25 Now Paul speaks of a mystery, lest his readers imagine that either he or they are capable of understanding the course of Israel's history simply by observation and insight. The term "mystery" (*mystērion*) as used in the NT does not mean "enigma," but the activity of God in salvation history made known to his people by revelation. Paul is not claiming revelation in the sense of those mentioned in 2 Corinthians 12:4, 7, but presumably in the sense of the guidance of the Spirit. The mystery relates to things hidden in the past (16:25), but now made known. In fact, the content of the mystery of Israel is stated immediately. It embraces Israel's hardening, which is "in part" in the sense that the believing remnant constitutes an exception and that the hardening is limited in duration, lasting only "until the full number of the Gentiles has come in." Therefore it also embraces what follows—the salvation of "all Israel."

26,27 The expression, "all Israel," when taken in the light of the context, must be understood of the nation Israel as a whole, in contrast to the present situation when only a remnant has trusted Christ for salvation. The language does not require us to hold that when this occurs every living Israelite will be included, but only that Israel as a nation will be saved.

Not all interpreters agree, however, on the meaning of "all Israel." It was the view of Calvin, for example, that the entire company of the redeemed, both Jew and Gentile, is intended. But "Israel" has not been used of Gentiles in these chapters, and it is doubtful that such is the case anywhere in Paul's writings, even in Galatians 6:16 (cf. Richardson, pp. 74–84). There may be grounds for speaking of the church as the new Israel, but so far as terminology is concerned, Israel means the nation or the godly portion of it (cf. 9:6). To be sure, Gentiles are included in the seed of Abraham (4:11, 12). Though this concept is applicable to the church at the present time, Paul is speaking of something definitely eschatological, actually to be fulfilled in the future, and he has not used the seed of Abraham concept in chapters 9 to 11 (it appears only in 11:1, where it has its literal, historical connotation). As Paul does not discuss the situation of those Jews who remain unbelievers during this age, so in v.26 he drops from view the Gentiles who have figured in vv.17–24.

Another suggested possibility is that "all Israel" refers to the total number of elect

Jews, the aggregate of the godly remnant that exists in each age of the church's history. This fails to come to grips with the climactic nature of Paul's argument, in particular the contrast between all Israel and the remnant as set forth, for example, in v.16a. It fails also to explain the use of the word "mystery" in v.25. "While it is true that all the elect of Israel, the true Israel, will be saved, this is so necessary and patent a truth that to assert the same here would have no particular relevance to what is the apostle's governing interest in this section of the epistle" (Murray, in loc.). Clearly "all Israel" stands over against "in part" by way of contrast.

It is tempting to the modern man to argue that since Israel has not acknowledged Jesus of Nazareth as the Messiah in great numbers, Paul's teaching here should be understood only as a hope, a hope that has not been realized. It is by a similar process of reasoning that some would rule out the related promise of the Lord's return. But a thousand years are as a day in the reckoning of God. The Christian period has not yet approached in length the time required for the fulfillment of the promise of Messiah's first coming.

Does our passage throw light on the time when Israel's national conversion is to be expected? Certainly not in terms of "that day or hour" (Matt 24:36), but rather in terms of the time when the full number of the Gentiles has come in (v.25). The "so" (v.26) is apparently intended to correlate with "until" (v.25), thereby acquiring temporal force (cf. 1 Cor 11:28 for a similar usage of *houtōs*). The NEB rendering in this passage is: "when that has happened"; and JB has "then after this."

The declaration concerning the future of Israel, made on apostolic authority, is now confirmed by citing Isaiah 59:20, 21 and 27:9. The interpretation is somewhat clouded by the fact that the Hebrew has "to Zion" and LXX "for" (on account of), whereas Paul has "out of." Liddon comments, "The change of preposition is probably an intentional variation from the [LXX and Heb.] text of Isaiah, suggested by Ps. xiv. 7, liii. 7, in order to bring into stronger relief the promises made to the Jewish people" (in loc.). The perplexity over the prepositions is largely cleared up by the supposition that Paul has chosen his own wording in order to hint that the conversion of Israel will occur at Messiah's return, when he will come out of Zion, i.e., from the heavenly Jerusalem (cf. Gal 4:26; Heb 12:22). It is hard to account for the wholesale conversion of Israel in any other way, since the activity of the Spirit of God has not produced any such mass movement of Israel during the course of this age. It is at least possible that Paul sensed a certain parallel between his own conversion and what he foresees for his people as a whole. Christ revealed himself to him directly, sweeping away his rationalizations and his self-righteousness.

The effect upon Israel is not couched in terms of material prosperity or martial invincibility, but purely in spiritual terms, in the forsaking of godlessness and the removal of sins by the Lord God. The reference to covenant suggests that Jeremiah 31:31-34 was in the mind of the apostle along with the passages from Isaiah.

28,29 Even though under the gospel economy Israelites as such are considered enemies (by God) for the sake of the Gentiles, yet all the time, when viewed from the standpoint of their national election, they are loved of God for the sake of the fathers (cf. v.16). God's promises are irrevocable and time will prove it. There is an evident parallel as well as contrast between "enemies" and "loved," so both must be referred to God. But as Leenhardt notes, the word "enemies" connotes "the condition of Israel before God rather than sentiments of animosity in God Himself" (in loc.). Likewise there is a parallel between "gospel" and "election," which forbids taking the latter word in the concrete sense of an elect people. Rather, it is the purpose or principle of election that is meant.

The gifts of God are doubtless the special privileges of Israel mentioned in 9:4, 5. These bear witness to the reality of the calling—the summons of Israel to a unique place in the purpose of God. By being first in the Greek sentence, the word "irrevocable" (v.29) is emphatic.

30-32 God's purpose must be implemented if it is to be effective. His mercy is the needed factor. Paul is addressing his Gentile readers here. In fact, the "you" is emphatic, as though to remind Gentile believers (who might be prone to think it strange that God has a glorious future in store for Israel) that they themselves were formerly disobedient toward God. It was Jewish disobedience in regard to the gospel that opened the gates of mercy for the Gentiles. It was the recurrence of a characteristic often displayed before. Israel had scarcely become a nation when the people rejected the good news about Canaan and as a result had to face years of wilderness wandering (Heb 4:6). The consequence of their disobedience to the gospel (Acts 14:2; 19:9) was still more tragic, for it meant shutting themselves out of the kingdom. This disobedience was stubborn unbelief, a confirmed negative attitude.

Again, to warn the Gentiles against being inflated over their present position in grace, Paul advances the reminder (v.31) that it was the very mercy received by the Gentiles that made the Jews more firm in their disobedience. This is graphically illustrated by the effect of the Jerusalem Council (Acts 15). While it gave marked encouragement to the Gentile mission by its decision, it deepened and strengthened Jewish opposition to the gospel. Yet God did not give up on his chosen people, but ever keeps in view his plan for their salvation and continues to extend his mercy. The second "now" in v.31 is somewhat perplexing in the light of the eschatological emphasis in vv.26, 27. It may refer to the present salvation of the remnant or it may even be intended to include the future along with the present and so anticipate the ultimate salvation of the nation. The conclusion of the whole matter is that God magnified his mercy by the very fact of disobedience, binding all men over to it (cf. 3:9) that he might have mercy on all. So disobedience does not have the last word (cf. Gal 3:22).

H. *Praise to God for His Wisdom and His Ways*

11:33-36

> [33]Oh, the depth of the riches, the wisdom and
>   the knowledge of God!
>   How unsearchable his judgments,
>   and his paths beyond tracing out!
> [34]"Who has known the mind of the Lord?
>   Or who has been his adviser?"
> [35]"Who has ever given to God,
>   that God should repay him?"
> [36]For from him and through him and to him
>   are all things.
>   To him be the glory forever! Amen.

In view of the assurance generated by v.32, it is no wonder that Paul, despite his burden for the Israel of his day, is able to lift his heart in adoring praise to God. We are reminded of Isaiah 55, where the ungodly and sinful man is urged to return to the Lord and find mercy, for God's thoughts and ways are not those of men but are infinitely higher and better. Instead of being vindictive, God is gracious. His plans defy the penetration of the human mind and his ways surpass the ability of man to trace them out. The Lord has not been obliged to lean upon another for advice (v.34). He has not had to depend on human assistance that would make him indebted to men (v.35). He is the source, the means, and the goal of all things (v.36).

While this exalted and moving ascription of praise has in view God's plans and operations in the history of salvation affecting the great segments of mankind, Jew and Gentile, the closing verse applies also to the individual life that pleases God. For that life has its source in God, lives by his resources, and returns to him when its course has been run. To God be the glory!

VII. Our Spiritual Service: The Practice of Righteousness (12:1–15:13)

Every reader of Romans is conscious of a distinct break in the train of thought as he moves from 11:36 to 12:1. The theological exposition (or argument) centering around the problem as to how sinful man can be put into right relationship with God is over. But there is more to be said, because when man is made right with his Maker, he needs to know what difference this makes in his relations with his fellowmen. He needs to know what is expected of him and how to apply his new resources to all the situations confronting him. This last main section of the Epistle is designed to meet these needs (cf. Eph 4:1).

Students of Scripture in recent years have begun to employ two terms that serve as convenient labels for the two broad types of instruction just noted. It will be recognized at once that these designations are borrowed from the sphere of grammar. They are "the indicative" and "the imperative." The one expression covers what God has done in terms of the gospel; it deals with divine provision. The other deals with what the Christian is expected to do by way of working out the salvation that has been given him (cf. Phil 2:12, 13), and consequently majors in exhortation. It is notable that the key word "righteousness," which has so dominated the book up to this point, occurs only once in the closing chapters (14:17) and then not in the forensic sense denoting right relationship with God but rather in the practical meaning of right relations with one's fellows. The hortatory element includes both commands and prohibitions and is spread over various areas of application, including Christian conduct toward fellow believers, toward society (especially in meeting hostile reactions), and toward the state.

A. The Appeal for Dedication of the Believer

12:1, 2

> [1]Therefore, I urge you, brothers, in view of God's mercy, to offer yourselves as living sacrifices, holy and pleasing to God—which is your spiritual worship. [2]Do not conform any longer to the pattern of this world, but be transformed by the renewing of your mind. Then you will be able to test and approve what God's will is—his good, pleasing and perfect will.

This introductory portion is a prelude to the discussion of specific duties of the believer. It sets forth the fundamental obligations one must meet before he is prepared to face the challenge of living as a believer in this world. Only an intelligent commitment of life in the light of God's gift of salvation will suffice.

1 "Therefore" establishes a connection with the entire foregoing presentation rather than with chapters 9 to 11 alone. The connection is particularly close with 6:13, 19, as a comparison of the terminology will show. The apostle begins now to "urge" his readers instead of simply instructing them. His choice of this word "urge" (*parakaleō*) is discriminating, seeing that its force lies between commanding and beseeching. It possesses something of the element of authority that is more forcefully expressed by "command," and has in it something of the element of appeal that attaches to "beseech."

"Mercy," rather than the familiar "mercies" of the KJV, is justified on the ground that the word used here (*oiktirmos*; cf. *eleos* in 11:30–32, also translated "mercy"), though plural in form, reflects the Hebrew *rahamîm*, which is a so-called intensive plural, meaning "great mercy" or "compassion." Sometimes it is used in LXX together with the more common *eleos*, as in Isaiah 63:15 and Hosea 2:19 (2:21 in LXX). It denotes that quality in God that moves him to deliver man from his state of sin and misery and therefore underlies his saving activity in Christ. Here "mercy" is the leverage for the appeal that follows. Whereas the heathen are prone to sacrifice in order to obtain mercy, biblical faith teaches that the divine mercy provides the basis for sacrifice as the fitting response.

Other problems of translation are somewhat more difficult. "Yourselves" is literally "your bodies" (*sōmata hymōn*). In the closely related discussion in 6:13 the original text does not have the word "body," but instead has "your members" (*melē hymōn*) and "yourselves" (*heautous*). Both are what the believer is to present to God for his service. Since the milieu of thought is so similar in 12:1, it is natural to conclude that "body" is intended to include both the person (the volition of the one making the dedication) and the bodily powers that are thus set apart for God's use. Though Greek thought was prone to consider the body the receptacle containing the soul, this was not the Hebraic concept, which viewed man as a unit. So it should be clear that Paul is not urging the dedication of the body as an entity distinct from the inner man. Rather, he views the body as the vehicle that implements the desires and choices of the redeemed spirit. It is essential for making contact with the society in which the believer lives. Through the body we serve.

One is reminded by "offer" and "sacrifices" that the apostle is using cultic language here (cf. 15:16). Before a priest in Israel could minister on behalf of others, he was obliged to present himself in a consecrated condition and the sacrifices he offered were to be without blemish (Mal 1:8–13). "Holy" is a reminder of that necessity for the Christian, not in terms of rite or ritual but as renouncing the sins of the old life and being committed to a life of obedience to the divine will (cf. 6:19). The body is not evil in itself; if it were, God would not ask that it be offered to him. As an instrument, it is capable of expressing either sin or righteousness. If the latter, then it is an offering "pleasing to God." The word "living" may glance by way of contrast to the animal sacrifices of the OT, which, when offered, no longer possessed life. But it is also a reminder that spiritual life, received from God in the new birth, is the presupposition of a sacrifice acceptable to him. Christian sacrifice, though made decisively and once-for-all (this is the force of "offer"), has in view a *life* of service to God. In Israel the whole burnt offering ascended to God and could never be reclaimed. It belonged to God.

Next the living sacrifice is equated with "spiritual worship." The exact sense is difficult to determine. "Spiritual" (NIV, RSV) may be an improvement on "reasonable" (KJV), since the latter term could be understood in the sense of adequate, seeing that no less a sacrifice could be offered in view of the sacrifice God has made in Christ for our salvation. The idea is rather that the sacrifice we render is intelligent and deliberate, perhaps to be understood in contrast to the sacrifices of the Jewish cultus in which the animals had no part in determining what was to be done with them.

"Worship" translates *latreia*, which Paul has already used for the entire Jewish cultus (9:4). Here he gives it a metaphorical turn. The problem to be faced is whether "worship" may not be too restricted a rendering, for worship in the strict sense is adoration of God, which does not fit well with the concept of "bodies" ("your bodies" is rendered "yourselves" in NIV). It is just at this point that the term "service" (KJV) has an advantage, since it covers the entire range of the Christian's life and activity (cf. Deut 10:12). Service is the proper sequel to worship.

2 The dedicated life is also the transformed life. Whereas v.1 has called for a decisive commitment, v.2 deals with the maintenance of that commitment. We need to "bind the sacrifice with cords . . . unto the horns of the altar" (Ps 118:27 KJV). Significantly, there is a shift in the tense of the verbs (from the aorist "offer") to the present tense, pointing up the necessity of continual vigilance lest the original decision be vitiated or weakened. The threat comes from "this world," whose ways and thoughts can so easily impinge on the child of God. Paul has used *aiōn*, essentially a time word, meaning "age," but it has much common ground with *kosmos*, the more usual term for "world." The believer has been delivered from this present evil age (Gal 1:4), which has Satan for its god (2 Cor 4:4). He lives by the powers of the age to come (Heb 6:5), but his heavenly calling includes residence in this world, among sinful men, where he is to show forth the praises of him who called him out of darkness into God's marvelous light. He is in the world for witness, but not for conformity to that which is a passing phenomenon (1 Cor 7:31).

Complementary to the refusal to be conformed to the pattern of this world is the command to be "transformed." The two processes are viewed as going on all the time, a continual renunciation and renewal. Our pattern here is Christ, who refused Satan's solicitations in the temptation and was transfigured (*metamorphoō*—the same word as that translated "transformed") in his acceptance of the path that led to Calvary (Mark 9:2, 3). As his mission could be summarized in the affirmation that he had come to do the Father's will (John 6:38), the Christian's service can be reduced to this simple description also. But he must "test and approve," refusing the norms of conduct employed by the sinful world and reaffirming for himself the spiritual norms befitting the redeemed. Aiding this process is "the renewing of your mind," which seems to mean that the believer is to keep going back in his thought to the original commitment, reaffirming its necessity and legitimacy in the light of the grace of God extended to him. In this activity the working of the Holy Spirit should no doubt be recognized (cf. Titus 3:5). It appears from the context that the believer is not viewed as ignorant of the will of God, but as needing to avoid blurring its outline by failure to renew the mind continually (cf. Eph 5:8-10). Dedication leads to discernment and discernment to delight in God's will. That there is an intimate connection between certifying the will of God and making oneself a living sacrifice is indicated by the use of "pleasing" in each case (cf. Phil 4:18; Heb 13:16).

B. *Varied Ministries in the Church, the Body of Christ*

12:3-8

> [3]For by the grace given to me I say to every one of you: Do not think of yourself more highly than you ought, but rather think of yourself with sober judgment, in accordance with the measure of faith God has given you. [4]Just as each of us has

one body with many members, and these members do not all have the same
function, [5]so in Christ we who are many form one body, and each member belongs
to all the others. [6]We have different gifts, according to the grace given us. If a
man's gift is prophesying, let him use it in proportion to his faith. [7]If it is serving,
let him serve; if it is teaching, let him teach; [8]if it is encouraging, let him encourage;
if it is contributing to the needs of others, let him give generously; if it is leadership,
let him govern diligently; if it is showing mercy, let him do it cheerfully.

3 The will of God, concerning which Paul has just spoken, is identical for all believers
in respect to holiness of life and completeness of dedication. But what that will involves
for each one with respect to special service in the church may be considerably diverse.
Since individual application is called for in appropriating the teaching, the apostle finds
it expedient to remind his readers of his authority to expound this subject even though
he is unknown to most of them and their gifts are unknown to him (cf. 1:5; Gal 2:9; Eph
3:7). But this reminder is not intended to erect a barrier between himself and them,
because what he has by way of authority and teaching ability is traced to divine grace,
the same grace that has bestowed spiritual gifts on them.

In addressing himself deliberately to "every one of you," Paul seems to be granting
that every believer has some spiritual gift (cf. v.6; 1 Peter 4:10). But the primary purpose
in getting the attention of each one is to drive home the necessity of appropriating and
using his gift with the utmost humility. After all, God was not obligated to spread his gifts
around so lavishly. Paul recognizes the danger that the possession of a gift could easily
result in a self-esteem that was nothing more or less than wretched pride (v.3). His
experience with the Corinthian church (1 Cor 12:14-31; 13:4; 14:12, 20) had alerted him
to this problem. He virtually equates humility with "sober judgment," as opposed to
thinking of oneself more highly than one should. In v.16 Paul comes back to this fundamental matter. Obviously, there is less danger of a person's depreciating himself than
of exaggerating his own importance.

Is there some gauge that will enable a person to estimate his position with respect to
spiritual gifts? Paul answers in the affirmative, pointing to "the measure of faith."
Though this is intimately related to sober judgment, its precise meaning is not easy to
determine. We may at once exclude the possibility that "faith" in this context means "the
faith" in the sense of a body of truth that is believed. Such a usage is familiar to us from
Jude 3, but Paul seems to avoid it. To him faith is what the Christian exercises. It is
subjective rather than objective. That this is so here is clear from the close of v.3. Faith
is God's bestowal. C.E.B. Cranfield, understanding "measure" in the sense of standard,
takes the phrase to mean that one's faith should provide the basis for a true estimation
of himself, since it reveals that he, along with other believers, is dependent on the saving
mercy of God in Christ (NTS 8 [July 1962] 345-351). To be sure, that ought to induce
humility. Godet understands "measure" in the sense of degree. "This gift, the measure
of the action to which we are called, is the divine limit which the Christian's renewed
mind should discern, and by which he should regulate his aspirations in regard to the
part he has to play in the church" (in loc.). This view brings "measure of faith" into close
agreement with "in proportion to his faith" (v.6). It should be added that faith, as used
in this passage, is hardly saving faith, but faith in the sense of grasping the nature of one's
spiritual gift and having confidence to exercise it rightly.

4,5 To offset the danger of individualistic thinking with its resulting danger of pride,
Paul refers to the human body—an illustration familiar from its earlier use in 1 Corinthi-

ans 12:12ff. Three truths are set forth: the *unity* of the body; the *diversity* of its members, with corresponding diversity in function; and the *mutuality* of the various members—"each member belongs to all the others."

The third item calls attention to the need of the various parts of the body for each other. They cannot work independently. Furthermore, each member profits from what the other members contribute to the whole. Reflection on these truths reduces preoccupation with one's own gift and makes room for appreciation of other people and the gifts they exercise.

6–8 "We have different gifts." Paul is not referring to gifts in the natural realm, but to those functions made possible by a specific enablement of the Holy Spirit granted to believers. The gift does not contradict what God has bestowed in the natural order and, though it may even build on the natural gift, it must not be confused with the latter.

Variety in the gifts should be understood from the standpoint of the needs of the Christian community, which are many, as well as from the desirability of giving every believer a share in ministry. With his eye still on the danger of pride, Paul reminds his readers that these new capacities for service are not native to those who exercise them but come from divine grace. Every time he delves into this subject he is careful to make this clear (1 Cor 12:6; Eph 4:7; cf. 1 Peter 4:10).

Although he has spoken of different gifts, Paul does not proceed to give anything like an exhaustive list (cf. 1 Cor 12:27, 28). He seems more intent on emphasizing the need for exercising the gifts and for exercising them in the right way—"in proportion to [one's] faith." He uses this expression only in connection with prophesying, but there is no reason to suppose it is not intended to apply to the other items as well.

What is meant by "in proportion to his faith" (v.6)? Theologians have tended to favor the translation "according to the analogy of the faith" (transliterating the Greek word *analogia* and stressing the definite article before "faith"). Upon this construction is built the Reformed principle that all parts of Scripture must be interpreted in conformity to the rest. This is a valid principle but hardly germane to this context. Another view of the matter, held by Godet (in loc.), for example, understands the phrase as referring to the hearers rather than to the prophets, so that, in framing the messages given them, those who speak should consider the stage of development attained by their audience. This view, too, may have merit, but against it is the fact that in this passage it is not spiritual gifts that are being treated for the edification of the hearers, as in 1 Corinthians 14, but the proprieties that should govern those who use the gifts.

The most satisfactory explanation is that "faith" retains the subjective force it has in v.3 and that the whole phrase has the same thrust as "measure of faith" there. A prophet is not to be governed by his emotions (1 Cor 14:32) or by his love of speaking (1 Cor 14:30) but by entire dependence on the Spirit of God.

Paul does not give a definition of prophecy here, but if we are to judge from the earlier reference to it in 1 Corinthians 14:3, 31, the nature of the gift is not primarily prediction but the communication of revealed truth that will both convict and build up the hearers. This gift is prominent in the other listings of gifts (1 Cor 12:28; Eph 4:11), where prophets are second only to apostles in the enumeration. That Paul says nothing of apostles in the Romans passage may be a hint that no apostle, Peter included, had anything to do with the founding of the Roman church (see Introduction, background).

"Serving" (v.7) is such a broad term that some difficulty attaches to the effort to pin it down. The Greek *diakonia* is sometimes used of the ministry of the word to unbelievers (Acts 6:4; 2 Cor 5:18), but the gifts in this passage in Romans seem intentionally restricted in their exercise to the body of Christ (it may be significant that there is no mention of evangelists as there is in Eph 4:11). Despite its place between prophesying and teaching, the narrower meaning of service as ministration to the material needs of believers is probable here. NEB and JB translate the word as "administration," perhaps hinting that the term should be taken as referring to the supervision of the giving of aid to the needy, which was specifically the province of the deacons. Even so, it should be recognized that others also could engage in a variety of helpful ministries to the needs of the saints (1 Cor 16:15). In fact, Paul inserts in the midst of a catalog of restricted terms dealing with gifts this very broad designation, "those able to help others" (1 Cor 12:28).

The gift of teaching (v.7) is mentioned next. It differed from prophesying in that it was not characterized by ecstatic utterance as the vehicle for revelation given by the Spirit. In 1 Corinthians 14:6 teaching is paired with knowledge, whereas prophecy is coupled with revelation. Probably the aim in teaching was to give help in the area of Christian living rather than formal instruction in doctrine, even though it must be granted that the latter is needed as a foundation for the former. Indeed the very structure of Romans attests this. Paul himself gives a notable example of teaching in vv.9–21. In the latter part of this section his considerable use of the OT suggests that early Christian teachers were largely dependent on it for their instruction.

"Encouraging" (v.8) is the translation of the Greek *paraklēsis*, which has a variety of meanings. Only the context can indicate whether the most suitable rendering is "encouragement" or "exhortation" or "comfort." All are closely related. In Acts 15:31 encouragement is certainly the idea conveyed. But in 1 Timothy 4:13 exhortation is clearly involved, evidently the application of the OT as it was read in the assembly during worship (cf. Acts 13:15). Assuredly some encouragement could be included, but exhortation seems to be the dominant meaning.

"Contributing to the needs of others" (v.8) has to do with spontaneous private benevolence (cf. 1 John 3:17, 18). This is evidently not intended as a repetition of "serving" (v.7), and this favors the view that the latter activity belongs to the public distribution of aid by the church to its needy. The only doubt concerning this interpretation resides in the word "generously" (NIV), which is a possible translation but hardly as likely as "with simplicity" (KJV)—that is, with singleness of heart, free of mixed motives, without regret (over having given so much). That wrong motivation could enter into giving is shown by the account of the sin of Ananias and Sapphira in Acts 5.

"Leadership" (v.8) is the translation of a word that means to stand before others, so the idea of governing derives readily from it. The need is for one to carry out his ministry "diligently." Even in church life some people are tempted to enjoy the office rather than use it as an avenue for service. A few interpreters, doubtless influenced by the items immediately preceding and following, favor the meaning of "giving aid," "furnishing care," etc., and this is possible. However, the exercise of leadership is the more common in NT usage (1 Thess 5:12; 1 Tim 3:4, 5; 5:17). "Diligently" fits well in either case.

"Showing mercy" does not pertain to the area of forgiveness or sparing judgment. It has to do with ministering to the sick and needy. This is to be done in a cheerful, spontaneous manner that will convey blessing rather than engender self-pity. Way renders it freely, "If you come with sympathy to sorrow, bring God's sunlight in your face" (Arthur S. Way, *Letters of St. Paul and Hebrews*. 6th edit. [London: Macmillan, 1926]).

C. Principles Governing Christian Conduct

12:9-21

> 9Love must be sincere. Hate what is evil; cling to what is good. 10Be devoted to one another in brotherly love. Honor one another above yourselves. 11Never be lacking in zeal, but keep your spiritual fervor, serving the Lord. 12Be joyful in hope, patient in affliction, faithful in prayer. 13Share with God's people who are in need. Practice hospitality.
>
> 14Bless those who persecute you; bless and do not curse. 15Rejoice with those who rejoice; mourn with those who mourn. 16Live in harmony with one another. Don't be proud, but be willing to associate with people of low position. Don't be conceited.
>
> 17Do not repay anyone evil for evil. Be careful to do what is right in the sight of everybody. 18If it is possible, as far as it depends on you, live at peace with everyone. 19Do not take revenge, my friends, but leave room for God's wrath, for it is written: "It is mine to avenge, I will repay," says the Lord. 20On the contrary: "If your enemy is hungry, feed him; if he is thirsty, give him something to drink. In doing this, you will heap burning coals on his head." 21Do not be overcome by evil, but overcome evil with good.

The presupposition here is the dedicated life, which enables one to discover and demonstrate the will of God. Relationship to fellow Christians is treated first (vv.9–13), then the stance to be assumed toward those who are without (vv.14–21).

9,10 Love is primary, but if it is not sincere, it is not real love but only pretense. When one recalls that Paul paused in his discussion of spiritual gifts to inject a chapter on love (1 Cor 13), it is altogether fitting that he should follow his presentation of spiritual gifts here in Romans with the same emphasis. The whole of the believer's conduct, in fact, should be bathed in love. If he fails to love his brother, doubt is cast on his professed love for God (1 John 4:19–21).

Love readily suggests purity. The two are found together in God, who is of too pure eyes to behold evil (Hab 1:13) and cannot be tempted by it (James 1:13). Hatred readily follows love—hatred, that is, of what is evil. The human attitude must follow the divine in this respect also, because it is the opposite of the command to love. The two belong together. To "cling to what is good" (v.9) is to be wedded to it. Total commitment leaves neither time nor inclination to court evil.

The apostle has called for love, but lest this be construed simply as an ideal, he now puts it in a living context (v.10). Love is to be shown to people, not lavished on a principle. He uses a special term denoting brotherly love (*philadelphia*). "Devoted" is appropriate, since it customarily denotes the family tie. Believers are members of the family of God.

"Honor one another above yourselves" (v.10). To honor is to accord recognition and show appreciation. Presumably, this is based not on some personal attractiveness that is perceived or usefulness that is known but rather on the fact that every Christian has Christ in his heart and is able to express him through his own individuality. Consequently, this recognition is based on the new creation (2 Cor 5:17) rather than on the old. One honors God when he recognizes his transforming work in human life. If the according of such honor seems to diminish the recognition of what God has done in one's own life, the problem is readily solved by the example of the Son's exalting of God the Father despite the Son's equality with him (John 10:30; Phil 2:4–6).

11,12 Paul now momentarily directs attention toward the Lord and his service before returning to horizontal relationship with the body of Christ (v.13). After converts have experienced the initial glow and ardor of Christian life there is often danger of their slipping back into a deadening spiritual inertia. To counter this, the apostle urges diligent endeavor fed by fervency of spirit. Such is the characterization of Apollos (Acts 18:25). On the other hand, it was the lack of such fire that brought down the rebuke of the Lord upon the Laodicean church (Rev 3:15, 16). In brief, the thrust here (v.11) is that the Lord's service calls for our best. Jesus is no ordinary master. Not the least element in his uniqueness is the confidence he instills in those who serve him that though he remains invisible, he is wonderfully real to the eye of faith, and this carries forward into the present the indelible influence of his life and ministry in the world during the days of his flesh. This in turn arouses the hope, tinged with joy, of seeing him in his glory and being united with him (1 Peter 1:7, 8). This hope sustains the servant of Christ, enabling him to be "patient in affliction" (tribulation), recalling what Paul had written in 5:3, 4. At this point, Paul's mention of prayer is natural, since it is the Christian's great resource when he is under stress and strain.

13 Even under persecution one should not allow himself to be so preoccupied with his own troubles that he becomes insensitive to the needs of other believers. Apparently, it is temporal need that is in view. To share with others is never more meaningful than when one is hard pressed to find a sufficient supply for himself. When this sharing takes place under one's own roof, it is labeled "hospitality." The Greek term (*philoxenos*) is more expressive than the English, for it means "love for strangers." Paul's word for "practice" (*diōkō*, "pursue") is strong (the same word is used in the sense of "persecute" in v.14), calling for an undiminished ardor in extending this courtesy to traveling believers. The Lord had encouraged his disciples to depend on such kindness during their missions (Matt 10:11). Without it, the spread of the gospel during the days of the early church would have been greatly impeded. With it, the "church in the house" became a reality (16:23; cf. 16:5). What sanctified this practice above all was the realization that in receiving and entertaining the traveler, those who opened their doors and their hearts were receiving and entertaining Christ (Matt 10:40; 25:40).

14-16 The material in these cases is not so easy to characterize as that in the foregoing and following paragraphs. It seems to describe the Christian's relations to their neighbors and friends (not excluding believers), as well as one reference to their opponents, whereas the next section definitely pictures the people of God bearing up under pressure from the unbelieving world. Perhaps the best thing is to view this portion in the light of Paul's word in Galatians 6:10 and consider it transitional.

Paul's injunction to bless persecutors rather than curse them undoubtedly goes back to the teaching of our Lord (Matt 5:44; Luke 6:28) through oral tradition. The teaching was incarnated in the Savior himself and became clearly manifested during his trial and his suffering on the cross. To persecute is literally "to pursue." Persecution could take various forms, running the gamut from verbal abuse and social ostracism to the use of violence resulting in death. A few years later, Roman Christians were to lose their lives in great numbers at the hands of Emperor Nero. Persecution in some form or another was so common in the experience of the early church that Paul is able to assume as a matter of course that it is a factor in the lives of his readers. If such treatment is not encountered in our society, we can at least cultivate the readiness to meet it and so fulfill the injunction in spirit. To bless one's persecutors involves praying for their forgiveness and for a change of outlook regarding the Christian faith. It can be done only by the grace of Christ.

One charge follows another without any apparent connection as Paul calls on his readers to share one another's joys and sorrows (v.15). It has often been noted that it is easier to fulfill the first half of this command than the second, because our natural inclination is to feel genuine sympathy for those in sorrow, but to share the joy of their rejoicing may present difficulty if the achievement or good fortune that prompts the joy is viewed with envy. This is one of the things that Philippians 4:13 is designed to cover. In general, however, people have less need for fellowship in times of joy than in times of grief, for if loneliness is added to sorrow, the trial is compounded. For an earlier statement of this teaching on sharing others' joys and sorrows under all circumstances see 1 Corinthians 12:26.

"Live in harmony with one another" (v.16) is not so literal a rendering as "have equal regard for one another" (NEB), but is warranted by the fact that the language closely resembles that of Philippians 2:2, which was written to dispel the discord in the church. As a means to attaining this harmony, Paul stresses the necessity of rejecting the temptation to think high thoughts about oneself, as though one were a superior breed of Christian, and of coming down off the perch of isolation and mingling with people "of low position" or of a humble frame of mind (the Gr. has simply "the lowly"). And lest one consent to do this while still retaining heady notions of his own superiority, Paul puts in a final thrust: "Don't be conceited" (v.16). Conceit has no place in the life ruled by love (1 Cor 13:4).

17-21 Here Paul takes his stand alongside the believer by giving him explicit counsel about how to face the hostile world. "Do not repay evil for evil" (v.17), for to do so would be to follow the inclination of the flesh. The remainder of the verse is open to more than one interpretation. It could mean that the Christian should be concerned to do what all persons understand to be right. But this presupposes no real difference between Christian and non-Christian in their evaluation. Consequently, the other explanation is preferable, namely, that believers are constantly under the scrutiny of unsaved persons as well as of fellow Christians, and they must be careful that their conduct does not betray the high standards of the gospel (cf. Col 4:5; 1 Tim 3:7). The verb "be careful" (*pronoeō*) is literally "to think of beforehand," which suggests that the conduct of believers ought not to be regulated by habit, but rather that each situation that holds prospect for a witness to the world be weighed so that the action taken will not bring unfavorable reflection on the gospel.

The charge to live at peace with everyone (v.18) is hedged about with two qualifying statements. "By this cumulation of conditions the difficulty of the precept is admirably brought out" (Field, in loc.). "If it be possible" suggests that there are instances in human relations when the strongest desire for concord will not avail. This, in turn, is explained by the statement "as far as it depends on you." In other words, if disharmony and conflict should come, let not the responsibility be laid at your feet. The believer may not be able to persuade the other party, but he can at least refuse to be the instigator of trouble. He can be a peacemaker (Matt 5:9) only if he is recognized as one who aims to live at peace with his fellows.

This peace-loving attitude may be costly, however, because some will want to take advantage of it, figuring that Christian principles will not permit the wronged party to retaliate. In such a case, what is to be done? The path of duty is clear. We are not to take vengeance. This would be to trespass on the province of God, the great Judge of all.

"Leave room for God's wrath" (v.19). Trust him to take care of the situation. He will not bungle. He will not be too lenient or too severe. Here Paul quotes Deuteronomy 32:35, whose context indicates that the Lord will intervene to vindicate his people when their enemies abuse them and gloat over them. God's action will rebuke not only the adversaries but also the false gods in which they have put their trust.

There is no suggestion that the wrath of God will be visited upon the wrongdoer immediately. On the contrary, that wrath is the last resort, for in the immediate future lies the possibility that the one who has perpetrated the wrong will have a change of heart and will be convicted of his sin and won over by the refusal of the Christian to retaliate (v.20). Here again Paul lets the OT (Prov 25:21, 22) speak for him. The course of action recommended is the positive aspect of what has been stated in v.17. "Burning coals" are best understood as "the burning pangs of shame and contrition" (Cranfield, in loc.). There is no definite promise at this point that the offender will be converted, but at least he will not be a threat in the future. Moreover, by going the second mile and showing unexpected and unmerited kindness, the believer may well have spared his companions from having the same experience he has endured. In that measure, society has benefited.

Guidance on the problem of coping with evil reaches its climax in the final admonition: "Do not be overcome by evil, but overcome evil with good" (v.21). In this context, "to be overcome by evil" means to give in to the temptation to meet evil with evil, to retaliate. To overcome evil with good has been illustrated in v.20. Many other illustrations could be given, such as David's sparing the life of Saul, who was pursuing him to snuff out his life. When Saul realized that David had spared his life, he said, "You have repaid me good, whereas I have repaid you evil" (1 Sam 24:17 RSV). The world's philosophy leads men to expect retaliation when they have wronged another. To receive kindness, to see love when it seems uncalled for, can melt the hardest heart.

Notes

11 It is reasonably certain that the variant reading καιρῷ (kairō), found principally in Western witnesses, arose by a misreading of κυρίῳ (kyriō, "Lord"), which was κῶ (kō), as κρῶ (krō), a contraction of καιρῷ (kairo, "opportunity").

D. The Duty of Submission to Civil Authority
13:1-7

> [1]Everyone must submit himself to the governing authorities, for there is no authority except that which God has established. The authorities that exist have been established by God. [2]Consequently, he who rebels against the authority is rebelling against what God has instituted, and those who do so will bring judgment on themselves. [3]For rulers hold no terror for those who do right, but for those who do wrong. Do you want to be free from fear of the one in authority? Then do what is right and he will commend you. [4]For he is God's servant to do you good. But if you do wrong, be afraid, for he does not bear the sword for nothing. He is God's servant, an agent of justice to bring punishment on the wrongdoer. [5]Therefore, it is necessary to submit to the authorities, not only because of possible punishment but also because of conscience.
> [6]This is also why you pay taxes, for the authorities are God's servants, who give

their full time to governing. [7]Give everyone what you owe him: If you owe taxes, pay taxes; if revenue, then revenue; if respect, then respect; if honor, then honor.

This is the most notable passage in the NT on Christian civic responsibility. It probably reflects the famous word of Jesus: "Give to Caesar what is Caesar's, and to God what is God's" (Matt 22:21). That Paul lived in conformity with his own teaching is apparent from his relation to various rulers as recorded in the Book of Acts. Pride in his Roman citizenship and his readiness to appeal to it in critical situations are also reflected in Acts. Because Paul realized that this subject had a definite bearing on the spread of the gospel (1 Tim 2:1ff.), he saw its relevance in this Epistle on the theme of salvation.

Some, however, have found it difficult to relate this thirteenth chapter to the flow of thought in Romans. It seems to them detached and so isolated from the material on either side of it as to suggest that it might even have come from a later period when such concerns were more pressing for the church. Nevertheless, it is possible to see in 13:1-7 an expansion and special application of the teaching about good and evil (12:17, 21) and living "at peace with everyone" (12:18). Perhaps the reference to "wrath" (*orgē*, 12:19) is intended to anticipate the same word in 13:5, where it is translated "punishment."

More important, however, is the broader connection in terms of thought. Here there are two pertinent elements. One is the natural connection with 12:1, 2, where the foundation is laid for Christian service in its various ramifications. The believer's relation to the state is one of those areas. Another and more specific connection with the forego-ing material is possible. Paul may be intent on warning the Roman church, which contained some Christian Jews as well as Gentile believers who sympathized with them over the plight of their nation, not to identify with any revolutionary movement advocat-ing rebellion against Rome (Marcus Borg in NTS 19 [Jan. 1973] 205-218). If this need was in Paul's mind as he wrote, then 13:1-7 may be considered a kind of postscript to chapters 9 to 11. This would put the apostle solidly behind the stance taken by our Lord, who was faced with pressure from Zealot elements in Palestine but refused to endorse their use of violence. Borg inclines toward the view that the expulsion of Jews from Rome by Claudius (Acts 18:2; Suetonius, *Claudius*, 25:4) was not due to Christian proclamation of Jesus as the Messiah which excited and divided the Jewish community at Rome, but to messianic agitation involving the expressed hope that the deliverer would bring release from the grip of Rome. If this is indeed the background, then Paul was not simply giving counsel of a general or universal nature (although applicable elsewhere), but was speaking to a definite historical situation that could have proved explosive from the Christian as well as the Jewish standpoint. Adjustment to the state was especially dif-ficult for the Jew because his people, from the days of the OT theocracy, looked to God as supreme and felt no tension in their own national life between the realms of politics and religion. There is also a possibility that the Jews who returned to Rome after the death of Claudius (including some Christian Jews) were hostile toward the state because of the way Claudius had treated them. These needed to be mollified.

1 The teaching that follows is addressed to "everyone." Presumably this means every believer rather than everyone in general, even though government is necessary for society as a whole. Paul could admonish only Christians. What he requires is submission, a term that calls for placing oneself under someone else. Here and in v.5 he seems to avoid using the stronger word "obey," and the reason is that the believer may find it impossible to comply with every demand of the government. A circumstance may arise

in which he must choose between obeying God and obeying men (Act 5:29). But even then he must be submissive to the extent that, if his Christian convictions do not permit his compliance, he will accept the consequences of his refusal.

Those to whom submission must be rendered are called "governing authorities" (v.1). The first word (*exousia*) is not a specific or technical term; it simply means those who are over others. With respect to the second word (*archōn* v.3), we find Josephus using it, as Paul does, with reference to Roman rulers, but specifically those who ruled in the name of Rome over the Jews in Palestine (*Jewish War* II, 350). (See note.)

Paul makes a sweeping statement when he says, "There is no authority except that which God has established" (v.1b). It is true even of Satan that what authority he exercises has been given him (cf. Luke 4:6). God has ordained this tension between authority and submission. "God has so arranged the world from the beginning—at the creation, by all means, if you like—as to make it possible to render him service within it; and this is why he created superiors and subordinates" (E. Käsemann, *New Testament Questions of Today* [Philadelphia: Fortress Press, 1961], p. 208).

It is probably significant that the name of Christ does not appear anywhere in the passage. The thought does not move in the sphere of redemption or the life of the church as such, but in the relation to the state that God in his wisdom has set up. While the Christian has his citizenship in heaven (Phil 3:20), he is not on that account excused from responsibility to acknowledge the state as possessing authority from God to govern him. He holds a dual citizenship.

2 Those who refuse submission are in rebellion against what God has ordained. To ground refusal on the fact that the believer is not of the world (John 17:14) is to confuse the issue, because the state cannot be identified with the world no matter how "worldly" its attitude may be. The world can be set over against God (1 John 2:16) but this is not true of the state as an institution, despite the fact that individual governments may at times be anti-God in their stance. Midway in v.2 Paul shifts from the singular ("he who rebels") to the plural ("those who do so"). If this is more than a stylistic variation, it may be intended to recognize that rebellion is not feasible at all unless it is instigated by collective action. Defiance of government is futile on an individual basis except as a demonstration of personal disagreement. Those who rebel "will bring judgment on themselves." By rendering judgment as "damnation," KJV suggests forfeiture of final salvation, which is wide of the mark. From the movement of thought, the judgment is to be conceived of as coming from God in the sense of bearing his approval, even though administered through human channels and in the sphere of human affairs. One may cite the words of Jesus, given in warning to one of his own: "All who draw the sword will die by the sword" (Matt 26:52). Sufficient illustration is provided by the Jewish war of revolt against Rome that was to begin within a decade of the time Paul wrote. This disastrous rebellion led to the sack of Jerusalem and the dispersion of the nation.

The question as to whether rebellion is ever justified (in the light of this passage) cannot profitably be examined till more of the paragraph has been reviewed.

3,4 Here we encounter the most difficult portion of the passage, for the presentation seems to take no account of the possibility that government may be tyrannical and may reward evil and suppress good. A few years after Paul wrote these words, Nero launched a persecution against the church at Rome; multitudes lost their lives, and not because of doing evil. Later on, other emperors would lash out against Christians in several waves of persecution stretching over more than two centuries. However, the empire did not persecute Christians for their good works, and not directly because of their faith, but rather, as Stifler observes, "because of . . . the mistaken notion that the peace and safety of the state were imperiled by the Christians' refusal to honor the gods" (in loc.).

One way to deal with the problem is to assume that Paul is presenting the norm, that is to say, the state as functioning in terms of fulfilling the ideal for government, which is certainly that of punishing evil and rewarding or encouraging good. If this is the correct interpretation, then we can understand why Paul warns against rebellion and makes no allowance for revolutionary activity. The way is then open to justify revolution in cases where rights are denied and liberties taken away, making life intolerable for freedom-loving men and women, since the state has ceased to fulfill its God-appointed function. However, Christians will not as a church lead in revolution, but only as citizens of the commonwealth. At the very least, under circumstances involving a collapse of justice, the Christian community is obliged to voice its criticism of the state's failure, pointing out the deviation from the divinely ordained pattern. Subjection to the state is not to be confused with unthinking, blind, docile conformity.

Another possibility is to introduce the principle of Romans 8:28 whereby God finds ways to bring good out of apparent evil, so that even in the event that the state should turn against the people of God in a way that could rightly be termed evil, he will bring good out of it in the long run. Käsemann remarks, "Sometimes the Lord of the world speaks more audibly out of prison cells and graves than out of the life of churches which congratulate themselves on their concordat with the State" (*New Testament Questions of Today,* p. 215).

The state is presented as "God's servant" to extend commendation to the one who does good and, conversely, to punish the wrongdoer. This certainly implies considerable knowledge on the part of the governing authority as to the nature of right and wrong, a knowledge not dependent on awareness of the teaching of Scripture but granted to men in general as rational creatures (cf. 2:14, 15). While "God's servant" is an honorable title, it contains a reminder that the state is *not* God and that its function is to administer justice for him in areas where it is competent to do so. Even as God's servant in the spiritual realm can err, so the state is not to be thought of as infallible in its decisions. Yet this does not entitle the individual to flout the state's authority when the decision is not to his liking.

The warning to the believer to avoid evil carries with it the admonition that if this warning is neglected, fear will be in order because the authority has the power to use the sword. This can hardly have to do with private misdoing that would rarely if ever come to the attention of those in power, but presumably refers to public acts that would threaten the well-being or security of the state. Consequently, even though traditionally the bearing of the sword is thought to signify the power of punishment, even to death, which the government rightly claims for itself in handling serious crimes, that understanding of the matter is somewhat questionable, because these words are addressed to Christians. Were Christians liable to descend to such things? Interpreters who have assumed that Paul's allusion to the sword refers to the *ius gladii* (the law of the sword) need to consider the new evidence to the effect that at the time of Paul this term had a very restricted application that would not fit our passage. A.N. Sherwin-White states, "For the first two centuries of the Empire the term referred only to the power given to provincial governors who had Roman citizen troops under their command, to enable them to maintain military discipline without being hampered by the provisions of the laws of *provocatio*" (*Roman Society and Roman Law in the New Testament* [Oxford: 1963], p. 10). *Provocatio* denotes right of appeal. So it is probable that Paul is warning believers against becoming involved in activity that could be construed by the Roman government as encouraging revolution or injury to the state. In that case he is not referring to crime in general. To engage in subversive activity would invite speedy retribution, as the word "sword" implies.

5 In bringing this portion of the discussion to a close, Paul advances two reasons why the Christian must be in submission to the state. One is the threat of punishment (the Gr. word is *orgē*, "wrath") if one does not put himself in subjection. This appeal is based on personal advantage, the instinct of self-preservation. To defy the state could mean death. The other reason is more difficult to determine. Pierce understands conscience (*syneidēsis*) to mean here, "the pain a man suffers when he has done wrong" (*Conscience in the New Testament* [London: SCM Press, 1955], p. 71). This is certainly what the word means in most other places, but it is questionable here, because the believer who goes so far as to defy the state could not be described as having a tender conscience; in fact, he has steeled his will and suppressed his conscience. More satisfactory is the statement of Christian Maurer: "*Syneidēsis* is responsible awareness that the ultimate foundations both of one's own being and also of the state are in God. Members of the community are to have neither a higher nor a lower estimation of the state than as a specific servant of God" (TDNT, 7:916). In other words, the Christian, by virtue of divine revelation, can have a clearer understanding of the position of the governing authority than an official of the government is likely to have. Let that knowledge guide him in his attitudes and decisions. This usage of the word "conscience" is found again in 1 Peter 2:19.

6,7 Building on his allusion to conscience, the apostle explains the payment of taxes on this very basis. The clearer the perception of the fact that the governing authority is God's servant, the greater appears the reasonableness of providing support by these payments. The man in authority may be unworthy, but the institution is not, since God wills it. Without financial undergirding, government cannot function. For the third time Paul speaks of rulers as God's servants, but this time he uses a different word, one that means workers for the people, public ministers. But the relationship to God is added in keeping with the emphasis made in v.4. Their work is carried on under God's scrutiny and to fulfill God's will. These public servants give their full time to governing; therefore they have no time to earn a living by other means. This is a reminder of the truth that "the worker deserves his wages" (Luke 10:7).

There is deliberate repetition in the sense that the paying of taxes is assumed (v.6), then enjoined (v.7). But in the repetition Paul adds an important ingredient, found in the word "give" (*apodote*). It is full of meaning, for literally it is "give back." When Jesus was interrogated on the subject of taxes, his questioners used the word "give," but in his reply he used "give back" (Mark 12:14, 17), suggesting that what is paid to the government in the form of taxes presupposes value received or to be received. It is quite possible that Paul, through familiarity with the tradition concerning Jesus' teaching, was aware of the language the Master had used and adopts it for himself. Some of the reluctance to pay taxes to the Romans that was associated with political unrest in Palestine may have infected Jewish believers at Rome, accounting for Paul's specific allusion to the subject. But on this point one cannot be sure, since the allusion comes in rather naturally during a discussion of the believer's relation to the state. Furthermore, the assumption is that the Roman Christians are already paying taxes (v.6).

The various items mentioned in v.7 are all classified as obligations. Since the Christian ethic demands the clearing of whatever one owes another (cf. v.8), no basis is left for

139

debate. The very language that is used supports the imperative form of the communication.

The word for "taxes" means tribute paid to a foreign ruler (it appears in Luke 20:22 in the incident concerning paying tribute to Caesar). "Revenue" pertains to indirect taxation in the form of toll or customs duties. It forms a part of the word for tax gatherer (*telōnēs*, Matt 10:3). "Respect" is defined by Liddon as "the profound veneration due to the highest persons in the state." He characterizes "honor" as "respect due all who hold public offices" (in loc.). It is just possible, however, that Paul intends the former term to refer to God, in which case it should be translated "fear" (cf. 1 Peter 2:17, where it is used in relation to God and in contrast to honor paid the supreme earthly ruler).

Notes

1 This term ἐξουσίαι (*exousiai*, "authorities") has become the center of a keen debate in recent years. Does it denote earthly rulers alone, or is it intended to refer also to invisible powers, as in Ephesians 1:21; 6:12? Oscar Cullmann has advocated the latter position, arguing that the plural form calls for this meaning and that Christ by his death and exaltation has triumphed over these powers of darkness, so that they are subject to him even when they influence earthly rulers (*Christ and Time* [London: SCM Press, 1951], pp. 191-210; *The State in the New Testament* [New York: Scribners, 1956], pp. 95-114). Though we cannot go into the pros and cons of this debate, suffice it to say that victory over the powers of the invisible world does not necessarily mean that Christ has pressed them into his service. If Paul had meant to include them, it seems logical that he would have made this clear by a more specific description. Beyond v.1 he shifts from the plural to the singular, which suggests that the plural is meant to refer to the emperor and subordinate rulers, whereas the singular indicates any official of the government with whom a believer might become involved. It is difficult, furthermore, to believe that Paul could advocate submission to unseen powers even in indirect fashion, since in Ephesians 6:12ff. he calls for the most strenuous resistance to them.

E. *The Comprehensive Obligation of Love*

13:8-10

> [8]Let no debt remain outstanding, except the continuing debt to love one another, for he who loves his fellow man has fulfilled the law. [9]The commandments, "Do not commit adultery," "Do not murder," "Do not steal," "Do not covet," and whatever other commandment there may be, are summed up in this one rule: "Love your neighbor as yourself." [10]Love does no harm to its neighbor. Therefore love is the fulfillment of the law.

Although Paul has previously put in an urgent call for love (12:9, 10), he now returns to this theme, knowing that he cannot stress too much this essential ingredient of all Christian service. The connection of the present paragraph with the foregoing section is indicated by the use of the word "debt," which has the same root as "owe" in v.7. There is a neat transition to the very highest demand on the child of God. He owes submission and honor to the civil authorities, but he owes all men much more.

8 "Let no debt remain outstanding." This translation has the advantage of avoiding the

danger of giving a wrong impression, such as might be conveyed by "Owe no man anything." If incurring any indebtedness whatever is contrary to God's will, the Lord would not have said, "Do not turn away from the one who wants to borrow from you" (Matt 5:42). On the other hand, to be perpetually in debt is not a good testimony for a believer, and to refuse to make good one's obligations is outrageous. Now comes the exception to the rule. There is a "continuing debt to love one another." One can never say that he has completely discharged it. Ordinarily, "one another" in the Epistles refers to relationship within the Christian community. But such is not the case here, for the expression is explained in terms of one's "fellow man" (literally, "the other person"). Since the passage goes on to refer to one's neighbor, we may be reasonably sure that the sweep of the obligation set forth here is intended to be universal. It is therefore a mistake to accuse the early church of turning its eyes inward upon itself and to a large extent neglecting the outside world. Granted that the usual emphasis is on one's duties to fellow believers, yet the wider reference is not lacking (Gal 6:10; 1 Thess 3:12). We may see something of a parallel in the fact that Jesus prayed for his own rather than for the world (John 17:9), since they were his one hope of reaching the world.

In saying that the one who loves has fulfilled the law, Paul presents a truth that parallels his statement in 8:4 about the righteous requirement of the law being fulfilled in those who live in accordance with the Spirit. The connecting link between these two passages is provided by Galatians 5:22, 23, where first place in the enumeration of the fruitage of the Spirit is given to love and the list is followed by the observation that against such fruit there is no law. So the Spirit produces in the believer a love to which the law can offer no objection, since love fulfills what the law requires, something the law itself cannot do.

9 When one seeks to know what the law requires, he is naturally referred to those precepts that pertain to human relationships, since love for one's neighbor is at issue, not love for God. Consequently, Paul lifts from the second table of the law certain precepts calling for the preservation of the sacredness of the family, the holding of human life inviolable, and the recognition of the right to ownership of property, concluding with the key item that is involved in the other three, viz., the control of one's desires (cf. 7:7).

One might object that these prohibitions belong to the sphere of justice rather than that of love, but this limited view is ruled out by the affirmation that these and other demands of the law are summed up in the positive command, "Love your neighbor as yourself." Incidentally, the original does not use "command" (NIV, "rule") here, but "word" (*logos*). However, this does not diminish the force of the term, since in the OT the Ten Commandments are sometimes called the "ten words" (e.g., Exod 34:28, Heb.).

Once again Paul follows the Lord Jesus in summarizing the horizontal bearing of the law by the use of Leviticus 19:18 (Matt 22:39). Jesus rebuked the narrow nationalistic interpretation of the word "neighbor" in the parable of the good Samaritan. The literal meaning of neighbor is "one who is near." Both the priest and the Levite found their nearness to the stricken man a source of embarrassment (Luke 10:31, 32), but the Samaritan saw in that same circumstance an opportunity to help his fellowman. In the light of human need, the barrier between Jew and Samaritan dissolved. Love provides its own imperative; it feels the compulsion of need.

10 "Love does no harm to its neighbor." This is an understatement, for love does positive good. But the negative form is suitable here, because it is intended to fit in with the prohibitions from the law (v.9). By concluding with the observation that love is the fulfillment of the law, Paul returns to the same thought he began with (v.8).

What, then, is the relationship between love and law? In Christ the two concepts, which seem to have so little in common, come together. To love others with the love that Christ exhibited is his new commandment (John 13:34). And if this love is present, it will make possible the keeping of all his other commandments (John 14:15). Love promotes obedience, and the two together constitute the law of Christ (Gal 6:2).

Notes

9 "You shall not bear false witness" (οὐ ψευδομαρτυρήσεις, *ou pseudomartyrēseis*) occurs in a few MSS, no doubt being added to conform to OT statements of the Decalogue.

F. *The Purifying Power of Hope*

13:11-14

> [11]And do this, understanding the present time. The hour has come for you to wake up from your slumber, because our salvation is nearer now than when we first believed. [12]The night is nearly over; the day is almost here. So let us put aside the deeds of darkness and put on the armor of light. [13]Let us behave decently, as in the daytime, not in orgies and drunkenness, not in sexual immorality and debauchery, not in dissension and jealousy. [14]Rather, clothe yourselves with the Lord Jesus Christ, and do not think about how to gratify the desires of your sinful nature.

The passage contains no explicit mention of hope. The same is true of love. But both are surely involved. Even as Paul turns to a new subject, he is loath to let go of the theme of love. So, with a final word about it, "And do this," he is ready to plunge into a delineation of the critical nature of the time that intervenes before the Lord's return. It is as though he is saying, "Show love while you can, and meanwhile keep girded with hope and sobriety for the consummation." If love singles out the Christian because he seeks to identify with others in their need, hope puts a gulf between the Christian and the worldling. He refuses to be conformed to this age that is satisfied with earthly things (cf. Phil 3:18-21). His summons is to self-discipline rather than to profligate living.

11 First, Paul sounds a call for alertness. The era between the advents is critical, because the promise of the return of Christ hovers over the believer. He must not be lulled to sleep by indulgence in pleasure or be influenced by the specious word of those who suggest that the Lord delays his coming or may not return at all. Paul does not say how near the day of the Lord's appearing is. As a matter of fact, he does not know. He is content to advance the reminder that "our salvation is nearer now than when we first believed" (v.11). To be sure, salvation is already an achieved fact for the believer (Eph 2:8) and a continuing fact as well (1 Cor 15:2, Gr.; 1 Peter 1:5). But it has also its future and final phase, as Paul here intimates (cf. 1 Peter 1:9). With this third aspect in mind, he says elsewhere that we "await a *Savior*" (Phil 3:20), for only then, at his return, will salvation be complete. The time of the appearing is subordinate to the fact of the appearing. "If primitive Christianity could note, without its faith being shaken thereby, that the 'end' did not come within the calculated times, that is just because the chrono-

logical framework of its hope was a secondary matter" (Leenhardt, in loc.). The believer is not like a child looking for a clock to strike the hour because something is due to happen then. He is content to know that with every passing moment the end is that much closer to realization.

12,13 The line of thought closely resembles the treatment in 1 Thessalonians 5:1-11. Even as darkness is symbolic of evil and sin, the light fittingly depicts those who have passed through the experience of salvation. Paul pictures the Christian as one who anticipates the day by rising early. His night clothes are the works of darkness, the deeds that belong to the old life. The garments to which he transfers, however, are unusual. They are likened to armor as in 1 Thessalonians 5:8. Evidently the purpose is to suggest that to walk through this world as children of light involves a warfare with the powers of darkness (cf. Eph 6:12, 13). Even though the day as an eschatological point has not yet arrived, the believer belongs to the day (1 Thess 5:8), anticipating by the very atmosphere of his transformed life the glory that will then be revealed (2 Cor 3:18; 4:4).

This is the basis for the plea, "Let us behave decently, as in the daytime." The Christian is to live as though that final day had actually arrived, bringing with it the personal presence of Christ. There should be no place, then, for the conduct that characterizes unsaved people, especially in the night seasons. Paul describes this manner of life (all too common in Corinth, where he was writing) in three couplets, the first emphasizing intemperance (which sets the stage for the other two), then sexual misconduct, followed by contention and quarreling. Here we learn the double lesson that one sin leads to another and that the committing of sin does not bring rest to the spirit but rather dissatisfaction that betrays itself by finding fault with others, as though they are responsible. The sinner tries hard to find a scapegoat.

14 In conclusion, the apostle returns to his figure of putting on clothing (cf. v.12), but now the garment is personalized. He urges his readers to put on the Lord Jesus Christ. This amounts to appropriation—the deliberate, conscious acceptance of the lordship of the Master—so that all is under his control—motives, desires, and deeds. A slight difficulty meets us at this point, since believers have already put on Christ, according to Galatians 3:27, at conversion and baptism. But there is always room for decisive renewal, for fresh advance. To be clothed with Christ should mean that when the believer comes under scrutiny from others, he enables them to see the Savior.

If, however, this putting on of Christ is done in a spirit of complacency, as though a life of godliness and uprightness will automatically follow, disappointment will result. The redeemed person must be attuned to the Savior. He must exercise ceaseless vigilance lest the flesh prevail. He must not give thought to how the desires of the old nature can be satisfied. Though the language differs from the teaching in chapter 6, the message is the same. If union with Christ is to be experientially successful, it must be accompanied by a constant reckoning of oneself as dead to sin and alive to God and his holy will.

G. *Questions of Conscience Wherein Christians Differ* (14:1-15:13)

It is uncertain to what extent Paul possessed definite information about the internal affairs of the Roman church. Consequently, it is difficult to know whether his approach to the problem of the "weak" and the "strong" is dictated by awareness of the precise nature of the problem in Rome or whether he is writing out of his own experience with other churches, especially the Corinthian congregation (1 Cor 8:1–11:1). His treatment in Romans is briefer and couched in more general terms, though there are obvious similarities, such as the danger that by his conduct the strong will cause the weak to stumble or fall, and the corresponding danger that the weak will sit in judgment on the strong. The differences are numerous: there is no mention in Romans of idols or food offered to idols; the word "conscience" does not appear; the strong are not described as those who have knowledge. On the other hand, we read in Romans of vegetarians and of those who insist on observing a certain day in contrast to others who look on all days as being alike. Neither of these features appears in 1 Corinthians.

Possibly the weaker brethren at Rome should be identified with the Jewish element in the church, because believing Jews might easily carry over their avoidance of certain foods from their former observance of the dietary laws of the OT. It is possible that information had reached Paul to the effect that with the return of Jewish Christians to Rome after the death of Emperor Claudius in A.D. 54 tension had developed in the church with the Gentile element that had been able for several years to enjoy without challenge its freedom in the matter of foods.

Judging from his discussion in 1 Corinthians, Paul would place himself among the strong. Yet he was careful not to become an occasion of stumbling to a weaker brother. He has words of warning and words of encouragement to both groups. His primary concern is to promote a spirit of unity in the church (15:5).

1. Brethren must refrain from judging one another.

14:1–12

> [1]Accept him whose faith is weak, without passing judgment on disputable matters. [2]One man's faith allows him to eat everything, but another man, whose faith is weak, eats only vegetables. [3]The man who eats everything must not look down on him who does not, and the man who does not eat everything must not condemn the man who does, for God has accepted him. [4]Who are you to judge someone else's servant? To his own master he stands or falls. And he will stand, for the Lord is able to make him stand.
>
> [5]One man considers one day more sacred than another; another man considers every day alike. Each one should be fully convinced in his own mind. [6]He who regards one day as special, does so to the Lord. He who eats meat, eats to the Lord, for he gives thanks to God; and he who abstains, does so to the Lord, and gives thanks to God. [7]For none of us lives to himself alone and none of us dies to himself alone. If we live, we live to the Lord; and if we die, we die to the Lord. So, whether we live or die, we belong to the Lord.
>
> [9]For this very reason, Christ died and returned to life so that he might be the Lord of both the dead and the living. [10]You, then, why do you judge your brother? Or why do you look down on your brother? For we will all stand before God's judgment seat. [11]It is written:
>
>> " 'As I live,' says the Lord,
>> 'Every knee will bow before me;
>>   every tongue will confess to God.' "
>
> [12]So then, each of us will give an account of himself to God.

1–4 "Eat" is the recurring word that characterizes this section. Diet practices differ and the differences are bound to be observed; they become a topic of conversation and a basis of disagreement. Paul's designation for the overscrupulous believer is "weak in faith," meaning that this man's faith is not strong enough to enable him to perceive the full liberty he has in Christ to partake. He is not troubled by questions of doctrine but is plagued by doubt as to whether it is right for him to eat some foods (cf. v.23). The injunction to those who do not share this weakness is to "accept him" (v.1). That this word (*proslambanō*) is capable of conveying the sense of warm wholeheartedness is shown by its use in Acts 18:26; 28:2. Such acceptance is impossible as long as there is any disposition to pass judgment on disputable matters. "The weak man should be accepted as the Christian brother he claims to be. One should not judge the thoughts which underlie his conduct. This is for God alone to do" (F. Büchsel in TDNT, 3:950). The weak brother must not be made to feel inferior or unwanted or "odd."

The specialized use of "faith" becomes clearer when Paul gives it a definite context (v.2). One man, obviously strong in faith, feels he can "eat everything" ("anything" would be a more cautious translation). Paul would concur that the believer has this freedom (1 Tim 4:3, 4). Another, weak in his faith, confines his diet to vegetables. No reason is advanced for this self-limitation. It could have been due to ascetic zeal. Some modern vegetarians believe they are healthier for not eating meat. Others have scruples about eating anything that has been consciously alive (perhaps unaware of research tending to establish that plants also have sensation). But the motive is a personal matter, and for that reason Paul does not make it an issue. He is solely concerned with specific practice and the reaction of the strong to this practice. The omnivorous man is apt to "look down" on the weak brother, an attitude that is not conducive to full fellowship. The weak brother may retaliate by condemning the one who has no inhibitions about his food. If so, the latter needs to reflect on the fact that God has accepted (same word as in v.1) this man (v.3). And why should he himself not do so?

To enforce the rebuke, Paul cites the relationship of a servant to his master (v.4). In ordinary life, it would be unseemly for anyone to attempt to interfere in a case involving the servant's actions. One might go so far as to inform the master of what the servant was doing, but even that could be regarded as an unjustified intrusion. Perhaps the analogy might be pushed to this extent: though reporting to the master might be inappropriate, one might conceivably pray to the Master in heaven about the conduct of the strong brother, asking the Master to deal with the case, while refraining from criticism directed at the brother himself. But the closing statement discourages such a line of thought. Paul affirms that the strong does not necessarily stand on slippery ground when enjoying his freedom in Christ. This assurance is grounded not so much on the discretion of the strong as on the power of Christ to sustain him. "The Apostle . . . is confident that *Christian* liberty, through the grace and power of Christ, will prove a triumphant moral success" (Denney, in loc.).

5–8 Here the recurring phrase is "to the Lord," indicating that whether one be thought of as "weak" or "strong," the important thing is that he conduct his life in the consciousness of God's presence, because God's approval is more significant than the approval or disapproval of fellow Christians. Eating is still in view, but alongside it Paul places a fresh topic—the holding of certain days as sacred.

5,6 Whether the question of regarding one day as more sacred than another refers to Sabbath observance or to special days for feasting or fasting is not easily determined. Since the early church in Jerusalem almost certainly observed the Sabbath (as well as the first day of the week) because of its Jewish constituency and the danger of giving offense to non-Christian Jews, and since the Roman church presumably had a good-sized minority of Jews, it is not impossible that Paul has the Sabbath in mind. Perhaps because the observance of the day was not being pressed upon the Gentile believers in the church in the way that Jewish sects challenged such believers elsewhere (Col 2:16), it was not necessary to identify the day explicitly. Even so, if the day of worship is in view, it is strange that any believer could be said to consider "every day alike." The close contextual association with eating suggests that Paul has in mind a special day set apart for observance as a time for feasting or as a time for fasting. The important thing is that one should "be fully convinced in his own mind" as to the rightfulness of his observance. More important still is the certitude of the individual involved that his motivation is his desire to honor the Lord in what he is doing. It is possible for the observant and the nonobservant to do this, as illustrated by the giving of thanks at mealtime (cf. 1 Tim 4:5). The one partaking can give thanks for the meat before him, while the one abstaining from meat can give God thanks for his vegetables. The latter should be able to do this without resentment toward his brother who enjoys richer fare.

7,8 Here we should not understand Paul as expressing a maxim applicable to all people, as though he intended to suggest that everyone has some sort of influence with others, even though in some instances it is more limited than in others. He is speaking of believers, as v.8 shows. The reason the Christian does not live to himself is that he lives to the Lord. This attachment, which is also an obligation, does not cease with death but carries forward into the next life (Phil 1:20). Paul has already affirmed that death cannot separate Christians from the love of God in Christ (8:38, 39; cf. 2 Cor 5:9). Their death is not merely a transfer from the arena of struggle to the realm of rest. Rather, it is to be viewed as an enlarged opportunity to show forth the praises of the Lord. Relationship to him is the key to life on either side of the veil.

9–12 Here Paul makes the point that both groups will have to answer to God in the coming day. So it is premature to pass judgment on one another (cf. 1 Cor 4:5), seeing that an infallible judge will assume that responsibility.

9 The Savior gave his life, laying it down in obedience to the will of God, and thereby purchased the church by his blood (Acts 20:28). But only after his resurrection could he assume the active headship of his people. Though the title "Lord" was appropriate to him in the days of his flesh (e.g., Mark 5:19), the title came into more frequent and more meaningful use after the resurrection, since that event established his claim to deity, his claim to Saviorhood, and his claim to universal dominion. His triumph included victory over death, so that even though his people may be given over to death's power temporarily, they have not ceased to be his, as the future bodily resurrection of Christians will demonstrate. He is in fact the Lord of both the dead and the living. The order in which these two divisions appear reflects the order in the previous statement about Christ in his death and return to life.

10–12 Against this background the apostle returns to direct address, first to the weak brother, then to the strong. The former is prone to judge, the latter to depreciate or even scorn. Both attitudes are virtually the same, because they involve improper judgment. The true judge is God, and his time for judging is coming, making man's judgment not only premature but also a usurpation of God's role. Notable is the ease with which Paul passes from the Lord (v.9) to God (v.10) in the same milieu of thought. The two are inseparable in their operations. In fact, God's judgment seat (v.10) is to be identified with the judgment seat of Christ (2 Cor 5:10). We see the same phenomenon in the quotation introduced here (v.11), which is a combination of Isaiah 49:18 and 45:23. In Philippians 2:10, 11 the same passages from Isaiah are utilized and the relationship between God and the Lord is made clear. In the summary of the situation (v.12) the note of judgment is retained, but the emphasis falls on the fact that each person must give account of *himself* (not of his brother) to God (cf. Gal 6:5). The same word for "account" (*logos*) occurs in Hebrews 4:13.

Notes

4 Some MSS have "God" instead of "the Lord." This change apparently crept into the text as copyists carried the mention of "God" over from v.3.
10 At the end of the verse "of Christ" occurs instead of "of God" in many witnesses, some of them early, apparently because of the copyists' desire to conform the statement to 2 Cor 5:10.

2. Brethren must avoid offending one another

14:13–23

13Therefore, let us stop passing judgment on one another. Instead, make up your mind not to put any stumbling block or obstacle in your brother's way. 14As one who is in the Lord Jesus, I am fully convinced that no food is unclean in itself. But if anyone regards something as unclean, then for him it is unclean. 15If your brother is distressed because of what you eat, you are no longer acting in love. Do not by your eating destroy your brother for whom Christ died. 16Do not allow what you consider good to be spoken of as evil. 17For the kingdom of God is not a matter of eating and drinking, but of righteousness, peace and joy in the Holy Spirit, 18because anyone who serves Christ in this way is pleasing to God and approved by men.

19Let us therefore make every effort to do what leads to peace and to mutual edification. 20Do not destroy the work of God for the sake of food. All food is clean, but it is wrong for a man to eat anything that causes someone else to stumble. 21It is better not to eat meat or drink wine or to do anything else that will cause your brother to fall.

22So whatever you believe about these things keep between yourself and God. Blessed is the man who does not condemn himself by what he approves. 23But the man who has doubts is condemned if he eats, because his eating is not from faith; and everything that does not come from faith is sin.

In this section, the appeal for the most part is directed to the strong brother, who is warned that his example may have a disastrous effect on the one who is weak by leading him to do what his spiritual development provides no ground of approval for. The discussion proceeds along the same line as before—what a Christian should include in his diet.

13–18 The opening statement gives the gist of what has been already said. Both parties have been guilty of passing judgment on one another. Then by a neat use of language, Paul employs the same verb "judge" (*krinō*) in a somewhat different sense ("make up your mind"). He is calling for a determination to adopt a course of action that will not hurt another brother, a decision once for all to avoid whatever might impede his progress in the faith or cause him to fall. Though Paul does not single out the strong brother, it appears that he must have him in mind in this admonition against putting a stumbling block in a brother's way. A stumbling block (*proskomma*) is literally something against which one may strike his foot, causing him to stumble or even fall. The second term (*skandalon*, rendered "obstacle" here) presents a different picture, that of a trap designed to ensnare a victim. It is used of something that constitutes a temptation to sin. Jesus applied this word to Peter when that disciple sought to deter him from going to the cross (Matt 16:23). In v.13 it could be taken as a stern warning against deliberately enticing a brother to do what for him would be sinful (cf. v.23). Even if such an act were motivated by the desire to get the brother out of the "weak" category, it would still be wrong.

Paul himself is convinced of something that the weak brother does not share, viz., that "no food is unclean in itself" (v.14). Elsewhere he affirms in a similar context that everything God created is good (1 Tim 4:4), an observation that rests on the record of creation (Gen 1:31). But in the passage before us the apostle seems to have reference to some utterance made by our Lord during his earthly ministry (note the human name "Jesus" here). We find it in Mark 7:15-23, where the Master declares that one is not rendered unclean by what goes into him but rather by what comes out of him, from his inner life. Mark adds the comment that in this pronouncement Jesus declared all foods "clean." But not everyone has been enlightened on this issue, and if one is convinced in his heart that some foods are unclean (e.g., in terms of the Levitical food laws), for him such foods remain unclean. Until he is convinced otherwise, it would violate his conscience to partake of them. Even the apostle Peter, who had been with Jesus and had heard his teaching, was in bondage on this point until some time after Pentecost (Acts 10:9-15).

Moreover, even if the strong brother does not try to convince the weak to change his habits, his own practice, since it is known, can be a stumbling block to the other, causing distress of soul. This distress may be viewed as reaction to the callous indifference of the strong brother. But it may contain a hint of something tragic, a sorrow of heart induced by following the example of the strong, only to find the conscience ablaze with rebuke and the whole life out of fellowship with the Lord. In such a situation, love is not operating.

Paul's basis of approach to the strong brother has changed from granting him his position on the grounds of his liberty to eat. Now the appeal is not to liberty but to love, which may call for a measure of sacrifice. If such sacrifice is refused, then the strong brother must face the responsibility for bringing spiritual ruin on the weak. Moule (in loc.) admirably sums up the situation. "The Lord may counteract your action and save your injured brother from himself—and you. But your action is, none the less, calculated for his perdition. And all the while this soul, for which, in comparison with your dull and narrow 'liberty,' you care so little, was so much cared for by the Lord that He died for it." A selfish insistence on liberty may tear down and destroy, but love, when it is exercised, will invariably build up (1 Cor 8:1).

"Do not allow what you consider good to be spoken of as evil" (v.16). Some understand this in terms of possible slander by the unsaved who find occasion to deride the Christian community for its squabbling over such minor matters. But the thought does not necessarily range beyond the circle of the redeemed. The good is naturally understood as the liberty to eat, since all foods are regarded as clean. This liberty, however, if resented because it has been flaunted in the face of the weak, can be regarded as an evil thing on account of its unloving misuse.

Then, with pastoral insight, Paul lifts the entire discussion to a higher level than mere eating and drinking (v.17). His readers, all of them, are the loyal subjects of Christ in the kingdom of God. In that sphere the real concerns are not externals such as diet but the spiritual realities motivating life and shaping conduct. Surely the strong will agree that if their insistence on Christian liberty endangers the spiritual development of the church as a whole, they should be willing to forgo that liberty. In this context "righteousness" (*dikaiosynē*) is not justification but the right conduct to which the believer is called in obedience to the will of God (cf. 6:13, 16, 18). This conclusion is supported by the fact that joy is an experiential term. Peace is sometimes peace *with* God (5:1), at other times the peace *of* God (Phil 4:7). The second meaning is appropriate to this passage (cf. v.19). Mention of the Spirit is understandable, because joy and peace are included in the fruit he produces in the believer's life. The list in Galatians 5:22 is not intended to be complete (see Gal 5:23), so we may legitimately claim practical righteousness as effected by his indwelling. Further confirmation of this interpretation is furnished by v.18, where Paul links these matters to the believer's service of Christ. The manifestation of the fruit of the Spirit is acceptable not only to God who provides it, but also to men who see it in operation and experience its blessings.

19–21 The entire church is urged to pursue peace (harmony between the two groups is the immediate application), which alone can provide the atmosphere in which "mutual edification" can take place. It will be recalled that "edification" (*oikodomē*) was Paul's key word in dealing with the problems created by the manifestation of spiritual gifts in the Corinthian situation (1 Cor 14:5, 12, 26). Mutual edification implies that the strong, despite their tendency to look down on the weak, may actually learn something from them. It may be that they will come to appreciate loyalty to a tender conscience and begin to search their own hearts to discover that they have cared more about maintaining their position than about loving the weaker brethren. Through the fresh manifestation of love by the strong the weak will be lifted in spirit and renewed in faith and life.

Having spoken of the edification (literally, the building up) of the saints, Paul reinforces his point by warning of the reverse process (v.20). To "destroy" the work of God is to tear it down, so that much time and painful labor will be required to restore the edifice to the point where it can function again as the instrument of the divine purpose. It is disheartening to realize that such colossal loss could be occasioned by a difference of opinion over food! Since all food can properly be regarded as clean, it is not wrong in itself for one to eat whatever he finds healthful or desirable. The wrong lies in his causing someone to stumble by his eating.

The "better" (literally, noble or praiseworthy) course is to do without meat under the circumstances and to refrain from drinking wine, if partaking would be a stumbling block to anyone. Paul extends the principle to include *anything* that might have this effect. For the first time in the discussion wine is mentioned, suggesting that a measure of asceticism may be in view here. The apostle may have anticipated this item by referring to drinking in v.17. In view of his strong stand taken in connection with a similar question involving the Corinthians (1 Cor 8:13), his counsel here (v.21) is not something new. He is simply commending to others what has for some time been the rule for himself.

22,23 Although the language of the opening statement of this section is general (cf. vv.1, 2), and could therefore apply to both groups, in all probability Paul is directing his

149

counsel chiefly to the strong, since it is the strong person who is warned to act on his confidence privately, where God is his witness. The natural explanation is that the exercise of his freedom in public would grieve the weak brother and raise a barrier between them, and this is the very thing to be avoided if at all possible. The strong is "blessed" (*makarios*, which can mean "fortunate" or "happy") in this private enjoyment of his freedom, because he is free from doubt and because no one who might be scandalized is looking on. In this way he is not faced with the danger confronting the weak brother—viz., that of condemning himself by approving something his conscience will not endorse. It should be granted that the language of v.22b can with equal propriety refer to the weak brother. But since the next verse is so definitely applicable to the weak brother, Paul is probably following his practice of having a word of encouragement or admonition for each party. This seems to be confirmed by the way he introduces his remark about the weak brother in v.23: "But. . . ."

It is important to understand "faith" here (v.23) in the same way it was used at the beginning of the chapter. Again, there is no question of saving faith, but only of confidence that one is free to make use of what God has created and set apart for man's good. In keeping with this, "condemned" does not refer to a future action of God excluding one from salvation, but, as the tense indicates, means that the person stands condemned by his own act as being wrong. The case of Peter comes to mind. In his actions at Antioch, "he stood condemned" (Gal 2:11 RSV). When Paul pointed out his fault, Peter had no defense. He was in the wrong and he knew it. To act in contradiction to conscience or to the known will of God inevitably brings this result. Christian experience shows that when a believer refuses to move in a certain direction because he lacks confidence that the step is in line with the will of God, he receives strength by the refusal so that it is much easier on other occasions to move on the basis of faith, even when to do so may be difficult because of possible misunderstanding by fellow Christians.

Notes

19 Though the indicative διώκομεν (*diōkomen*, "we pursued") has strong support (ℵ A B, et al.), the subjunctive διώκωμεν (*diōkōmen*, "let us pursue"), expressing exhortation, seems to be the better choice here.
22 An alternate reading calls for the tr. "Do you have faith?" at the beginning of the sentence. Either reading makes tolerably good sense.
23 See note on 16:25–27, p. 171.

3. *The unity of the strong and the weak in Christ*

15:1–13

¹We who are strong ought to bear with the failings of the weak, and not to please ourselves. ²Each of us should please his neighbor for his good, to build him up. ³For even Christ did not please himself but, as it is written: "The insults of those who insult you have fallen on me." ⁴For everything that was written in the past was written to teach us, so that through endurance and the encouragement of the Scriptures we might have hope.

⁵May the God who gives endurance and encouragement give you a spirit of unity among yourselves as you follow Christ Jesus, ⁶so that with one heart and mouth you may glorify the God and Father of our Lord Jesus Christ.

7Accept one another, then, just as Christ accepted you, in order to bring praise to God. 8For I tell you that Christ has become a servant of the Jews on behalf of God's truth, to confirm the promises made to the patriarchs 9so that the Gentiles may glorify God for his mercy, as it is written:

"For this reason I will praise you
among the Gentiles;
I will sing hymns to your name."

10Again, it says,

"Rejoice, O Gentiles, with his people."

11And again,

"Praise the Lord, all you Gentiles,
and sing praises to him, all you peoples."

12And again, Isaiah says,

"The root of Jesse will spring up,
one who will arise to rule over the nations;
the Gentiles will hope in him."

13May the God of hope fill you with great joy and peace as you trust in him, so that you may overflow with hope by the power of the Holy Spirit.

Two fairly distinct motifs run through this portion. In vv.1–6 the appeal to both the strong and the weak is grounded on the example of Christ who did not please himself but gladly accepted whatever self-denial his mission required. In vv.7–13 Christ is again the key. He has graciously accepted both Jew and Gentile in accordance with the purpose of God. To refuse to accept each other is to resist that purpose in its practical outworking.

1–4 As Paul draws the discussion to a close, he openly aligns himself with the strong. They are the ones who hold the key to the solution of the problem. If they are interested simply in maintaining their own position, the gulf between the two groups will not be narrowed and the weak will continue to be critical and resentful. But if the strong will reach out the hand of fellowship and support, this will be a bridge. So to the strong belongs the responsibility of taking the initiative. "Ought" is not to be watered down as though it means the same thing as "should." It speaks not of something recommended but of obligation. The word "bear" was used earlier when the apostle enjoined the Galatian believers to "carry [bear] each other's burdens, and in this way ... fulfill the law of Christ" (Gal 6:2). Let the strong, then, bear the burden of the scrupulousness of the weaker brethren. But if they do this in a spirit of mere resignation or with the notion that this condescension marks them as superior Christians, it will fail. When the strong bear with the weak, they must do it in love—the key to fulfilling the law of Christ. The temptation to be resisted by the strong is the inclination to please themselves, to minister to self-interest. This is the very antithesis of love. For example, were a strong brother to indulge his liberty openly in the presence of a weak brother, this would be labeled self-pleasing, for it would do nothing for the other but grieve or irritate him.

2 Indeed, the refusal to live a life of self-pleasing should characterize every believer, whether strong or weak, and should extend beyond the narrow circle of like-minded people to all with whom we come in contact—in short, to our neighbor, whoever he is.

As Hodge remarks, what is called for here is not "a weak compliance with the wishes of others" (in loc.). It is rather a determined adjustment to whatever will contribute to the spiritual good of the other person. The present injunction is akin to Paul's own principle of making himself all things to all men in order to win as many as possible to the Lord (1 Cor 9:19–23). There is no conflict between such a principle and his refusal to "please men" (Gal 1:19), since in the latter context he is merely setting himself against any trimming of the gospel message designed to avoid giving offense to those resisting revealed truth. The goal to be achieved here is the good of the other person, his edification (cf. 14:19). This leaves no room for anything like mere ingratiation.

3 For the first time in this letter Paul holds Christ before his readers as an example. Christ was faced with the same problem that continues to confront his followers. Should they please themselves, go their own way, speak what people want to hear; or should they resolve to be guided by their commitment to do the will of God? Christ's own affirmation is recorded for us: "I always do what pleases him" (John 8:29). The cost was heavy. "The insults of those who insult you [God] have fallen on me" (quoting Ps 69:9). Even in Israel, through the years, God's servants had suffered reproach and insult when they attempted to warn their countrymen that their sin and rebellion were inviting the judgment of God. The first half of Psalm 69:9 is quoted in John 2:17 in connection with the cleansing of the temple—"Zeal for your house will consume me." This is generally interpreted to mean that the opposition stirred up by Jesus would lead eventually to his death. To espouse the cause of God fervently is to arouse the passions of sinful men. See John 15:25, quoted from the same psalm (69:4), where Jesus acknowledged that human hatred had dogged his steps, but unjustly. Our Lord did not on this account discontinue his faithful ministrations that were designed to help those about him. Paul would have his readers realize that similarly they are to seek the good of others even if they are misunderstood or maligned in doing so.

4 Having cited Psalm 69, a portion evidently regarded in the early church as messianic, the apostle is led to refer to the Scriptures in a more general way as useful for the instruction of NT believers—in fact, as deliberately planned for their edification. The very phenomenon of quoting from the OT speaks loudly of the dependence of the church on the course of redemption history reflected there. Things both new and old enter into Christian faith. The example of Christ was bound to influence the church to revere and use the OT, and this was made easier because at the beginning its constituency was largely Jewish-Christian. As for the Gentiles, in many cases at least, they had become familiar with the OT in the synagogue (Acts 13:44–48) before hearing the gospel and putting their trust in the Lord Jesus. The use of the Scriptures promotes "endurance" and supplies "encouragement." Both may be learned by precept and example from these records of the past. These two elements are intimately connected with hope, for the endurance is worthwhile if it takes place on a course that leads to a glorious future, and the encouragement provides exactly that assurance.

5,6 Endurance and encouragement are ultimately God's gift, though they are mediated through the Scriptures. They tend, however, to be individually appropriated, some realizing them to a greater degree than others. So Paul prays for a spirit of unity (likemindedness) that will minimize individual differences as all fix their attention on Christ as the pattern for their own lives (cf. v.3). This does not mean that believers are intended to see eye-to-eye on everything, but that the more Christ fills the spiritual vision, the greater will be the cohesiveness of the church. The centripetal magnetism of the Lord can effectively counter the centrifugal force of individual judgment and opinion. Though this unity will help the church in its witness to the world, Paul is more interested here in its effect on the worship of the people of God—"with one heart and mouth" glorifying the God and Father whom Jesus so beautifully glorified on earth.

7 As he moves forward to the conclusion of his treatment of the strong and the weak, Paul, good teacher that he was, pauses to summarize what he has already stated. "Accept one another" picks up the emphasis of 14:1, where the same verb occurs, but here the charge is directed to both groups rather than to the strong alone. Then, in line with 15:3, 5, he brings in the example of Christ once more and states that bringing praise to God is the grand objective, in agreement with v.6. It is not fully clear whether this final phrase relates grammatically to the command to receive one another or to the fact that Christ has received them. As far as the sense of the passage is concerned, it could apply to both.

8–12 From the three elements that constitute v.7 Paul now singles out the second— Christ's acceptance of all who make up his body—and proceeds to enlarge on it, first in relation to the Jewish Christians (v.8) and then in relation to the Gentiles (vv.9–12). The central thrust is to show that in these two directions Christ has fulfilled the anticipations of the OT.

"Christ has become a servant of the Jews" (v.8). This simple, brief statement epitomizes the earthly ministry of our Lord, who announced that he was sent only to the lost sheep of the house of Israel (Matt 15:24) and restricted the activity of his disciples during those days to their own nation (Matt 10:5, 6). The word "servant" reminds us to what lengths Jesus was prepared to go to minister to the needs of Israel (cf. Mark 10:45). This dedicated limitation of ministry to his own people was in the interest of "God's truth" in the sense of God's fidelity to his word, more specifically his promises made to the patriarchs (cf. 9:4, 5). God pledged himself to provide for Abraham a progeny that would culminate in Christ himself as the Redeemer (Gal 3:16). This was a salutary reminder to the Gentile element in the church (the strong) that God had given priority to Israel, lest Jewish believers should be slighted or depreciated. As noted earlier, a similar motive underlies Paul's treatment of the Jewish question in chapters 9 to 11.

Once that point has been made, however, Paul brings out the truth that all the time God's purpose was not exclusively directed toward the nation of Israel (cf. Gen 12:3), since ever and again in the Scriptures the Gentiles are viewed as embraced in the saving mercy of God and responding to it. Consequently, the Jewish believer of Paul's time should not think it contradictory for God to lavish his grace on the nations through the gospel.

There is an element of progression in the marshaling of quotations from the OT. The first (from Ps 18:49) pictures David as rejoicing in God for his triumphs in the midst of the nations that have become subject to him. In the second (from Deut 32:43), the position of the Gentiles is elevated to participation with Israel in the praise of the Lord (according to LXX). In the third and fourth quotations the Gentiles, no longer pictured in relation to Israel, are seen in their own right, whether as praising the Lord (Ps 117:1) or as hoping in him whom God has raised up to rule over the nations (Isa 11:10).

13 As he had done at the close of the first section in this chapter (v.5), Paul again expresses his desire that God will meet the needs of his readers. Although eschatology in a formal, structured sense has little place in Romans, its subjective counterpart, hope,

is mentioned more often than in any other of his letters, especially in this portion (vv.4, 12, 13).

The expression "the God of hope" (v.13) means the God who inspires hope and imparts it to his children. He can be counted on to fulfill what yet remains to be accomplished for them (5:2; 13:11). Likewise, in the more immediate future and with the help of Paul's letter, they can confidently look to God for the working out of their problems, including the one Paul has been discussing. Hope does not operate apart from trust; in fact, it is the forward-looking aspect of faith (Gal 5:5; 1 Peter 1:21). Paul in his pastoral zeal is not satisfied with anything less than a rich, abounding experience of hope, even as he expects from them an overflowing of love (Phil 1:9; 1 Thess 3:12; 4:10), of pleasing God (1 Thess 4:1), and of thanksgiving (Col 2:7). The reason for this is that the God who is supplicated here has so wonderfully abounded in the exercise of his grace (5:15) that he can be expected to enable his people to increase in the manifestation of Christian graces, especially as this is insured "by the power of the Holy Spirit" who indwells and fills the inner life.

VIII. Conclusion (15:14–16:27)

A. *Paul's Past Labors, Present Program, and Future Plans*

15:14–33

[14]I myself am convinced, my brothers, that you yourselves are full of goodness, complete in knowledge and competent to instruct one another. [15]I have written you quite boldly on some points, as if to remind you of them again, because of the grace God gave me [16]to be a minister of Christ Jesus to the Gentiles with the priestly duty of proclaiming the gospel of God, so that the Gentiles might become an offering acceptable to God, sanctified by the Holy Spirit.

[17]Therefore, I glory in Christ Jesus in my service to God. [18]I will not venture to speak of anything except what Christ has accomplished through me in leading the Gentiles to obey God by what I have said and done—[19]by the power of signs and miracles, through the power of the Spirit. So from Jerusalem all the way around to Illyricum, I have fully proclaimed the gospel of Christ. [20]It has always been my ambition to preach the gospel where Christ was not known, so that I would not be building on someone else's foundation. [21]Rather, as it is written:

"Those who were not told about him will see,
and those who have not heard will understand."

[22]This is why I have often been hindered from coming to you.

[23]But now that there is no more place for me to work in these regions, and since I have been longing for many years to see you [24]I plan to do so when I go to Spain. I hope to visit you while passing through and to have you assist me on my journey there, after I have enjoyed your company for a while. [25]Now, however, I am on my way to Jerusalem in the service of the saints there. [26]For Macedonia and Achaia were pleased to make a contribution for the poor among the saints in Jerusalem. [27]They were pleased to do it, and indeed they owe it to them. For if the Gentiles have shared in the Jews' spiritual blessings, they owe it to the Jews to share with them their material blessings. [28]So after I have completed this task and have made sure that they have received this fruit, I will go to Spain and visit you on the way. [29]I know that when I come to you, I will come in the full measure of the blessing of Christ.

[30]I urge you, brothers, by our Lord Jesus Christ and by the love of the Spirit, to join me in my struggle by praying to God for me. [31]Pray that I may be rescued from the unbelievers in Judea and that my service in Jerusalem may be acceptable

to the saints there. [32]Then by God's will I can come to you with joy and together with you be refreshed. [33]The God of peace be with you all. Amen.

The remainder of this chapter can be regarded as complementary to the introduction of the letter, since there is a similar prominence of personal matters Paul feels will be of interest to the believers at Rome. In both portions, however, his own affairs are invariably regarded as important only as they relate to the gospel of Christ of which he is such a committed minister.

14-16 Paul now reflects on the character of his readers and what he can expect his letter to accomplish for them. If his assessment of them seems unexpectedly favorable after his admonition in the last chapter and a half, we need not conclude that he was beginning to chide himself for being too hard on the brethren. Study of his Epistles reveals that he had a sense of fairness that led him to strike a just balance between pointing out deficiencies and finding things he could honestly commend. Concerning the church at Rome, since he has acknowledged their strong faith (1:8), it is now in order to add some other things he has picked up from various sources of information, including people mentioned in the closing chapter. In reference to v.14, George Edmundson writes, "Such a declaration implies a conviction based upon trustworthy evidence, otherwise his readers would be the first to perceive that here was only high-flown language covering an empty compliment" (*The Church in Rome in the First Century* [London: Longman, Green and Co., 1913], p. 15).

The first item is goodness. Having just written of the Holy Spirit, Paul undoubtedly has in mind the goodness that is the fruit of the Spirit (Gal 5:22). So it is not a native disposition but the moral excellence wrought into the texture of life by the Spirit's indwelling. He may give it prominence as the quality needed to carry out the recommendations directed to both groups in the previous discussion. Desire to do the right thing by another is essential, but it must be coupled with knowledge of what is rightly expected of the believer. Paul goes so far as to call his readers "complete" in this area and therefore "competent to instruct one another" (v.14). Such language shows his confidence that the Roman church, which had been in existence for at least a decade, had been well taught (cf. 6:17). At the same time this relative maturity did not make his contribution superfluous, because it served to confirm what they knew, underscoring it with apostolic authority, making them the more capable of instructing each other. This word "instruct" (*noutheteō*) reflects more than the imparting of information. "Inculcate" comes close to expressing its force (cf. Col 3:16, "counsel," and 1 Thess 5:14, "warn"). In the absence of resident pastors, brethren were the more under obligation to exercise such a ministry among themselves. Paul's use of the term at this point reflects the admonition in the preceding chapter.

Though he was not the founder of the Roman church, Paul has been outspoken, and he proceeds to explain this lest he be thought immodest or tyrannical or simply tedious in going over things he now admits they were already aware of. He is simply doing his duty, fulfilling the commission God in his grace has granted him as a minister of Christ (vv.15, 16). Furthermore, his boldness has been in evidence "on some points" (v.15) but has not pervaded the letter as a whole. Since in this connection he emphasizes his call to go to the Gentiles, one may assume that most of his readers were Gentiles (cf. 1:13) and would be especially interested in this allusion. Redeemed Gentiles are his special offering, a sacrifice acceptable to God (cf. Isa 66:18-20). His own function as a priest pertains directly to the proclamation of the gospel and the winning of Gentiles to Christ.

It remains for them to make their own personal commitment to God (12:1). He is not claiming, of course, that he has won his readers to Christ, but is speaking generally. Directly, he will refer to his labors in the East that have involved precisely this sort of ministry. Before doing this, he pauses to note that the acceptability of Gentiles to God comes not only from their reception of the gospel of Christ but also from the ministry of the Holy Spirit that sets them apart to God as the people of his possession (cf. 1 Cor 6:11). This initial sanctification makes possible the progressive spiritual development that spans the two great foci of justification and final redemption (1 Cor 1:30). This setting apart by the Spirit is a natural consequence of the new birth by the Spirit and is closely connected with it.

17–22 Paul refuses to boast in his ministry to the Gentiles. He restricts his glorying to Christ Jesus (cf. Gal 6:13, 14), the one he serves as a minister (cf. v.16). This relationship means not only that the glory goes to the Savior, but also that as the minister of Christ Paul must depend on him for everything that is accomplished in connection with his mission. Paul is only the instrument by which God brings Gentiles to obey him in faith and life (cf. 1:5). Christ is the one ultimately responsible as he continues to work through his servant (cf. Acts 1:1). The ministry has consisted both of word and deed ("what I have said and done," v.18). As far as the ministry of the word is concerned, it is sufficient at this stage in the letter to express the content of it as the gospel of Christ, since he has been explaining the gospel from almost the first word he has written. So he enlarges on the other aspect of his ministry.

"Signs and miracles" (v.19) served to accredit the messenger of God and validate the message he brought. It was so in the ministry of Jesus (Acts 2:22) and in that of the original apostles (Acts 5:12). Paul is able to certify the same for himself (cf. 2 Cor 12:12). A "sign" is a visible token of an invisible reality that is spiritually significant. The same act may also be a "wonder," something that appeals to the senses and is recognized as a phenomenon that needs explanation. In the OT, God's presence and power were indicated through such means, especially at the time of the Exodus and during the wilderness sojourn. However, "the power of the Spirit" was required to persuade people to make the connection between the miracles and the message and so believe the gospel and be saved. Israel saw countless miracles, both in OT times and during the ministry of Jesus, but often without profit. Stephen supplied the explanation for this fruitlessness: They resisted the Spirit (Acts 7:51).

How well has Paul fulfilled his task in proclaiming the gospel as a minister of Christ? He now affords his readers a glimpse into his activity over many years (v.19b). There is no account of churches founded or the number of converts or the sufferings entailed in all this service. Paul is content to draw a great arc reaching from Jerusalem to Illyricum (a Roman province northwest of Macedonia) to mark the course of his labors. Years—perhaps as many as ten—were spent in Syria and Cilicia before his ministry in Antioch that led in turn to travels in Asia Minor and Greece and establishing congregations in those areas. Luke's account of Paul's final visit to Macedonia and Achaia before going up to Jerusalem for the last time is very brief (Acts 20:1, 2). Yet it is at least possible that a visit to Illyricum or its border was made before settling down at Corinth for the winter. The Egnatian Way would have made travel easy from Thessalonica to the Adriatic Sea. Paul mentions Illyricum probably because he was closer to Italy there than he had ever been before. We can picture him anticipating in Illyricum the day when he would be free to cross the water and set foot in Italy, making contact with the Roman church.

The statement "I have fully proclaimed the gospel of Christ" is not intended to mean that he had preached in every community between the two points mentioned but that he had faithfully preached the message in the major communities along the way, leaving to his converts the more intensified evangelizing of surrounding districts. His ministry in Jerusalem was brief and met with great resistance, for he was a marked and hated man for abandoning the persecution of the church that he had carried on with such vigor in Jerusalem (Acts 9:28, 29). But the very fact that it was attempted at all displayed his determination to fulfill that part of his commission that included Israel (Acts 9:15). His habit of visiting the synagogues wherever he went points in the same direction.

From this brief outline of his missionary activity, the apostle turns to the drive that kept him ceaselessly at his task (v.20). He had a godly "ambition" to preach the gospel where Christ was not known. Such an item was not contained in his call to service except by implication in connection with reaching the Gentiles, so it represents his desire to shoulder the responsibility for blazing a trail for the gospel no matter how great the cost to himself. He longed to preach "in the regions beyond" (2 Cor 10:16). This man could not be an ordinary witness for his Lord. Somewhat parallel is his insistence on preaching the gospel without charge, supporting himself by the labor of his hands (1 Cor 9:18). Verse 20 should be taken in close connection with vv.18, 19 as providing a reason for the passing of so many years without a visit to Rome: Paul had been fully occupied elsewhere. When conditions in the Corinthian church detained him so long, it burdened him that he was not free to pursue his ambition to move on to another area. His dislike of building on another's foundation did not come from an overweening sense of self-importance that could be satisfied only when he could claim the credit for what was accomplished. Actually, he preferred to work with companions, as the Book of Acts attests, and he was always appreciative of the service rendered by his helpers. His statement about "not . . . building on someone else's foundation" requires no more explanation than that he was impelled by the love of Christ to reach as many as possible. He felt deeply his obligation to confront all men with the good news (1:14). This is confirmed by the quotation (v.21) of Isaiah 52:15. Isaiah was a favorite source for Paul's quotations, especially the sections dealing with the Servant of the Lord and his mission, to which this citation belongs.

Concluding this section of the letter is the observation that Paul's delay in coming to Rome was the result of his constant preoccupation with preaching the gospel elsewhere (v.22). Now his readers will understand why he has not come from Jerusalem, the holy city, directly to Rome, the royal city, with the message of reconciliation and life in Christ.

23–29 Only as we take into account the restless pioneer spirit of Paul can we understand how he could claim to have "no more place . . . to work" in the regions where he had been laboring. Plenty of communities had been left unvisited and several groups of believers could have profited from a visit, but his eyes were on the western horizon to which they had been lifted during his stay at Ephesus (Acts 19:21). In view of his mention of "many years," perhaps we may believe that his desire to go to Rome had been born even earlier, though not crystallized into resolve till the successes at Ephesus showed him that a move to more needy fields was in order. Others could carry on after he had laid the foundation.

Now a still more remote objective than Rome comes into view. Spain (v.24) marked the frontier of the empire on the west. So the stay in Rome is seen as limited. Though Paul looks forward to fellowship with the believers there, in line with his earlier statement (1:11, 12), he hopes to go beyond. Openly, he announces his hope that the Roman church will assist him in making the Spanish campaign a reality. This sharing will naturally include their prayers on his behalf, their financial cooperation, and possibly some helpers to go with him to the limits of the West. If Paul were ever to reach Spain, he would no doubt feel that he had realized in his own ministry a measure of fulfillment of the Lord's Great Commission that bade his followers go to the ends of the earth (Acts 1:8).

Whether Paul actually reached Spain is not certain. The strongest positive evidence is found in First Clement V.7, a late first-century writing: "He [Paul] taught righteousness to all the world, and when he had reached the limits of the West he gave his testimony before the rulers, and thus passed from the world." Spain fits "the limits of the West." The remainder of the statement applies more naturally to Rome, but may be intended to refer to a later period in Paul's life.

The contemplated trip to Spain by way of Rome will have to be postponed until another mission is accomplished, namely, his impending visit to Jerusalem. So three geographical points lie commingled in the mind of the apostle: Rome as the goal of much praying, hoping, and planning; Jerusalem as the necessary stop on the way; and Spain as the ultimate objective. One can see how necessary the journey to Jerusalem was in his thinking, since otherwise the lure of the West might take precedence over everything else. So Paul explains just how important this trip to the mother church is, that his readers will understand that he is not dilatory about visiting them.

The principal reason, no doubt, for his having to remain in the East so long is the situation necessitating this final trip to Jerusalem. Paul's churches were made up mainly of Gentile converts. While the Hebrew-Christian element in the church, strongest in Jerusalem, had an interest in the growing work among the Gentiles (Acts 11:21, 22; 15:4), some were concerned that these Gentiles were not being required to accept circumcision in accordance with the OT provision for receiving proselytes into Israel (Exod 12:48) and were not keeping the various ordinances of the Levitical law, such as avoiding foods listed as unclean (Acts 15:1, 5). A further concern was the rapid growth of the Gentile churches, while growth in Jerusalem and Judea had diminished because of persecution and other factors. Jewish believers might be outnumbered before long.

As the leading apostle to the Gentiles, Paul found this situation troubling. What could be done to cement relations between the Jewish and Gentile elements in the church? He was led to conclude that the answer might well lie in a great demonstration of love and desire for unity on the part of his churches toward the mother church in Jerusalem. This could take the same form as the gift of assistance to the poor Christians there that Barnabas and Paul had brought years before on behalf of the Antioch church (Acts 11:27–30). The gratitude of the recipients was real and lived on in the memory of Paul. One cannot help surmising that the quick trip Paul himself made to Jerusalem as reported in Acts 18:22 was undertaken with the definite purpose of conferring with the leaders of the church there about the plan taking shape in his mind—namely, to enlist the cooperation of all his churches in raising a fund to help the mother church, which had a hard time caring for its poorer members. At an earlier period he had expressed eagerness to help the leaders at Jerusalem in ministering to their needy (Gal 2:10). Shortly thereafter he began to inform his congregations of the plan and their responsibility to participate in it (1 Cor 16:1; cf. 2 Cor 8–9). Soon after writing to the Romans, he made preparation for the trip to Jerusalem, in which he was accompanied by representatives of the various churches bearing the offerings that had been collected over a period of time (Acts 20:3, 4).

According to Paul's remarks (v.27), this contribution could be looked at from two standpoints: as a love-gift ("they were pleased to do it") and as an obligation ("they owe it to them"). The latter statement is then explained. Had it not been for the generosity of the Jerusalem church in sharing their spiritual blessings (the gospel as proclaimed by people from Jerusalem and Judea, as seen in Acts 10; 11:19–22; 15:40, 41), the Gentiles would still be in pagan darkness. So it was not such a great thing that they should reciprocate by sharing their "material blessings" (v.27). Some have seen another aspect of this element of obligation. Bruce, in loc., writes:

> Here indeed the question suggests itself whether the contribution was understood by Paul and by the Jerusalem leaders in the same sense. For Paul it was a spontaneous gesture of brotherly love, a token of grateful response on his converts' part to the grace of God which had brought them salvation. But in the eyes of the Jerusalem leaders it perhaps was a form of tribute, a duty owed by the daughter-churches to their mother, comparable to the half-shekel paid annually by Jews throughout the world for the maintenance of the Jerusalem temple and its services.

This must remain a conjecture, though it gains somewhat in plausibility by the fact that Luke's report of the arrival of Paul and his companions in Jerusalem says nothing about any word of thanks by James and the elders for the offering they brought (Acts 21:17ff.).

Paul mentions only those of Macedonia and Achaia as taking part in the contribution (he calls it a *koinōnia*, a participation, v.26) perhaps because he was in Achaia at the time of writing and had recently passed through Macedonia (2 Cor 8–9 reflects the last stages of preparation by these churches). From 1 Corinthians 16:1 and Acts 20:4, it is clear that believers in Asia Minor participated also.

Evidently Paul looks forward to a great feeling of relief when he will be able to convey the monetary offering into the custody of the Jerusalem church. It will mark the completion of an enterprise that has taken several years. He speaks of the gift as "this fruit" (v.29), probably meaning that the generosity of the Jerusalem church in dispersing the seed of the gospel to the Gentiles will now be rewarded, the offering being the fruit of their willingness to share their spiritual blessings.

The completion of the service to be performed at Jerusalem will free Paul to make good on his announced purpose to visit the saints at Rome. He looks forward to it as a time when the blessing of Christ will be poured out upon all. It will be a time of mutual enrichment in the Lord. KJV has "the fulness of the blessing of the gospel of Christ," but the added words are not sufficiently attested to warrant inclusion in the text. Paul's expectations were somewhat shadowed, as it turned out, by the emergence of a group in the Roman church that he characterizes in Philippians 1:15 as motivated by envy and rivalry, but his initial welcome was hearty, despite his coming as a prisoner (Acts 28:15).

30–33 At the time of writing, Paul was aware of stubborn Jewish opposition to him and his work. The attempt on his life when he was about to leave for Jerusalem (Acts 20:3) clearly shows that his apprehension was justified. He had experienced deadly peril before and knew that prayer was the great resource in such hazardous times (2 Cor 1:10, 11). So he requests prayer now (v.30), the kind involving wrestling before the throne of grace that the evil designs of man may be thwarted (cf. Eph 6:18–20). In doing so, he enforces his request by presenting it in the name of Him whom all believers adore—the Lord Jesus Christ—and adding, "by the love of the Spirit." This could mean the love for one another that the Spirit inspires in believers (Gal 5:22). But since the phrase is coupled apparently equally with that of the person of Christ, it is probably better to understand it as the love that the Spirit has (cf. 5:5). The warmth of the expression is enough to warn us against thinking of the Spirit rather impersonally as signifying the power of God. Paul had already affirmed the Spirit's deity and equality with Father and Son (2 Cor 13:14).

The request for prayer includes two immediate objectives. One was deliverance from nonbelieving Jews in Judea. This group had forced his departure from the city at an earlier date (Acts 9:29, 30) and there was no reason to think they had mellowed. The other objective concerned the attitude of the Jerusalem church to the mission that was taking him and his companions to the Jewish metropolis. Evidently the opposition of the Pharisaic party in the church (Acts 15:5) had not ceased, despite the decision of the council (Acts 15:19–29). This opposition, as it related to Paul, was nourished by false rumors concerning his activities (Acts 21:20, 21). So there was reason for concern. It would be a terrible blow to the unity of the church universal if the love-gift of the Gentile congregations were to be spurned or accepted with only casual thanks. The body of Christ could be torn apart.

These two items are intimately related to the successful realization of his hope of reaching Rome safely, coming with joy because of the goodness of God in prospering his way and finding refreshment in the fellowship of the saints (v.32). Yet he knew that all this had to be conditioned on God's will (cf. 1:10). As it turned out, that meant that he would reach Rome, but not as a free man. Yet that very circumstance enabled him to demonstrate the all-sufficient grace and power of Christ (Phil 1:12–14; cf. 2 Tim 4:17). However strife-torn may be his lot in the immediate future, he wishes for his friends the benediction of the God of peace (v.33; cf. v.13).

Notes

19 "Of the Spirit" ($\pi\nu\epsilon\acute{\nu}\mu\alpha\tau\sigma\varsigma$, *pneumatos*) has the support of B. The other principal reading, $\pi\nu\epsilon\acute{\nu}\mu\alpha\tau\sigma\varsigma$ $\theta\epsilon\sigma\hat{\nu}$ (*pneumatos theou*), is found in P[46] $\aleph$, et al., but $\theta\epsilon\sigma\hat{\nu}$ (*theou*) may well be a scribal addition.

29 "The blessing of Christ" has the support of the leading MSS. Later witnesses have "the blessing of the gospel of Christ," an apparent expansion.

B. *Warning Concerning Schismatics, Personal Greetings, and Doxology* 16:1–27

16:1, 2

> I commend to you our sister Phoebe, a servant of the church in Cenchrea. [2]I ask you to receive her in the Lord in a way worthy of the saints and to give her any help she may need from you, for she has been a great help to many people, including me.

Paul has referred to his hope of coming to the believers at Rome (15:32) but he has also mentioned a circumstance that prevented his immediate departure (15:25). Another person, however, is about to leave for the imperial city, so Paul takes this opportunity to commend her to the church. It was customary for believers who traveled from place to place to carry with them letters of commendation (2 Cor 3:1) roughly similar in function to letters of transfer used today when Christians move from one church to another. Here "sister" refers to a woman who is a believer rather than to a blood relative.

"Phoebe" means "bright" or "radiant," a well-known epithet of the Greek god Apollo. She belonged to the church at Cenchrea, located some seven miles from Corinth and serving as the seaport of the city for commerce to the East. Paul had sailed from this port when he went from Corinth to Ephesus several years before (Acts 18:18). It was one of the communities to which the gospel spread from Corinth during and after Paul's original ministry in that city (2 Cor 1:1).

Phoebe is called a "servant" of this church. The same word can be rendered "deaconess" (RSV, JB). Men were serving as deacons about this time (Phil 1:1), and before long women were being referred to in a way that suggests they held such an office in the church (1 Tim 3:11), though the word "deaconess" is not used in that passage. In any event, Paul is not stressing office but service, as we gather from v.2.

Phoebe, it seems, had stopped at Corinth on her way from Cenchrea to Rome. A logical inference from what is said about her is that Paul is sending his letter in her care. She is accustomed to serve, so this will be in character for her. Many had reason to thank God for her assistance in the past, Paul among them. Possibly, like Lydia, she was a businesswoman as well as being active in Christian work and would need help in connection with her visit to the great metropolis.

Notes

2 The word "help" ($\pi\rho o\sigma\tau\acute{a}\tau\iota\varsigma$, *prostatis*) as applied in the last clause of v.2 to the service of Phoebe is not the same as that used for assistance to be given her; it is a somewhat rare term used nowhere else in the NT, conveying the idea of affording care and protection (for papyri examples, see MM). One may conclude that she was outstanding in her ministry of aiding and befriending others.

16:3–16

[3]Greet Priscilla and Aquila, my fellow workers in Christ Jesus. [4]They risked their lives for me. Not only I but all the churches of the Gentiles are grateful to them.
[5]Greet also the church that meets at their house.
Greet my dear friend Epaenetus, who was the first convert to Christ in the province of Asia.
[6]Greet Mary, who worked very hard for you.
[7]Greet Andronicus and Junias, my relatives who have been in prison with me. They are outstanding among the apostles, and they were in Christ before I was.
[8]Greet Ampliatus, whom I love in the Lord.
[9]Greet Urbanus, our fellow worker in Christ, and my dear friend Stachys.
[10]Greet Apelles, tested and approved in Christ.
Greet those who belong to the household of Aristobulus.
[11]Greet Herodion, my relative.
Greet those in the household of Narcissus who are in the Lord.
[12]Greet Tryphaena and Tryphosa, those women who work hard in the Lord.
Greet my dear friend Persis, another woman who has worked very hard in the Lord.
[13]Greet Rufus, chosen in the Lord, and his mother, who has been a mother to me, too.
[14]Greet Asyncritus, Phlegon, Hermes, Patrobas, Hermas and the brothers with them.

¹⁵Greet Philologus, Julia, Nereus and his sister, and Olympas and all the saints with them.
¹⁶Greet one another with a holy kiss.
All the churches of Christ send greetings.

Certain preliminary observations are in order before plunging into these greetings to individuals. It has seemed strange to some Pauline scholars that he would know so many people in the imperial city, seeing that he had never been there. Clearly, he must have met them or at least heard of them elsewhere. Travel, however, was facilitated by peaceful conditions in the empire, by the fine network of Roman roads connecting the principal centers, and by available shipping in sailing season. With regard to references to travel in early Christian documents, Sir William Ramsay comments, "Probably the feature in those Christian writings which causes most surprise at first to the traveller familiar with those countries in modern times, is the easy confidence with which extensive plans of travel were formed and announced and executed by the early Christians" (HDB, extra volume, pp. 396, 397).

But on the assumption that many if not most of those mentioned in chapter 16 were obliged to leave Rome because of the edict of Claudius expelling the Jews (Acts 18:2) and that they crossed Paul's pathway, returning to Rome after the death of the emperor, a problem is created by the almost complete lack of Semitic names (Mary in v.6 is an exception). However, this is not an insuperable difficulty. "We have sufficient evidence from papyri and inscriptions which indicates that both in the diaspora as well as in Palestine, the changing of personal names was a common practice. The Jews acquired not only Greek, but Latin and Egyptian appellations as well" (K.P. Donfried in JBL 89:445). Paul's relatives (vv.7, 11) were Jews, but do not bear Jewish names.

An element of doubt may remain, however, because most of Paul's letters lack personal greetings. How are we to account for so many here? A clue is provided by his letter to the Colossians, which also contains greetings and is written to a church he did not personally establish. In his letter to the Romans Paul is taking advantage of all the ties he has with this congregation that he hopes to visit in the near future. To send greetings to individuals in churches where he knew virtually the entire congregation would expose Paul to the charge of favoritism. But the congregation at Rome was not such a church.

Since his letter to the Philippians was in all probability written from Rome, the greetings he sends from those of Caesar's household (Phil 4:22) to the believers at Philippi may well have been from slaves and freedmen serving in the imperial establishment, people who had been converted before Paul wrote to the Roman church. That this is so seems evident from the fact that many of the names in Romans 16 appear also in the burial inscription of households (establishments) of emperors of that period, notably those of Claudius and Nero (the reigning emperor when Paul wrote). J.B. Lightfoot made a study of the inscriptions available in his time (*Saint Paul's Epistle to the Philippians* [London: Macmillan, 1879], pp. 171–178) and concluded that even though it is not demonstrable that the individuals mentioned in Romans 16 are identical with those whose names occur on the inscriptions, at least it can be said that "the names and allusions at the close of the Roman Epistle are in keeping with the circumstances of the metropolis in St. Paul's day" (ibid. p. 177). So the appropriateness of this chapter as a close for the letter is confirmed.

3–5 First to be greeted are Priscilla and her husband, Aquila. Paul's friendship with them went back several years to his mission at Corinth, when they gave him hospitality, encouragement, and cooperation in the Lord's work (Acts 18:2). Their usefulness is confirmed by his taking them with him on leaving Corinth (Acts 18:18). When he left Ephesus for Jerusalem, they remained in Ephesus to lay the groundwork for his long ministry there (Acts 18:19) and were used of God in the life of Apollos (Acts 18:24-28). It was during the mission at Ephesus that these "fellow workers" proved their mettle and personal devotion to Paul. They "risked their lives for me" (v.4). Probably the reference is to the dangerous riot that broke out, endangering the apostle's life (Acts 19:28-31; cf. 1 Cor 16:9, 2 Cor 1:8-10). Their presence with him at Ephesus just prior to this incident is confirmed by 1 Corinthians 16:19; cf. v.8). At that time they had a church in their house, so it is not surprising to find that the same is true of their situation in Rome. Their return to the imperial city fits in with their earlier residence there (Acts 18:2), even though Aquila came originally from Pontus. He had a Roman name meaning "eagle." It is quite likely that their return to Rome was encouraged by Paul, so that they could prepare for his arrival by acquainting the church with his work in some detail and with his plans for the future (cf. Acts 19:21). It may have been their business interests that dictated the return of this couple to Ephesus at a later time (2 Tim 4:19), but the work of the Lord must have engrossed them along with their occupation. It has been observed that Priscilla and Aquila represent a splendid image of Christian married life. "Neither Luke nor Paul ever thinks of either of these apart from the other; their names are as truly wedded as their lives" (Herbert S. Seekings, *Men of the Pauline Circle* [London: Chas. H. Kelly, 1914], p. 99). Since several women are mentioned in this chapter, it is well to note that in addition to single women who served Christ, there was a married woman whom Paul encouraged to labor in the gospel along with her husband. Paul's habit of naming Priscilla first seems to testify to her great gifts and usefulness in the kingdom of God.

Epaenetus ("praiseworthy") is the next to be greeted (v.5). It is understandable that Paul should speak of him as "my dear friend" (literally, "my beloved"), since this man was the first convert to Christ in connection with the mission to the province of Asia, of which Ephesus was the leading city. Actually Paul calls him the firstfruits of that area, which hints that many more were expected to follow as the full harvest, and this indeed came to pass. This individual, however, naturally held a special place in the heart of the missionary. If the statement is somewhat differently rendered as "the first of Asia's gifts to Christ" (JB), then the emphasis falls more on what Epaenetus meant to the believers who came after him. His dedication to the work of the Lord as well as his faith may be implied. The presence of Epaenetus in Rome, in view of travel conditions, creates no more difficulty than that of Priscilla and Aquila.

6-16 Mary (Miriam) is a Semitic name borne by several women in the NT. Paul indicates his precise knowledge of her, testifying to her hard work for the saints, but without any hint as to the nature of the work. Emphasis falls rather on her willingness to grow weary in serving them. If Paul had been writing to Ephesus, as some assert, it is doubtful that he would have made this precise observation; it would have exposed him to the criticism of playing favorites. He could safely make the comment, however, in writing to a church where he knew a limited number of people.

Andronicus and Junias (v.7) are Latin and Greek names respectively. Three things out of the four said about them create difficulty for the interpreter. What is the meaning of "relatives"? The identical word (*sungeneis*) is found in 9:3, but there it is qualified by the addition, "according to the flesh," indicating that the meaning is fellow Israelite. Here in Romans 16 other Jewish people are named (e.g., Aquila and Mary) who are not described in this way. Yet even so this may be the best conclusion if one adds mentally—"who are also Christians." To take the word in the ordinary sense of "relative" is difficult, since Paul gives the impression that he suffered the loss of all things for Christ's sake (Phil 3:7), which should embrace kindred. Added to this is the improbability of his having three kinfolk in Rome (cf. v.11) and three more in Corinth (v.21). Sir William Ramsay suggests that all these were fellow tribesmen in the sense that the Jews at Tarsus were organized into a "tribe" by the civil authorities, as in other leading communities where Jews were prominent (*The Cities of St. Paul* [New York: A.C. Armstrong and Son, 1908], pp. 175–178). A possible objection to this solution is that Greek has a word for fellow tribesmen—and it is not used here.

Paul adds that these have been in prison with him. Since such an experience befell him many times (2 Cor 11:23), the expression in this case is doubtless intended to be taken literally, even though we are left uninformed as to the circumstances.

The pair are further described as "outstanding among the apostles." We cannot well reduce the word "apostle" to "messenger" in this instance, however suitable it may be in Philippians 2:25, and it goes without saying that Andronicus and Junias do not belong in the circle of the Twelve. What is left is the recognition that occasionally the word is used somewhat broadly to include leaders in Christian work (cf. 1 Thess 2:7). To interpret the statement as meaning that these men were outstanding in the estimation of the apostles scarcely does justice to the construction in the Greek. Evidently their conversion to the faith occurred in the early years of the history of the church, so they have had ample time to distinguish themselves as leaders.

Ampliatus (v.8) is a Latin name. Again, as in the mention of Epaenetus (v.5), Paul confesses to a very warm personal attachment, demonstrating the reality and depth of Christian friendship that developed between him and others who remain rather obscure to us. Paul was a man who gave himself to the people among whom he served and to those who worked alongside him.

Urbanus (v.9), another Latin name, means "refined" or "elegant." Paul seems to indicate that this man helped him at some time in the past and that he assisted others also in the work of the Lord ("*our* fellow worker").

Regarding Stachys (v.9), Paul contents himself with indicating, as with Ampliatus, a very close bond of affection.

Apelles (v.10) was a fairly common name, but this man has an uncommon pedigree, for he is one who is "tested and approved in Christ." This was Paul's desire for Timothy (2 Tim 2:15) and for himself (1 Cor 9:27).

Something of an enigma confronts us in trying to identify those who belong to the household of Aristobulus (v.10). Lightfoot identified Aristobulus as the grandson of Herod the Great, who lived in Rome and apparently died there (*Philippians*, pp. 174, 175). If this is correct, Aristobulus was either not a believer or had died before Paul wrote, since he is not personally greeted. Those addressed would then be his slaves and employees who had become Christians. On the other hand, if this identification is incorrect, we must think of an otherwise unknown figure whose family is mentioned here. The former alternative is somewhat favored by the fact that the next person to be greeted (v.11) is Herodion, a name suggestive of association with, or admiration for, the family of Herod. Even though no actual relationship may have existed, the placing of the two names with Herodian association so close together may support Lightfoot's thesis. That Herodion was a Hebrew Christian is evident from the use of the word "relative."

Regarding the household of Narcissus (v.11), Lightfoot judges that again contemporary history furnishes a clue.

Here, as in the case of Aristobulus, the expression seems to point to some famous person of the name. And the powerful freedman Narcissus, whose wealth was proverbial ... whose influence with Claudius was unbounded, and who bore a chief part in the intrigues of this reign, alone satisfies this condition. ... As was usual in such cases, his household would most probably pass into the hands of the emperor, still however retaining the name of Narcissus. (ibid., p. 175)

Similar in name, Tryphaena and Tryphosa (v.12) were likely sisters. It was not uncommon then, as now, to give daughters names with a certain resemblance (cf. Jean and Joan). Possibly they belonged to an aristocratic family, since "dainty" and "delicate" (or "luxuriating"), as their names mean, would seem to fit this category. If so, their Christian convictions led them to put aside any tendency to live a life of ease. They are given an accolade for being hard workers in the Lord's cause.

To these two Paul adds another, probably a single woman. Persis (v.12) means simply "a Persian lady." She was close to Paul—a "dear friend." Possibly from their correspondence he was able to know enough about her efforts to commend her as having worked "very hard" in the Lord.

A person bearing the name of Rufus (Latin for "red," v.13) is mentioned in Mark 15:21, where it is indicated that he was one of the sons of Simon, the man who was compelled to bear the cross of Jesus. On the supposition that Mark's Gospel was composed at Rome, all is clear: Rufus is referred to in Mark because of being well known to local readers, being a member of the Roman church. He is designated here as "chosen in the Lord," which is awkward if the usual meaning "elect" is intended, since the whole Roman church would qualify also. Possibly the word is here intended to connote the idea of "choice," "noble," or "eminent." There may also be a hint that the incident involving his father brought him a certain fame among believers at Rome. This possibility is heightened if he was a tried and true Christian workman.

Paul cannot think of Rufus without turning his thought to the mother. Though she remains unnamed, she was special in the eyes of the apostle, because she evidently perceived his loneliness after the loss of his family when he became a Christian (Phil 3:8) and resolved to mother him. This required great understanding and tact, but Paul sensed her loving purpose and did not resent her ministrations. Where this occurred remains unknown (Syrian Antioch is a possibility), but her presence in Rome made him look forward with special anticipation to his visit. Incidentally, the Mark 15:21 reference serves as a confirmation that chapter 16 is genuinely a part of the Roman Epistle rather than being intended for the church at Ephesus, as some scholars contend.

In vv.14, 15 two groups of believers are mentioned without accompanying descriptions or commendations. Apparently Paul's ties with them were less strong than his ties with those previously mentioned. Lightfoot notes that the name of Hermes (v.14), famous as the messenger of the gods, was often borne by slaves. (Hermas is a variation.) In connection with both groups, a greeting is extended to the believers associated with them. This appears to indicate a church in the house in both cases. Rome was a large place, making it probable that there were circles of believers in several sections of the city. They would certainly maintain communication and, when necessity dictated, could arrange to meet together.

The admonition to share a holy kiss (v.16) may well be intended in this case to seal the fellowship of the saints when the letter has been read to them (cf. 1 Cor 16:20; 2 Cor 13:12; 1 Thess 5:26). The reminder that it is a "holy" kiss guards it against erotic associations. It was a token of the love of Christ mutually shared and of the peace and harmony he had brought into their lives.

Desiring to encourage warm relations among churches as well as among individuals within them, Paul takes the liberty of extending the greeting of the churches he has founded in the East.

In summary, two observations concerning the greetings should be made, since the church at Rome was destined to become the strongest in all Christendom. First, as Lightfoot has pointed out, several of these names appear in inscriptions of the period at Rome in reference to slaves of the imperial household. If many of Paul's friends were actually slaves, this may seem a rather inauspicious beginning for an influential church. But slaves in the Hellenistic age were often people of education and outstanding ability. Frequently they were able to gain their freedom and play a larger role in society. The very fact that at Rome believers were found in the service of the emperor (Phil 4:22) augured well for the growth of the church in subsequent days. Yet it should be remembered that God's grace, not man's nobility, is the important thing. See 1 Corinthians 1:26–31.

Another feature of this list of names is the prominence of women in the life of the church. They occupied various stations—one a wife, another a single woman, another a mother—and all are represented as performing a valuable service for the Lord. Evidently Paul esteemed them highly for their work's sake. His relation to them and appreciation for them makes suspect the verdict of those who would label him a misogynist on the basis of such passages as 1 Corinthians 14:34 and 1 Timothy 2:11–15.

16:17–20

> 17I urge you, brothers, to watch out for those who cause divisions and put obstacles in your way, contrary to the teaching you have learned. Keep away from them. 18For such people are not serving our Lord Christ, but their own appetites. By smooth talk and flattery they deceive the minds of naive people. 19Everyone has heard about your obedience, so I am full of joy over you; but I want you to be wise about what is good, and innocent about what is evil.
>
> 20The God of peace will soon crush Satan under your feet.
>
> The grace of our Lord Jesus be with you.

17,18 This warning concerning schismatics raises questions that cannot be answered with certainty. How can we account for its position between greetings from Paul to members of the Roman church and greetings from those who are with him? Could it be an insertion from a later time? This is improbable, for if both groups of greetings were originally one unit, it is doubtful that anyone would destroy this unity by placing something between them. The language and style are certainly Pauline. Is it not simply that at this point the danger Paul speaks of gripped him so powerfully that he felt urged to mention it at once? Dodd (in loc.) may be right in thinking that here Paul took the pen from his secretary and wrote this final admonition himself. That v.20b contains the usual benediction found in his letters is somewhat favorable to this conclusion.

Is it possible to identify the troublemakers? Could this passage be intended to glance back at the problem of the strong and the weak already discussed in 14:1–15:13? One conceivable link is the word "obstacles" (v.17), found also in 14:13. However, the general tone of vv.17–20 is so much sharper than the earlier one that any relationship is dubious. If the church read it as related to the foregoing discussion, it could well have been offensive and could have undone the good Paul's irenic approach had already accomplished.

What sort of people were those the apostle singles out here? Were they already in the church at Rome, or were they simply in the offing? Dealing first with the latter question, one gets the impression that they had not yet come on the scene but posed a threat of doing so. If they had already been active in Rome, those who corresponded with Paul, such as the spiritually discerning Priscilla and Aquila, would surely have given information to enable him to point out specifically the nature of the danger the false teaching of these schismatics presented. Observe that Paul does not specify the particular content of the doctrine of these interlopers. Apparently he is counting on the instruction given the Roman church by others (6:17), buttressed by his own teaching in this letter, to enable his readers to recognize the propaganda as spurious when they hear it, even though it may be sufficiently attractive to some to cause division in the church.

By contrast, Paul is much more pointed in identifying the motives and tactics of these people, which suggests that his warning is based on his missionary experience that had brought him into contact with false teachers who tried to build their own work on the foundation he had laid (Phil 3:18, 19; Acts 20:29, 30). Some of them may even have kept track of Paul's movements and, being aware of his plan to visit Rome, were hoping to arrive there before him. If they could gain a foothold in this influential church, it would be a notable success.

17,18 "Watch out." Alertness to the danger is the main consideration, because failure to be on guard could result in being deceived. "Obstacles" (*skandala*) is too general a term to yield anything specific for our knowledge of the propagandists. Whatever they did, their activity could affect the whole church; therefore they should not be identified with those in 14:13, where the singular "obstacle" (*skandalon*) occurs, seeing that these were a problem to only one segment of the congregation.

As an antidote to the corrupting influence that may threaten the Roman believers, the apostle points them to "the teaching you have learned" (v.17). This is hardly to be identified solely with the contents of this letter, but is more particularly intended to refer to the instruction they have already received in the basics of the faith (cf. 6:17). This should serve as the touchstone enabling them to discern error. But such counsel is not enough. As a practical measure, it is necessary to "keep away from them," giving no opportunity for inroads into the congregation. Religious errorists covet opportunities for "friendly discussion."

Paul speaks of "such people" (v.18) rather than "these people," a slight distinction, perhaps, but nevertheless an important one, confirming the opinion already given that he does not have in mind a group he could name or identify precisely, but a class he has become all too familiar with in his travels. They may talk about the Lord but they do not serve him. Rather, they serve "their own appetites" (cf. Phil 3:18, 19; 1 Tim 6:3–5). With their smooth talk and flattery intended to deceive, they brand themselves as sophists and charlatans. Those they aim to reach are the "naive," the simpleminded folk so innocent of ulterior motive themselves that they imagine others are like them. Their gullibility can be their downfall (cf. "the simple" in the Psalms, a class distinguished both from "the wise" and "the foolish").

19 Here, despite the warning, the apostle affirms his confidence that his readers will be able to handle the situation (cf. a similar expression in 15:14 after dealing with the weak and the strong). This assurance is based chiefly on their "obedience" (cf. 1:5; 6:16), which is so well known in the church at large as to make it almost inconceivable that there will be a failure in the matter under discussion. An appeal to one's record always puts a person on his mettle. So Paul strikes a balance: on the one hand, he has joy as he thinks of the good name of this congregation; on the other hand, he wants to make sure that they are discerning, able to spot trouble and avoid falling into it.

20 Perhaps the mention of "what is evil" leads Paul to think of the instigator of it, namely, Satan, and of the One who blocks his efforts and will thwart his hoped-for triumph. God is the God of peace (cf. 15:33; Phil 4:9; 1 Thess 5:23), who is concerned to preserve harmony among his people and protect them from divisive influences. He is able to defeat the adversary who delights to sow discord among Christians. Though Paul's statement in v.20 has often been taken as a reference to the Second Advent, it is doubtful that this is the intent. "Paul means . . . not that the victory will be near, but that it will be speedily gained, once the conflict is begun. When the believer fights with the armour of God (Eph VI), the conflict is never long. Victory will result from two factors, the one divine (*God shall bruise*), the other human (*under your feet*). God communicates strength; but it passes through the man who accepts and uses it" (Godet, in loc.). The word "crush" suggests that Paul has in mind the "promise" of Genesis 3:15 as the background for his statement.

The benediction, as usual, magnifies the grace of our Lord. The odd feature, however, is that it does not conclude the letter. Did Paul intend to stop here, or did he as an afterthought decide to allow his companions to send greetings when they requested the privilege?

16:21–23

21Timothy, my fellow worker, sends his greetings to you, as do Lucius, Jason and Sosipater, my relatives.

22I, Tertius, who wrote down this letter, greet you in the Lord.

23Gaius, whose hospitality I and the whole church here enjoy, sends you his greetings.

Erastus, who is the city's director of public works, and our brother Quartus send you their greetings.

Paul usually had co-workers and friends around him. This occasion is no exception, and they take this opportunity to send greetings. Timothy, named first, had been Paul's helper on the mission to Macedonia and Achaia (Acts 17–18) and his assistant in handling problems in the Corinthian church (1 Cor 4:17; 16:10).

The next three persons named (v.21) are called "relatives," raising the same problem of interpretation faced in vv.7, 11. Though Lucius could be an alternate form for Luke, this is not the spelling Paul uses for the beloved physician (Col 4:14). And if "relative" is the proper meaning of the word so rendered here, Luke is excluded from this group anyway, because he is distinguished from Paul's Jewish-Christian companions (Col 4:11). It seems likely that Luke *was* with Paul at Corinth (Acts 20:5), so the temptation is strong to identify him with Lucius. Yet it should probably be resisted. Jason could be the individual who entertained Paul and his two helpers at Thessalonica (Acts 17:5). But here, too, there is uncertainty because he is not named as a representative of the Thessalonian church traveling to Jerusalem (Acts 20:4). Sosipater, on the other hand, could be the Sopater mentioned in that passage, since these are forms of the same name (cf. Hermes-Hermas in v.14). His home was in Berea.

At this point (v.22) Paul's amanuensis, who by this time had become thoroughly wrapped up in the message and had developed a feeling of rapport with the Roman

Christians, asks for the privilege of adding his personal greeting. His name, Tertius, is Latin, meaning "third." Though it was Paul's habit to dictate his letters except for the close (2 Thess 3:17), we may be sure he was careful to use believers rather than public secretaries who would do their work without any spiritual concern. We also may be sure that people like Tertius would undertake the task as work for the Lord, so that it would cost the apostle nothing.

Resuming his closing remarks, Paul passes on the greeting of Gaius, with whom he had been staying while he wintered at Corinth (v.23). Evidently his man had a commodious house that he made available for the meetings of the congregation. He seems to have been one of the early converts in Paul's mission to the city (1 Cor 1:14), and the very fact that Paul made an exception in his case by personally baptizing him suggests that his conversion was a notable event due to his prominence. Because of Paul's remark that the whole church enjoyed Gaius's hospitality, it is tempting to suppose that he is the man (Titius Justus) who invited believers into his home after the break with the synagogue (Acts 18:7). This involves the supposition that Paul is giving only a part of his name and that Luke provides the rest (Romans had three names). At any rate, the mention of Gaius as Paul's host is strong evidence that the apostle was writing from Corinth rather than from Cenchrea or from some point in Macedonia.

Erastus (v.23) also, a notable figure because of his public office, sends a greeting. Oscar Broneer, who has done considerable excavating at the site of ancient Corinth, reports in *The Biblical Archaeologist* XIV (Dec. 1951) p. 94:

> A re-used paving block preserves an inscription, stating that the pavement was laid at the expense of Erastus, who was *aedile* (Commissioner of Public Works). He was probably the same Erastus who became a co-worker of St. Paul (Acts 19:22: Rom. 16:23, where he is called *oikonomos*, "chamberlain" of the city), a notable exception to the Apostle's characterization of the early Christians: "Not many wise men after the flesh, not many mighty, not many noble are called" (1 Cor 1:26).

One should add, however, that the correlation with the Erastus named in Acts 19:22 is uncertain.

Nothing more is known of Quartus than what is stated here. He was probably a member of the Corinthian church and may have had some contact with the congregation in Rome.

Notes

---

24 This verse is omitted by leading witnesses, including P[46] ℵ A B C. It is included by Western witnesses (D G, et al.), which omit it at v.20.

16:25–27

²⁵Now to him who is able to establish you by my gospel and the proclamation of Jesus Christ, according to the revelation of the mystery hidden for long ages past, ²⁶but now revealed and made known through the prophetic writings by the command of the eternal God, so that all nations might believe and obey him— ²⁷to the only wise God be glory forever through Jesus Christ! Amen.

Since Paul has already given his usual benediction of grace (v.20) found at the close of all his letters, we must see some explanation for the doxology here. The greetings in vv.21-23 may have seemed to Paul a somewhat ill-fitting close, leading him to write this magnificent doxology that draws into itself words and concepts found in his earlier Epistles and gives special emphasis to the leading matters broached in the preceding chapters of the present letter. Whereas a benediction is the pronouncing of a blessing from God on his people, a doxology is an ascription of praise to him. This one is rather lengthy, so much so that the final verse is separated from the rest by a dash in order to indicate a resumption of the thought with which the passage begins and to bring it to a proper conclusion.

25 The opening words express confidence in God's ability to do what is needful for the readers. The same formula is found in Ephesians 3:20 (cf. Jude 24). In the introduction (1:11) Paul wrote that he was looking forward to his ministry at Rome as a means of strengthening the congregation. Now he acknowledges that in the ultimate sense only God can bring this result (*stērizō* the Greek word for "strengthen," tr. "establish" in NIV, is the same in both places). As an instrument for establishing the saints, nothing can compare with the gospel. Paul is not being egotistical or possessive in calling it "my gospel" (cf. 2:16; 2 Tim 2:8). Lagrange rightly raises the question whether he could ask God to confirm readers in his gospel if it were different from that preached by others. Doubtless the possessive pronoun points up the fact that in Paul's case it came by direct revelation (1:1; cf. Gal 1:12), though confirmed as to its actual historical content by leaders of the Jerusalem church (1 Cor 15:1-11). Another term for the gospel is the "proclamation of Jesus Christ," by which we should understand not the preaching done by the Lord Jesus while on earth and probably not his preaching through his servant Paul (2 Cor 13:3 uses this conception, but with emphasis on authority), but rather the preaching that has Jesus Christ as its message (cf. 1:2, 3). This is the only time the word "proclamation" (*kērygma*) occurs in Romans, but Paul had used it earlier (1 Cor 1:21; 2:4; 15:14).

"Proclamation" follows upon "revelation," and both stand in contrast to "mystery" and "hidden." There is a similar tension between mystery and revelation in 1 Corinthians 2:7-10. In fact, this is usual in the apostle's reference to mystery. What is hidden in the divine purpose ultimately becomes revealed and is then the property of all his people. The only other allusion to mystery in Romans (11:25) is more restricted in its scope than in the present passage. How long was the mystery hidden? "For long ages past" may possibly be intended to embrace the OT period (though the Scriptures contained data on the gospel, according to 1 Cor 15:3, 4). The most natural reference, however, is to "eternity past" (cf. 2 Tim 1:9; Titus 1:2), and this is confirmed by the matching description of the deity as "the eternal God" (v.26).

26 "Now revealed" recalls 3:21 (where the same root word is used in the Greek). "Made known through the prophetic writings" raises again the problem faced in v.25 concerning the meaning of the "long ages." This somewhat favors referring these ages to the precreation setting. Of course, it is true that the presence of prophetic material in the OT did not necessarily mean that people understood it as referring to Christ (Luke 24:44, 45). The OT prophets themselves were puzzled by the messianic element in their own predictions (1 Peter 1:10-12). Prophets were active in NT days, engaged not only in exhortation and comfort (1 Cor 14:3) but also in revelation (1 Cor 14:29, 30; Eph 3:5). But all this was on an oral basis; so it seems necessary to refer "prophetic writings" to the OT. No doubt Paul is taking a backward glance at what he had set down at the beginning of the letter concerning the gospel as promised by God through his prophets in the Holy Scriptures (1:2).

"The command of the eternal God" points to the Great Commission, which includes all the nations as embraced in the divine purpose (Matt 28:19). This emphasis recalls the language Paul used in speaking of his own commission (1:1, 5; cf. Titus 1:3). Colossians 1:25-27 is in the same vein. Paul had a special concern to reach the Gentiles (11:13).

27 God is described under two terms. "Only" (cf. 1 Tim 1:17) may well be intended to recall the line of thought in 3:29, 30. He is God of both Jew and Gentile, with a provision for both groups in the gospel of his Son. "Wise" invites the reader to recall the outburst of praise to God in his wisdom (11:33) that brings to a close the long review of his dealings with Israel in relation to his purpose for the Gentiles. Wisdom is also allied to the hidden/revealed tension noted in v.25, as we gather also from 1 Corinthians 2:6, 7. So the God whose eternal purpose has been described as hidden and then manifested in the gospel of his Son, draws to himself through his Son the praise that will engross the saints through all the ages to come. The silence that for so long held the divine mystery has given way to vocal and unending praise.

Notes

25-27 The doxology presents problems. One of these is the varying position it holds in the MSS. Although most of them have it at the end of the letter, a few place it after 14:23, one after 15:33, and a few others after 14:23 and also after 16:24. Marcion, the second-century heretic, refused to include the doxology as well as the two final chapters.

Another source of difficulty is the style and content of this portion. It has been said that nothing like it is to be found elsewhere in Paul's acknowledged writings (Eph 3:20, 21 and 1 Tim 1:17 are held by many scholars to be post-Pauline). It must be granted that a few terms do not occur elsewhere in the Pauline corpus: "eternal God," "prophetic," and "hidden" (lit. "kept in silence"), though a synonym for the latter is fairly frequent in Paul, used, as here, in contrast to "revealed" or "manifested."

On the other hand, most of the items in these three verses agree very well indeed with Paul's teaching in his letters, and especially with his teaching in Romans, as we have already seen. Hence, there is no insuperable difficulty in ascribing the doxology to him. For more detailed treatment, see Bruce pp. 26-29, 281, 182; Barrett pp. 10-13.